THE POLAR REGIONS

For Alison

THE POLAR REGIONS

AN ENVIRONMENTAL HISTORY

ADRIAN HOWKINS

polity

First published in 2016 by Polity Press

Polity Press
65 Bridge Street
Cambridge CB2 1UR, UK

Polity Press
350 Main Street
Malden, MA 02148, USA

ISBN-13: 978-0-7456-7080-5

A catalogue record for this book is available from the British Library.

Typeset in 10.75 on 14 pt Janson Text by
Servis Filmsetting Ltd, Stockport, Cheshire
Printed and bound in Great Britain by Clays Ltd, St Ives plc

The publisher has used its best endeavors to ensure that the URLs for external websites referred to in this book are correct and active at the time of going to press. However, the publisher has no responsibility for the websites and can make no guarantee that a site will remain live or that the content is or will remain appropriate.

Every effort has been made to trace all copyright holders, but if any have been inadvertently overlooked the publisher will be pleased to include any necessary credits in any subsequent reprint or edition.

For further information on Polity, visit our website:
politybooks.com

CONTENTS

ACKNOWLEDGMENTS

My academic interest in the Polar Regions began as a graduate student at the University of Texas. I would like to thank my doctoral supervisor Roger Louis, and my committee members Diana Davis, Bruce Hunt, Jonathan Brown, and Tony Hopkins, for their teaching, support, and for their willingness to supervise a dissertation on the history of Antarctica. In Austin it was a great pleasure to be part of an intellectually stimulating graduate student cohort that included Pablo Mijangos, Cory Conover, Chris Albi, Heather Peterson, José Barragán, Brandon Marsh, Mike Anderson, and many other wonderful friends and colleagues. Texas might not be the most obvious place to start writing about the history of the Polar Regions, but I like to think that there are a number of overlaps with the "it ain't braggin' if it's true" mentality of America's second largest state.

At Colorado State University my interest in the environmental history of extreme environments has developed in a vibrant intellectual atmosphere. I am particularly grateful to my friends and colleagues at the Public Lands History Center, who have encouraged me to think about history in a way that is fundamentally collaborative and engaged with wider publics. Mark Fiege has taught me more than he can know about being an environmental historian, and has offered constant support and encouragement with this project. Jared Orsi has been extremely generous in reading my work, offering insights with an uncanny ability to say the right thing at the right time. Ruth Alexander, Janet Ore, Sarah Payne, and Maren Bzdek have each done much to broaden my appreciation and understanding of the field of history. I would also like to thank the other members of the CSU History Department, especially my two departmental chairs, Doug Yarrington and Diane Margolf, who have been patient and supportive of my frequent requests to travel to distant places. The CSU History Department and College of Liberal Arts have both been generous in providing financial support for my research. In my classes I have learned as much from my students as they have learned from me, and I would like to thank them all for tolerating my idiosyncratic interests and laughing at my attempted jokes.

In summer 2013 I received a McColl Fellowship from the American Geographical Society Library in Milwaukee to conduct research for this project. Marcy Bidney, Jovanka Ristic, Susan Peschel, and Robert Jaeger made this one of the most productive and enjoyable research experiences of my career. I have also benefitted from the assistance of many other archivists and librarians at institutions around the world, including the University of Alaska Anchorage; the University of Alaska Fairbanks; the Byrd Polar Research Center; the US National Archives at College Park, Maryland; the Denver Public Library; the British Antarctic Survey; the Scott Polar Research Institute; the British National Archives; the Argentine Foreign Ministry Archive; the Argentine Antarctic Institute; the Chilean Foreign Ministry Archive; the National Library of Australia; the Australian Antarctic Division; the University of Waikato; the Victoria University of Wellington; Gateway Antarctica at the University of Canterbury; and the New Zealand National Archives in Wellington and Christchurch.

A few years ago, I wrote a short essay in the journal *Environmental History* titled "Have You Been There? Some Thoughts On (Not) Visiting Antarctica" in which I considered the importance environmental historians place on visiting the places we study. Since writing that essay I have had several opportunities to visit the Polar Regions. I would like to thank Diana Galimberti and Mariano Curiel for giving me my first opportunity to travel to Antarctica as a history lecturer, guide, and Zodiac driver with the tourist company Antarctica XXI. I am extremely grateful to Diana Wall, for introducing me to the McMurdo

Dry Valleys Long Term Ecological Research project in Antarctica. Visiting the Dry Valleys has been one of the highlights of my life, and I would like to thank Diane McKnight and everyone associated with the project for making me feel so welcome, as well as the National Science Foundation's Office of Polar Programs for making this research possible (Grant ANT-1115245). In Alaska—the one state bigger than Texas—Dave Shaw was a fantastic guide on a trip I made to the Arctic National Wildlife Refuge with the Arctic Wild Company. My friends Sam and Tasha Caughey, Lars Mjaerfoss, and Pia Veldt Larsen have accompanied me on trips to Arctic Norway. It has been a tremendous privilege to be able to visit some of the places I write about in this book, but I try to keep reminding myself of the many issues raised by the nagging question, "Have you been there?"

I made my first venture into comparative polar history with Brandon Luedkte, and I would like to thank him for encouraging me to start looking to the north as well as to the south. Klaus Dodds, Peder Roberts, Lize Marié van Der Watt, Mark Carey, Alessandro Antonello, Ron Doel, Jim Fleming, Anita Guerrini, Cornelia Lüdecke, Daniela Liggett, Consuelo Leon, Mauricio Jara, Andrés Zarankin, Ximena Senatore, Tom Griffiths, Graeme Wynn, Ryan Jones, Brett Bennett, Paul Sutter, Tina Adcock, and Nigel Milius have all been especially helpful in helping to lay the intellectual foundations for this book. At Polity Press I would like to thank Andrea Drugan and Elliott Karstadt for encouraging this project and being fantastic editors. The anonymous reviewers provided many useful ideas and suggestions. It is impossible to thank everyone by name for the conversations, shared ideas, research support, and general assistance that has been given to me as part of writing this book, but I am truly grateful to you all. Any errors of fact or interpretation are my responsibility alone.

Finally, and most important, I would like to thank my family for the love, support, and patience that have made this book possible. I like to think that the real origins of this project began with family walks with my Mum, Dad, and sister across Dartmoor National Park in southwest England. Whether by accident or design these walks instilled in me a passion for extreme environments that has never gone away. I met my wife Alison Hicks while we were students at the University of St. Andrews. Alison shares my love of wild landscapes, and we spent many happy weekends climbing mountains in the Scottish Highlands. Since then we have continued to explore the world together, visiting places as far away as Nuuk in Greenland and Hobart in Tasmania. Alison has been a true inspiration for my work, and I dedicate this book to her.

Introduction

LANDS OF DARKNESS AND LIGHT

Sailing across Prince William Sound in southern Alaska early in the summer of 2014, it is difficult to imagine that twenty-five years earlier this was the site of one of the world's high-profile environmental disasters. Sea otters bob up and down, seabirds fly around, and the presence of fishing boats suggests healthy fish populations beneath the surface of the waters. The forests that cover the surrounding mountain slopes appear to be flourishing and the beaches along the shoreline look pristine. Mixed in with the locals and seasonal workers, a handful of tourists appear to be enjoying the crossing, sipping coffee and taking pictures. Even on a rainy day, this is one of the most beautiful places in the world. From the ferry there is no visible sign of the eleven million gallons or more of crude oil that spilled from the gashed hull of the *Exxon Valdez* after it ran aground shortly after midnight on March 24, 1989—Good Friday—polluting the waters and killing wildlife in one of the cruelest imaginable fashions.[1]

Following the oil spill, attempts at containment were largely ineffective, and cleanup efforts after the disaster often exacerbated the contamination. In the days, weeks, and months that followed, thousands of oily corpses were collected and put into freezers, creating a grisly archive of the disaster. Dead seals, otters, and seabirds were the most visible victims; entire ecosystems were smothered in toxic crude oil.

The oil spill divided local communities. Recriminations focused on the alcohol consumption of the captain and the willful disregard for the environment shown by the oil companies. Members of local communities launched multimillion–dollar lawsuits against Exxon Corporation, and substantial payouts were made. But few people were truly satisfied with the outcome. Alaska Native artist Mark Webber carved a totem of shame to condemn the disaster and mock those held responsible. Particularly grating for Webber was the chairman of Exxon's promise that "we will make you whole again."[2]

Scraping beneath the surface, it is still possible to find evidence of the lasting environmental impact of the *Exxon Valdez* disaster twenty-five years after the event. The museum in the nearby fishing town of Cordova—where the fishing industry was severely affected by the spill—contains a jar of oily sand collected from Eleanor Island in February 2014. The contents of the jar and the accompanying pictures serve as a reminder of the long-term consequences of the spill. It is difficult to attribute causation in complex ecosystems, but according to the museum's display, loons, harbor seals, sockeye salmon, and a number of other species have returned to prespill numbers, while AT1 (or transient-type) killer whales, Pacific herring, and pigeon guillemots have shown no sign of recovery.[3] The museum in Valdez confirms the decline of herring and guillemots, but has no mention of killer whales.

The oil that spilled into Prince William Sound came from Prudhoe Bay, above the Arctic Circle on Alaska's North Slope. It had traveled 800 miles to the south through the Trans-Alaska Pipeline, one of the most expensive and environmentally controversial feats of civil engineering ever conducted in the United States.[4] Completed in 1977, the pipeline created a physical connection between the Arctic North and the town of Valdez, the most northerly ice-free port in the United States. For a while, legal challenges issued by environmentalist organizations had been successful in delaying the construction of the pipeline. But too many economic and political forces were lined up in favor of Arctic oil production to hold up the construction for long. For the Federal government in Washington D.C., Arctic oil brought down gas prices and reduced reliance on Middle Eastern oil in the wake of the oil crisis of the mid 1970s. For the state of Alaska, oil revenues offered a panacea to the economic struggles that had befallen it since state-hood in 1959.[5] For Alaskan indigenous communities, the need for the pipeline had helped facilitate the passage of the 1971 Alaska Native Claims Settlement Act, which granted land and money in partial compensation for losses suffered following the arrival of Europeans.[6] For oil companies and the oil workers who flocked to Alaska, this was a financial bonanza unprecedented in recent U.S. history.[7] In contrast, environmentalists viewed the exploitation of Arctic oil as epitomizing the unthinking greed of modern economic growth and its blatant disregard for the natural environment.[8] The *Exxon Valdez* disaster proved that their worst fears could come true.

For all the debates and recriminations caused by the 1989 oil spill in Prince William Sound, a case could be made that the most important legacy of the disaster occurred not in the Arctic but rather on the opposite side of the world, in Antarctica. Although regulations for transporting crude oil were tightened in the aftermath of the event, oil continued to flow through the Trans-Alaska Pipeline and onward across the ocean. In Antarctica, in contrast, the *Exxon Valdez* disaster made a significant contribution to agreement on a long-lasting prohibition of mineral exploitation of any sort. Members of the Antarctic Treaty System had spent most of the 1980s negotiating a minerals regime for Antarctica that sought to facilitate and regulate extractive activities along the lines of those taking place at Prudhoe Bay.[9] The environmental disaster that occurred in Prince William Sound contributed to the decisions made by the delegations of several countries to rethink this position. Instead of ratifying the Convention for the Regulation of Antarctic Minerals Activities (CRAMRA), members of the Antarctic Treaty instead signed the 1991 Madrid Environmental Protocol, which prohibited any form of economic mineral extraction throughout Antarctica for a period of at least fifty years. As a result of this agreement, the entire southern continent became, by many measures, one of the most protected environments anywhere on the planet.

It is impossible to say whether the Madrid Protocol would have been signed if crude oil had not spilled from the hull of the *Exxon Valdez* into Prince William Sound. Antarctic politics during the 1980s were fraught and unpredictable. Inside the Antarctic Treaty System, the seven states that claimed sovereignty over parts of the southern continent clashed repeatedly with other member states that refused to recognize these claims; at the same time, Britain, Argentina, and Chile continued to dispute the ownership of the Antarctic Peninsula region. Outside the Treaty System, an alliance of nonaligned countries led by Malaysia derided member states as an "imperial club" and called for Antarctica to be handed over to the United Nations.[10] Their argument was based on the "common heritage of mankind" principle, in which every country had a stake in the world's shared natural resources. Environmental organizations such as Greenpeace and the Antarctic and Southern Ocean Coalition (ASOC) were campaigning vociferously against a minerals regime on the basis that Antarctica was the world's last remaining wilderness and it should not be put at risk for short-term economic gain. It is perfectly possible to imagine a scenario whereby the member states of the Antarctic Treaty abandoned the minerals negotiations in favor of an environmental protocol simply to keep the peace and keep themselves in control. But the *Exxon Valdez* disaster certainly contributed to the decision to abandon the minerals negotiations and sign the Madrid Protocol, and the chronological coincidence is compelling. In giving his testimony to the Senate Committee on Foreign Relations hearing on legislation relating to the protection of the Antarctic environment in July 1990, Senator Al Gore directly referred to the events in Prince William Sound: "Last year, the *Exxon Valdez* disaster in Prince William Sound provided vivid, heartbreaking illustrations of the devastating consequences of an environmental disaster in a pristine wilderness."[11]

Writing about the *Exxon Valdez* oil spill in in an essay titled "Landscapes of Abundance and Scarcity," the environmental historian William Cronon notes:

> Remote as it may have seemed from the day-to-day lives of most Americans, the wrecked Exxon supertanker could not have been more intimately entangled with [the] central questions of western environmental history.... Not even Alaska was safe, not even Alaska was far enough away to remain an unsullied landscape of frontier freedom and wilderness escape. Even there, abundance could give way to scarcity, forcing those who had counted on the promise of plenty to confront

the consequences of its loss. It was not the first such failed promise in western history, and would surely not be the last.[12]

An examination of the history of Antarctica alongside the history of the Arctic offers a different perspective on the already contested legacy of the *Exxon Valdez* oil spill. On the one hand, the freezers full of corpses serve as a reminder of the worst that humans can do to damage the world we live in. On the other hand, the connections between the oil spill at Prince William Sound and the Madrid Protocol in Antarctica suggests that some good can come out of even the worst environmental disaster. Whether this connection can be the cause for hope very much depends on individual perspective, but it certainly complicates a one-directional declensionist narrative, in which the only story is environmental degradation.

The connections between the *Exxon Valdez* oil spill in the far north and the signature of the Madrid Environmental protocol in the far south exemplify the three central arguments that will be made by this book. First, it argues that the histories of the Arctic and Antarctica are deepened and enriched by studying them together. Despite being located at opposite ends of the planet and being significantly different in many ways, the environmental histories of the Polar Regions share much and have often been closely connected. Second, the environmental histories of the Arctic and Antarctica offer good opportunities for thinking about important environmental themes. In much the same way that the ugliness of the crude oil spilled from the *Exxon Valdez* was highlighted by the beauty of Prince William Sound, a study of the Polar Regions brings into stark relief themes such as resource exploitation, the militarization of nature, conservation, and anthropogenic climate change. This makes them good places for thinking about the theory and practice of environmental history. Third, a careful study of the environmental histories of the Polar Regions reveals these histories to be characterized by contrast and contradiction. These are not histories with a simple message of good and bad, but rather a messy enmeshing of geographies of hope and geographies of despair. As places of inherent contradiction, the Polar Regions have much to contribute to the way we think about the environment generally.

What Are the Polar Regions?

In many parts of the world the Polar Regions occupy a position at the periphery of popular imagination. The Arctic and Antarctica are places that epitomize the unknown and faraway. Many people might struggle to say which Polar Region is located to the north and which to the south; even more would probably have difficulty identifying the respective habitats of penguins and polar bears. Once in a while the Polar Regions may intrude into everyday life, as happened so dramatically with the *Exxon Valdez* disaster. More often, the Arctic and Antarctica exist in the background of popular culture. The success of the recent BBC documentary *Frozen Planet* suggests a popular interest in the natural history of the Polar Regions.[13] Stories of polar exploration—now often blogged and tweeted in real time—retain much of their capacity to fascinate, however derivative they may have become.[14] In recent years anthropogenic climate change and the consequent melting polar ice causing rising sea levels around the world has brought the Arctic and Antarctica a little closer to the center of popular consciousness. But for most people, most of the time, the Polar Regions remain places that they are unlikely to think much about and that they will almost certainly never visit.

For a much smaller number of people, the Polar Regions are an everyday reality. Over two million people live north of the Arctic Circle, and a total of over thirteen million live in a more broadly defined "Circumpolar North."[15] A substantial minority of these Arctic populations are indigenous peoples with their cultural roots and histories strongly connected to the northern landscape. For Inuit, Sami, Chukchi, and other ethnic groups of the far north, the Arctic is truly home, and elaborate knowledge systems have developed to make sense of the polar environment.[16] In contrast, nobody lives permanently in Antarctica and there are no Antarctic citizens. Although there are multiple ways of knowing Antarctica's environment, science is by far the dominant paradigm and there is no indigenous worldview. For a small handful of people—mostly scientists, logistics staff, members of the military, and tourism operators—the southern continent is an everyday reality. But sooner or later they all go home to somewhere else. In any given winter there are fewer than one thousand people living south of the Antarctic Circle, making its population less than one-twentieth of a percent of the Arctic.

For a third group of people, mostly living in a handful of countries fairly close to the Arctic or Antarctica, the Polar Regions are neither completely alien nor completely familiar. In Norway, for example (parts of which do lie north of the Arctic Circle), the Arctic and Antarctica occupy important places in conceptions of national identity, not least because the Norwegians Fridtjof Nansen and Roald Amundsen played such prominent roles in the history of polar exploration. In Chile and Argentina it is a legal requirement for all published maps to include inserts of their respective sovereignty claims to Antarctica, and in both countries the ownership of an overlapping pie piece of the southern continent is a recurring, if not unproblematic, cause of national pride.[17] Canada has cultivated a northern identity, in part to differentiate itself from its southern neighbor.[18] Over the course of the twentieth century Australians and New Zealanders have used Antarctica as a space to assert their increasing independence from Great Britain. The British themselves have a particular fascination with the Polar Regions, as demonstrated by Francis Spufford's *I May Be Some Time: Ice and the English Imagination* (1996).[19] A similar cultural affinity for one or both Polar Regions—sometimes with unsavory racial connotations—might be found at different times in the histories of Russia, Germany, Japan, the United States, and South Africa.[20] But even in the countries that have shown a special interest in the Polar Regions, the majority of people have little direct connection with either the Arctic or Antarctica.

This diversity of perspectives raises important questions about insider and outsider status in the research and writing of history. The contrast between the lived-in Arctic and the almost entirely uninhabited Antarctic presents this dichotomy in a particularly stark form. But within the Arctic itself (and to a much lesser extent Antarctica as well), there are important gradations. A number of excellent "insider" histories of the Arctic exist, and have been excellent resources.[21] But this book is a history of the Polar Regions written from the outside looking in.

The fact that the Arctic and Antarctica mean such different things to different people also exacerbates the problem of definition: what exactly are the Polar Regions and where are they located? When most people do think about extreme northerly and southerly latitudes, it is likely that the first image that comes to mind is a vast expanse of ice and snow. For much of the Arctic and Antarctica, such an image is entirely appropriate. "To enter Greater Antarctica," writes the environmental historian Stephen Pyne, "is to be drawn into a maelstrom of ice. Ice is the beginning of Antarctica and ice is its end."[22] Even in the Arctic, where there is a lot less continental ice, images of ice and snow work well as a definition for much of the year. The use of snow and ice to define the Polar Regions has even led some people to talk about the glaciated regions of the Himalayas as a "Third Pole."[23] Defining the Polar Regions as places with large quantities of frozen water, however, quickly breaks down. If the Himalayas can be referred to as a Third Pole, why not refer to every significant glaciated part of the world as polar? Within many parts of the Arctic, snow and ice cover are seasonal: areas that are covered in snow for most of the year can become flower-strewn meadows for a brief summer season, and many maritime regions of both the Arctic and Antarctica freeze in the winter and thaw in the summer. Some degree of stability is required for any definition of a place to have utility, and snow and ice are fundamentally—and increasingly—unstable.

Another way of defining the Arctic and Antarctica might take an ecosystems approach. As a result of the low angle of the sun, the terrestrial parts of the Polar Regions are generally low-energy ecosystems, characterized by relatively slow growth and low biomass. In the north, the tree line is often seen as the most useful definition of the Arctic: the cold, dry conditions north of this line do not support the growth of trees. The tree line works as a definition for Antarctica, but is a little absurd since there are no trees of any sort, and only two species of vascular plant exist anywhere on the continent. It might also extend Antarctica northwards into parts of Patagonia and various sub-Antarctic islands. In the Southern Ocean the Antarctic convergence is used as a political boundary by the Convention on the Conservation of Antarctic Marine Living Resources (CCAMLR).[24] The convergence is the point in the ocean where the cold waters of the Southern Ocean meet the warmer waters of the Atlantic, Pacific, and Indian Oceans. The Antarctic Convergence is marked by a dramatic shift in temperature of 2 to 3 degrees Celsius accompanied by a significant change in ecology, with the nutrient-rich waters of the Southern Ocean supporting abundant ecosystems of a quite different character than those found further north. The Arctic Ocean is similarly colder than the neighboring bodies of water, but the situation is complicated by it being a largely closed basin. While an ecosystem approach to defining the Polar Regions has some utility, it suffers from several of the same flaws as a climatic definition. Ecosystems are inherently unstable, and both the tree line and the Antarctic Convergence are fluctuating boundaries. "Polar" ecosystems may be found in other parts of the world, especially in high mountain regions. Most significant, the largely lifeless polar ice sheets of Greenland and Antarctica differ as much from many parts of the seasonally abundant Arctic tundra as the Arctic tundra differs from a tropical forest. This diversity makes a mockery of a coherent definition of the Polar Regions as a whole based on a shared ecology.

A somewhat more satisfactory definition of the Polar Regions focuses on latitude. In both north and south, the Polar Regions are the places where the sun never rises for at least one day in winter and never sets for at least one day in summer. Maps locate these lines at approximately 66.33°N (the Arctic Circle) and 66.33°S (the Antarctic Circle).[25] Although these lines have a somewhat imaginary quality, they do mark a physical reality. In this definition, the Polar Regions are characterized by extreme seasonality. In wintertime, the Arctic and Antarctica are dark, frozen, vitamin-deficient places and there is no escape from the unrelenting cold. In the summertime solar energy radiates through polar landscapes, bringing a semblance of warmth and life. A definition based on latitude explicitly excludes "The Third Pole" of the Himalayas and other glaciated regions of the world. It also has the advantage of being largely stable, changing only slightly over the course of geological time. This is important for historians, since it allows for significant changes to take place within the Polar Regions without the definition of the places themselves changing. A definition based on latitude also allows for a great deal of variation both within and between the Arctic and Antarctica, both in terms of the environment and the human history.

Even a definition based on latitude, however, is problematic. In Antarctica, a large part of the Peninsula region juts north of the Antarctic Circle toward South America; in the Arctic large parts of

Greenland, including its capital city Nuuk, are located south of the Arctic Circle. While 66.33°N and 66.33°S form convenient lines for thinking about what comprises the Polar Regions, these boundaries are not absolute. Anywhere located in high northern or southern latitudes and consequently characterized by extreme seasonality might be considered "polar," especially if that is how people think about it. This flexibility inevitably creates some fuzzy areas at the edges, as demonstrated by the concept of a "Circumpolar North."[26] Should Alaska's Prince William Sound, for example, be considered part of the Arctic? What about northern Scotland? If the island of South Georgia is included in discussions of Antarctica, then why not Patagonia or Tierra del Fuego, parts of which are located at similar latitudes? Boundary issues such as these can be opportunities for exploring the interactions of culture and environment that come together to create place. The Arctic and Antarctica have never simply been points on a map, but rather cultural constructions that have changed and developed over time. Engaging with the historical complexity of the interactions between nature and culture is arguably the best approach to the problem of defining the Polar Regions.

Despite obvious differences between the histories of the Polar Regions considering the Arctic and Antarctica together can be productive. While the early human histories of the regions are very different, both raise questions about the interaction between myth and history and the cultural construction of place. Histories of sealing and whaling in the Polar Regions cannot be fully understood without thinking about interconnections between the two regions in terms of shared markets, technology transfer, and the development of a global resource frontier. From the late eighteenth century explorers often traveled to both Polar Regions in pursuit of knowledge and the common goal of "conquering nature" in its most extreme form, and they took their experiences of one place with them into the other. From the late nineteenth century the Arctic and Antarctica became sites for economic development projects at various levels of viability and often with imperial connotations; once again experiences in the far north shaped activities in the far south and vice versa. The politics of the twentieth-century Cold War encompassed both ends of the planet, with two economic systems vying with each other to demonstrate a strategic and rhetorical mastery of polar nature. In the second half of the twentieth century—as demonstrated by the connections between the *Exxon Valdez* disaster and the signing of the Madrid Environmental Protocol—environmental organizations have often thought about the Polar Regions together, at the same time as oil and mining companies have looked toward both the Arctic and Antarctica as largely untapped resources. Most recently, the Polar Regions have become central to the science and politics of global climate change as research conducted in the Arctic and Antarctica has played an important role in identifying the reality of anthropogenic climate change. In turn, the Polar Regions have come to be seen as intensely vulnerable to rising temperatures, and melting polar ice could have dire consequences for the entire planet. These connections, and many others, make a combined approach a useful way to think about the history of the Polar Regions.

Pairing the histories of the Polar Regions is not unproblematic. Politically, it is important to acknowledge that an emphasis on "bipolarity" might privilege the countries with political and scientific interests in both Polar Regions (the United States, Russia, Norway, and Britain). Culturally, there has been a general tendency to privilege the north over the south, perhaps reflecting something of a broader Northern Hemisphere literary and artistic dominance.[27] The nature writer Barry Lopez, who was captivated by the far north, for example, found himself "informed by indifference" by the McMurdo Dry Valleys of Antarctica.[28] In conflating the Polar Regions, certain environmental characteristics are privileged above others. Shared images of snow, ice, and cold trump major differences in geography, such as the fact that the Arctic is an ocean surrounded by continents and Antarctica a continent surrounded by oceans. This raises interesting questions about why different people and cultures tend to focus on certain environmental characteristics over others, but also creates a problem: environmental similarity may be assumed where it does not exist.[29]

From a social perspective there are clearly major difficulties raised by comparing the populated Arctic with the unpopulated Antarctic. As in many other parts of the world, narratives of "empty lands" and "wilderness" have frequently been used in the north rhetorically to depopulate territories and claim them for imperial powers. Care needs to be taken that a connection with unpopulated Antarctica does not simply perpetuate these strategies.[30] It is easy to label the aboriginal peoples of the Arctic as "traditional communities" or a "people without history."[31] This creates a static version of the Arctic past that a comparison with Antarctica may seem to support. In order to overcome these categories the Arctic scholars David Anderson and Mark Nuttell have suggested that the notion of "cultivated places" offers one of the best ways to think about the history of the far north.[32] This idea creates an obvious contrast with Antarctica, parts of which have never been visited by people.

These problems of juxtaposition might usefully be seen as opportunities. By recognizing that there is little inherently "natural" about studying the Polar Regions together, a comparative approach encourages connections to be made between the Arctic and Antarctica and other parts of the world. The history of indigenous peoples in the Arctic North has much in common with the history of indigenous peoples in other parts of the world, and their experiences of colonialism can usefully be thought about within the framework of settler colonial studies.[33] It is interesting, for example, to think of the Polar Regions in relation to other "frontier spaces" such as the U.S. West, Patagonia, the Russian steppe, or the Australian outback.[34] The history of science in the Polar Regions can be studied alongside the history of science in other extreme environments such as deserts, oceans, and outer space. In many cases, connections with other parts of the world make more sense than direct connections between the Arctic and Antarctica. But without starting with some form of comparative perspective, these global connections may also get overlooked.

Places for Environmental History

In the introduction to *Northscapes: History, Technology, and the Making of Northern Environments* (2013) Dolly Jørgensen and Sverker Sörlin write: "In the circumpolar north, environmental history has co-evolved with economic, diplomatic, and geo-political history to an extent that is true of few other regions in the world."[35] While the explicit exceptionalism of this argument can be challenged, Jørgensen and Sörlin make a good point that these connections are more obvious in the history of the Arctic than in many other locations. Both the Arctic and Antarctica are excellent places for "doing environmental history" for three connected reasons.[36] First, the strangeness of the Polar Regions offers new perspectives from which to view familiar subjects. Second, the role of the environment in the human history of the Arctic and Antarctica cannot be ignored. Third, as a consequence of the obvious role of the environment, the Polar Regions offer useful places for expanding our understanding of the field of environmental history beyond subjects traditionally considered "environmental." It is not only economic history, diplomatic history, or geopolitics that have "co-evolved" with environmental history, but also social history, the history of exploration, the history of science, and arguably every other historical subfield. While these connections are often difficult to notice in places where the environment is taken for granted, in the Arctic and Antarctica the polar environment intrudes quite obviously on almost every facet of human behavior. An environmental history of the Arctic and Antarctica thus has much to contribute to the theory and practice of the field more broadly.

In a classic essay on literary history, the philosopher Carlo Ginzburg discusses the intellectual strategy of "making things strange."[37] The Polar Regions offer the estrangement that Ginzburg describes. For example, while the morality of imperial claims to sovereignty over productive territory in the tropics or temperate regions is often challenged, the economic motivations for claiming land that could be used for sugar plantations or sheep stations can seem so obvious that they might be taken for granted. A similar claim to an apparently worthless swathe of territory in the Polar Regions, however, immediately raises fundamental questions about the nature of imperialism: why bother with making sovereignty claims to an unproductive expanse of ice? Similarly, the idea of "wilderness" has been extensively challenged by environmental historians in recent years, in part for its rhetorical depopulating of inhabited regions. But the fact that Antarctica and some parts of the Arctic have no permanent populations offers an opportunity to rethink some of these criticisms, and to ask whether there might be some parts of the world where genuine wilderness does in fact exist.[38] On a superficial level, the act of making things strange may appear to reinforce the idea that the Arctic and Antarctica are "Poles apart" as historian Phillip Quigg termed Antarctica.[39] But it is a strategy that relies for its utility on connections and similarities with the rest of the world, thereby undermining any notion of exceptionalism.

The Polar Regions make evident that the role of the environment in human history cannot be ignored. Writing about Antarctica, the Australian environmental historian Tom Griffiths notes: "This is a place where 'the environment' is so dominant and overwhelming that it can never be tamed or taken for granted."[40] The simple fact that people cannot survive unsupported for long in these places focuses attention on the environment. The intense seasonality of the Polar Regions imposes an obvious chronology onto the human history: in the darkness of winter, human activity has tended to be extremely limited, while summertime can bring short bursts of activity. The most interesting parts of many adventure narratives from the Arctic and Antarctica are often not the adrenaline-filled descriptions of falling into a crevasse or surviving a shipwreck, but the seemingly mundane accounts of everyday life. In these circumstances, the material environment is an ever-present reality, and the constant struggle to stay warm, get enough food, and perform basic tasks in environmental conditions that are extremely hostile to human survival provide the narrative. The material environment plays an important role in all human history, but in many places this role gets ignored and taken for granted.[41] In contrast, it is difficult to find any book written about the history of the Arctic or Antarctica that does not put some emphasis on the extreme environment and the consequences of this hostility for the people living, working, and traveling in these places.

The Polar Regions have much to contribute to ongoing debates within environmental history about the scope and definition of the field. As a consequence of the fact that the environment cannot be ignored, environmental history in the Arctic and Antarctica goes far beyond subjects that have traditionally been considered "environmental," and encompass almost every facet of human activity. For geographers and philosophers speculating about the existence of lands in the far north and the far south in a time before systematic exploration, the hostility of polar environments and their spatial locations functioned as a barrier to knowledge and allowed for an obvious blurring of myth and history. In the histories of sealing and whaling it is easy to focus attention on the environmental destruction wreaked by these often rapacious industries, but historical studies of the Arctic and Antarctica can also ask how and why environmental perceptions of the Polar Regions changed at particular points in time to help bring about the rise and fall of natural resource extraction activities. Histories of exploration are rarely presented as environmental histories, but the expeditions that traveled to the Arctic and Antarctica from the late eighteenth century provide excellent case studies of the interactions among human activity, human ideas, and the material environment, which are at the heart of the field of environmental history. Economic histories of the Polar Regions are often so obviously connected to the material environment that this fact often goes unstated: successful development projects almost always require the production of some sort of tradable commodity. The Arctic and Antarctica offer useful locations for thinking about an environmental history of the Cold War that goes beyond how conflict between communist and capitalist powers changed and damaged the environment to think about how a competition for control of the environment was at the very center of this ideological conflict.[42] Disputes between developers and environmentalists are often the subjects of what might be defined as "traditional" environmental history, but a broader definition of the field encourages a political analysis that goes much further than who is for or against the protection of the environment.

A recurrent theme in an expanded definition of environmental history is how the material environment as well as environmental perceptions fit into contests for political power. The Polar Regions offer useful locations for thinking about this question, especially in their histories of imperialism and resistance to imperialism. Since at least the late eighteenth century, imperial powers have used the idea of "improvement" to legitimate policies of occupation and control in many parts of the world.[43] The underlying assumption that the production of useful knowledge about the material environment can justify and facilitate political claims might be thought of as an assertion of "environmental authority."[44] In the Arctic, imperial powers have repeatedly sought to improve the lives of indigenous peoples through highly problematic policies of forced settlement, nontraditional education, and—at least sometimes—integration into a market economy. In Antarctica, assertions of environmental authority have focused on understanding and regulating the environment "for the good of humanity," in forms such as attempts to control the whaling industry or the production of scientific knowledge about anthropogenic climate change. In the history of the Polar Regions, resistance to environmental authority has taken many forms. In the Arctic the championing of Indigenous culture or "Traditional Ecological Knowledge," often has an explicitly anti-imperial intent. In the history of Antarctica it is possible to identify an "environmental nationalism" that rejected the notion that the production of scientific knowledge can justify political claims, and instead made use of the environment in other ways to help legitimate their own assertions of sovereignty. However, in both Polar Regions science remains the dominant paradigm, and states continue to assert their environmental authority. Thinking about connections between the material environment, environmental perceptions, and political power not only expands a definition of the field of environmental history but also provides a powerful tool for understanding contemporary power dynamics, both in the Polar Regions and beyond.

Lands of Darkness and Light

The Arctic and Antarctica are places where myth and history merge, where environmental preservation and exploitation coexist, and where repeated attempts to conquer nature have resulted in an environment that remains largely unconquered. The Polar Regions offer extreme examples of human fallibility in the exploitation and abuse of nonhuman nature, but at the same time there are episodes in the histories of the Arctic and Antarctica that offer cause for environmental optimism and hope. High latitudes have generally been peripheral to global wars and conflicts, but both the Arctic and Antarctica played important roles in the Cold War, the most threatening conflict in global history. The Arctic and Antarctica are the coldest places in the world, but in recent years they have become strongly associated with global warming through images of melting icebergs, stranded polar bears, and overheating penguins. In these and many other ways, the human histories of both the Arctic and Antarctica can be thought of as exemplifying darkness and light; these histories have been as "polarized" as their physical environments.

Contrast and contradiction are magnified by studying the two Polar Regions together. In the case of the *Exxon Valdez* oil spill, the environmental disaster in Prince William Sound led to relatively little change in the Arctic, but contributed to a radical shift in the politics and economics of the entire Antarctic continent. Similar contrasts can be identified in many other aspects of the environmental history of the Polar Regions. In the historiography of polar exploration, for example, heroic narratives from Antarctica often contradict starkly the more debased stories from the Arctic, where a lot more people died and where honesty often appeared in short supply. In the Arctic, a number of scientific research projects—especially those dealing with indigenous health—have left a deeply troubling legacy, while scientific research in Antarctica has generally been accepted as being conducted "for the good of mankind." What has proved to be the case in the Arctic has not always been true in Antarctica.

Contrast and contradiction provide a frame for this environmental history of the Polar Regions. By setting up each chapter as a dichotomy of contradicting ideas, the inherent tensions within these histories can be explored. The first chapter, "Myth and History," examines the environmental histories of the Arctic and Antarctica from prehistory roughly up to 1800. It thinks about how myths can become part of history, and how historical events and people can assume mythical status. Such blurring posits the importance of culture in the construction of place, as well as demonstrating how environmental perceptions can have powerful political significance. Chapter Two, "Scarcity and Abundance," studies diverse histories of marine resource extraction in the Polar Regions from the late eighteenth century to the twentieth century. Histories of marine resource extraction connect the Polar Regions to wider global markets, informing wider debates about resource frontiers and the tragedy of the commons.[45] These histories of sealing and whaling and other kinds of harvest in the Arctic and Antarctica also highlight the important role played by the material environment in shaping the historical development of the two Polar Regions.

Chapter Three, "Nature Conquered, Nature Unconquered," examines the history of the exploration of the Polar Regions from the mid-nineteenth century up to the early twentieth century. The history of polar exploration helps to interpret how exploration fits into the field of environmental history, by highlighting the interactions between the material environment, environmental perceptions and human activities. Constant themes in the history of exploration in both north and south during this period were nation-building and imperialism, through the idea of "conquering nature." Very often, the same people and institutions were involved in the exploration of both the Arctic and Antarctica. The histories of economic development in the Arctic and Antarctica, which are examined in Chapter Four, "Dreams and Realities," were often motivated by shared assumptions. In much the same way that histories of polar exploration were connected to the politics of imperialism, there were racialized and gendered dimensions to all of these schemes. The economic development of the Arctic and Antarctic history should be included more fully in environmental histories of imperialism.

From the mid 1940s into the 1990s, the Polar Regions played important roles in the Cold War. Chapter Five, "War and Peace," holds that the Arctic and Antarctica are informative to thinking about an environmental history of this era. At both ends of the planet, communism competed with capitalism to demonstrate a superior ability to conquer nature and assert environmental authority, and this competition had both rhetorical and geopolitical dimensions. Despite these similarities, the Cold War histories of the two Polar Regions were in other ways very different. The Arctic was the front line in the confrontation between the Soviet Union and the United States, and consequently became a highly militarized region with significant consequent environmental change. In Antarctica, in contrast, the International Geophysical Year (IGY) of 1957–58 helped lead to the signing of the 1959 Antarctic Treaty, which created a "continent dedicated to peace and science," and which offers a rare example of Soviet-American détente. These differences serve to undermine any lingering sense of political or environmental determinism associated with the environmental history of the Cold War. Chapter Six, "Preservation and Exploitation," lays out how the diplomatic and political histories of the Polar Regions have become increasingly entangled with explicitly environmental issues, taking up questions of preservation and exploitation. Resource extraction, environmentalism, climate change, and even tourism in the Polar Regions all have political implications that go beyond the question of whether you are for or against the preservation of the polar environment. Once again, the recent histories of the Arctic and Antarctica have often been quite different. But in both Polar Regions, studies of subjects that might be considered "traditional" environmental history rapidly led into other questions that reveal the expansive nature of the field and the futility of trying to put limits on what constitutes environmental history.

The conclusion, "Geographies of Despair and Hope," emphasizes contrasts and contradictions to create a space for constructive discussion. The Arctic and Antarctica have always been dynamic rather than static places; their futures abound in possibilities. The field of environmental history is rightfully proud of its activist origins, even as it moves away from many of its more dogmatic tendencies.[46] In the face of ongoing environmental crises, environmental historians continue to engage with the world and seek relevance in their work. Moving away from a good *or* bad approach to the history of the Polar Regions toward an approach that considers both the good *and* the bad together brings additional nuance and complexity to these histories. In its treatment of the Lands of Darkness and Light, this environmental history of the Polar Regions encourages an ongoing engagement with contemporary issues facing the Arctic and Antarctica, and hopes in all humility for additional answers in future.

1

MYTH AND HISTORY
The Polar Regions Up to 1800

Few things differentiate the Arctic from Antarctica more than the scale and chronological scope of their early human histories. By the year 1800, people had been living, traveling, and hunting north of the Arctic Circle for thousands of years. Only some islands, inland regions, and the extreme far north had no human populations. In contrast, the first recorded sightings of Antarctica did not take place until 1820; the size and hostility of the Southern Ocean barred the presence of people. It would not be until the middle of the twentieth century that the first permanently occupied settlements would be built on the Antarctic continent. While large parts of the Arctic therefore have a history of human occupation stretching into the deep past, at the turn of the nineteenth century the Antarctic continent remained completely unseen and unknown. A case could be made that prior to 1800, everything in Antarctica was myth while the Arctic already had a long human history.

In contemporary western culture, the word "myth" is often used to imply something that is not true while the word "history" is usually assumed to have some relationship to what actually happened. While such a distinction has been widely challenged and would not be recognized by many cultures around the world, it is a dichotomy that retains much of its power, at least in the west. Rather than suggesting a stark distinction between Arctic history and Antarctic myth, a study of the two Polar Regions up to 1800 reveals myth and history to be much more fluid than is often believed. In many parts of the Arctic, the elaborate myths that are told about a place are fundamental to the way people make sense of their environment. It makes little sense in this context to ask what is true and what is not, since myths are a fundamental part of the history. In Antarctica speculation about the existence of a southern continent existed long before the first recorded sighting, and this speculation has become part of the history. In particular, very few books on the history of Antarctica begin without some reference to the classical geographies of Aristotle and Ptolemy that hypothesized the existence of a southern continent.[1]

Myths and histories are seldom politically neutral, and the way we perceive the distant past shapes the recent past and the present. By telling stories about Greek and Roman speculation, for example, Europeans have created for themselves a longstanding connection with Antarctica that goes back more than ten times further than the continent's known existence. In the twentieth century, such a historical connection proved politically useful for the European countries that sought to assert their ownership of the southern continent. In both north and south, in the triumphalist stories of Enlightenment explorers such as Captain Cook, the act of exploration is presented as the replacing of the unknown with the known, myth with history. Over time, however, the historical deeds of these explorers often become myths in their own right through frequent retelling and embellishment.[2] In the Arctic, European colonialism often began with the appropriation of indigenous myths. Colonial anthropologists such as Knud Rasmussen sought to rationalize and make sense of Arctic belief systems, rather than taking them purely on their own terms. Colonial powers sought to replace indigenous myths with supposed Christian and scientific truths, thereby creating disconnects with place and the environment and facilitating land removal and political control. Historical resistance to such a process has often focused not on direct competition, but on the perpetuation and valorization of the myths that connect people to the land.

The blurring of myth and history has important implications for the field of environmental history. It highlights the importance of perception in human interaction with the natural world. In seeking to understand the role of the environment in human history, environmental historians have tended to privilege the place of scientific understanding over other ways of making sense of the natural world. Modern scientific understanding of climate change and ice ages, for example, are used to explain how people first arrived in Arctic North America. While there is certainly nothing wrong with this approach, it is important to acknowledge that it is neither fully objective, nor politically neutral. Although tremendously powerful, science offers just one way among many of making sense of the natural world. The early human history of the Polar Regions offers a useful reminder that history—including the history of science—can become myth as easily as myth can become history. This in turn calls for a degree of humility in the way we go about seeking to understand the past.

One of the recurring themes associated with attempts to integrate human history with an understanding of the natural world is the idea of environmental determinism.[3] In this reading, the environment becomes the all-powerful determinant of what happens in human history. The history of Norse settlers in Greenland offers one of the most debated case studies of environmentally induced "collapse."[4] On the one hand, there is much that is compelling in placing such a heavy emphasis on the role of the environment: it would seem to make sense, for example, that as the climate cooled in the fourteenth century life got a lot harder for the communities living in southern Greenland. On the other hand, an overemphasis on the causal power of the environment can obscure the complex interplay among environmental perceptions, human actions, and the material environment. In the case of Greenland, a careful examination suggests that multiple factors played into the abandonment of the settlement. Environmental determinism can remove human agency from history, often with racial and colonial undertones. Emphasizing the role played by human perceptions through myths and histories sets up a more dynamic, and arguably much more interesting, approach to the environmental histories of the Arctic and Antarctica.

Inuit Creation Myths

Early in the twentieth century an Iglulik Inuit named Ivaluardjuk living in the far north of Canada told a story about the creation of the world:

During the first period after the creation of the earth, all was darkness. Among the earliest living beings were the raven and the fox. One day they met, and fell into talk, as follows: "Let us keep the dark and be without daylight," said the fox. But the raven answered: "May the light come and daylight alternate with the dark of night." The raven kept on shrieking: "qa·›rn, qa·›rn!" ... And at the raven's cry light came, and day began to alternate with light.[5]

In this particular story, light came from darkness, not as the result of some elemental struggle between good and evil, or at the will of some omnipotent god, but as a consequence of an altercation between a fox and a raven. Besides its obvious anthropomorphism, the story is perhaps most notable for its somewhat mundane quality: in Ivaluardkuk's telling, there is nothing particularly spectacular about the creation of the world and the origins of darkness and light.[6]

The Arctic environment had a bearing on how stories such as Ivaluardjuk's were told. During the active months of summer there were fewer opportunities for community storytelling with people scattered in different directions.[7] But during the darkness of the polar night there was plenty of time for such entertainment. Many of the elaborate oral cultures of the Inuit developed sitting around blubber lanterns in *iglu*, typically built of rocks, earth, and driftwood. Despite people's intimate familiarity with winter darkness and the several attractions of this time of year, the polar night could be a deeply depressing time.[8] People were cut off from the vitamin-enhancing rays of the sun and deprived of many of the activities of summer. In these conditions, the telling of stories was crucial to people's ability to get through the winter. They also created community through the sharing of common values. As a consequence of the important role played by oral culture, storytellers occupied an important place in the community, and were often associated with shamanism.

At the same time as the Arctic environment shaped the way stories were told, the stories themselves were filled with descriptions of the natural environment and explanations for how it came to be. Cold, snow, and ice fill the stories, and Arctic animals populate the landscape. In these narratives, people are very much part of this environment and there is little conception of a stark division between humans and nature.

In the middle of his story about the fox and the raven Ivaluardjuk interrupted the narrative to explain: "Eskimos interpret the cry of the raven qa·›rn, roughly as qa·›q, which means dawn and light." This interjection gives the story a "just so" quality of accounting for why things are as they are in the natural world. The anthropomorphizing was not uncommon, which is in keeping with wider beliefs of environmental harmony and reciprocity.[9]

The man who recorded Ivaluardjuk's story was the famous Danish anthropologist and explorer Knud Rasmussen, known to some as the "father of Eskimotology."[10] At the time, Rasmussen was near the beginning of his famous Fifth Thule Expedition from 1921 to 1924, which traveled 20,000 miles across northern North America over a three-and-a-half year period, visiting almost every significant Inuit community en route. Rasmussen had been born in 1879 in the West Greenlandic town of Ilusissat, then known as Jacobshavn. His father was a Danish missionary, and his mother was one-quarter Inuit. He grew up speaking Kalaallisut, the Greenlandic dialect of Inuit, and his partial Inuit heritage was something Rasmussen would later be very proud of. His linguistic ability and cultural affinity for the Greenlandic people helped to give him entry into the lives of the northern peoples.

Rasmussen had got his start in polar exploration as a member of Mylius-Erichson's poorly funded and badly planned Danish Literary Expedition to the Cape York district in the far north of Greenland from 1902 to 1904. Cut off from the rest of the island by the ice sheet, this area remained largely isolated from wider Greenlandic culture, and outside Danish colonial control. Rasmussen was struck by the fact that the "Polar Eskimos" spoke more or less the same language that he had grown up speaking further to the south, and he immediately developed an emotional connection to the people who formed the most northerly community anywhere in the world. Over the years that followed Rasmussen returned on numerous occasions to the Cape York region. "No hunter exists up there," he could boast, "with whom I have not hunted, and there is hardly a child whose name I do not know."[11] He helped to establish a Christian mission, and then set up a trading station, which he named Thule, taking the classical Greek name for the most faraway place in the world.

Rasumussen saw his work as having the colonial purpose of securing

Figure 1 and Figure 2   *Anguisinaog, storyteller from Baille Island, and poster of Rasmussen speaking event (Source: American Geographical Society Library [(47a) 523 No. 12145 S])*

the far north of Greenland for Denmark in the face of interest from the United States, Germany, and Norway. His attitude toward the Inuit was shaped by a benevolent paternalism, and he believed that the Danes would be the best protectors of the native peoples of the Arctic. Exploration and discovery were important justifications for sovereignty, and Rasmussen used the profits from the trading station to fund expeditions around northern Greenland, which become known as the Thule Expeditions. The Fifth Thule expedition, in which the meeting with Ivaluardjuk took place, was his first venture into Arctic North America. With the aid of his fellow scientists Kaj Birkett-Smith, Therkel Mathiassen, and Peter Freuchen, and a group of Greenlandic assistants that included the seamstress Anarulunguaq and her cousin Miteq, Rasmussen's ambitious aim was to study "the great primary problem of the origin of the Eskimo race."[12]

By putting himself in the same environmental conditions as his research subjects, Rasmussen the anthropologist assumed for himself a privileged position from which to understand and interpret Eskimo myths. He became an expert in the eyes of many of his readers because he had been there and lived for an extended period of time with the people he studied. His mixed background, and his willingness to endure the everyday hardships of Arctic life over a sustained period, to some extent overcame the insider-outsider dichotomy. He became something of a go-between, helping to create, at least temporarily, a middle ground between Danish and Inuit culture.[13] In his writings, Rasmussen frequently lamented many elements of the onset of modernity into the Arctic. But he seemed largely oblivious to the fact that his own activities were partly responsible for facilitating this transition. In particular, the arrival of the Christian faith through missions such as Rasmussen's created a crisis of authority within traditional belief systems by demanding an immediate end to traditional practices.[14] Rasmussen sought purity in the Arctic, and was disappointed when he did not find it: "I had expected to find these people living in quite a primitive state," he wrote of the Caribou Eskimo, "and in this respect, was disappointed beyond measure."[15] Similar desires to find an untouched purity in polar landscapes would later be taken up by environmentalists and environmental organizations with an interest in protecting both the Arctic and Antarctica.[16]

In the years that followed Rasmussen's pioneering expedition, the discipline of anthropology as it existed in the early twentieth century has come in for sustained criticism for its implicit racism and associations with imperialism.[17] "Traditionally, Western scholars have done fieldwork in order to study 'the other' and they have used bilingual interpreter/translators to analyze the material they have gathered," writes Yupiaq scholar George P. Kanaqlak Charles, "then they have looked upon the persons as the object of their research and not as authorities of their own culture."[18] Taken out of their context, stories like Ivaluardjuk's account of the creation of light and darkness can become meaningless parodies of the Inuit worldview.[19] In particular, a textual rendition largely severs the connection with place and environment that is so vital for making sense of the story.

While the work of Knud Rasmussen, and other anthropologists working in the Arctic such as Franz Boas, should certainly be given some credit for helping to preserve the oral culture of the Inuit, their primary aim was not to collect these stories for their own sake. Instead, Rasmussen and other academics sought to use these stories to learn about the Inuit. He viewed their religious beliefs as a response to the harsh environment and rationalized Inuit mythology as "faith out of fear."[20] In particular Rasmussen sought to use the stories to learn something about the scientific origins of the Inuit people. He recounted a number of other creation stories from different parts of the Arctic, which bore a marked similarity to Ivaluardjuk's tale of the fox and the raven. In the region of northern Canada he labeled the Barren Lands, for example, Rasmussen wrote down a story of a fox and a raven leading to the creation of the world.[21] In this telling, the fox wanted continued darkness so that he could continue to hunt by night. As trickster figures, the Fox and Raven feature prominently in numerous creation stories across the Arctic and sub-Arctic North.[22]

By putting together as much evidence as possible from stories like Ivaluardjuk's, as well as from linguistic differences, social customs, and material culture (they collected 20,000 artifacts),[23] the Fifth Thule Expedition's study of language and folklore contributed to what might be thought of as a modern, scientific creation myth of the Inuit. Rasmussen showed that there were remarkably strong linguistic and cultural similarities between the people he met living in Greenland, Canada, and Alaska. This made the Inuit the most dispersed indigenous people of a homogenous culture anywhere in the world.[24] Cultural and linguistic unity also suggested a common origin. Building on the work of H. P. Steensby, Rasmussen himself believed that cultural and linguistic differences between the Inuit peoples living in the interior and those on the coast revealed that they had originally come from Native American Indians living in the interior of North America.[25] The fact, for example, that the inland tribes had no knowledge of coastal ways of life suggested to Rasmussen that Inuit must have migrated to the coastline from the continental interior.

Rasmussen's ideas in some ways challenged the dominant nineteenth-century belief that the Inuit were remnants of an ancient Stone Age culture that had been living in the Arctic since time immemorial.[26] Writing in *My Life With the Eskimo*, for example, the explorer and anthropologist Vilhjalmur Stefansson noted:

Their existence on the same continent as our populous cities was an anachronism of ten thousand years in intelligence and material development. They gathered their food with weapons of the men of the Stone Age, they thought their simple, primitive thoughts and lived their insecure and tense lives—lives that were to me the mirrors of the lives of our far ancestors whose bones and crude handiwork we now and then discover in river gravels or in prehistoric caves.[27]

The findings of the Fifth Thule Expedition suggested that Inuit society was much more dynamic and more recent than Stefansson proposed. But in other ways the findings of Rasmussen's expedition fitted with a widespread belief at the time that nobody would want to live in such an extreme environment and so must have been forced there by more aggressive peoples to the south: "Nothing short of persecution," wrote the British Arctic explorer John Barrow in 1846, "could have driven them to take up their abode in these extreme parts of the globe."[28]

The most sophisticated presentation of the results of Rasmussen's expedition came from the archeologist Therkel Mathiassen. The Fifth Thule Expedition identified the remains of a "Thule Culture," which was richer, more sophisticated, and more uniform than the people they encountered.[29] Mathiassen proposed the Inuit had moved eastward across the North American Arctic and into Greenland from coastal Alaska starting roughly one thousand years ago from a homeland in the Bering Straits region. This relatively recent migration accounted for the fact that there had been relatively little time for linguistic change and the Inuit of Greenland could understand the Inuit of Alaska. Mathiassen's theory presented a picture of a dynamic society taking advantage of the abundance of the Arctic, rather than being forced to live in the region against their will.[30] His ideas also raised interesting questions about what had caused the apparent cultural decline of Inuit communities in their recent history.

In the decades that followed the Fifth Thule Expedition, however, archeologists turned back to the nineteenth-century idea of a longterm occupation of the Arctic by the Inuit. This was driven by the discovery of archeological remains described as "paleo-Eskimo" dating back at least several thousand years.[31] The term "paleo-Eskimo," however, is now thought to be erroneous, since these cultures were probably culturally and linguistically distinct.[32] Today it is believed that these remains came from the Tuniit peoples who became the first permanent and widespread occupants of the Arctic around 5,000 years ago.[33] Archeological evidence suggests that these people came from the region between Lake Baikal and Chukotka in Siberia.[34] They most likely crossed the Bering Sea on the shifting winter sea ice.[35] The Tuniit developed into the so-called Dorset Culture, which flourished from 500

BCE to CE 1500, hunting seals and walrus. Their lives may have been made more difficult by the medieval warm period melting sea ice where they hunted seals, although one Tuniit group survived on Southampton Island until the early twentieth century.[36]

The discovery of more information about the Tuniit has allowed for a revival of Therkel Mathiassen's theory that the Inuit arrived in the Arctic about a thousand years ago and fairly rapidly displaced the people they found living there as a result of powerful Mongolian-style recurved bows, and the consequent ability to hunt a wider range of animals. In recent years the question has turned to what drove the Inuit's eastward migration. One theory is that environmental factors drove the Inuit to follow the migration of the bowhead whales. The archeologist Robert McGee challenges this theory by arguing that sea-ice conditions still formed a 600-mile barrier between the western and eastern Canadian Arctic, which the bowhead whales would not have been able to cross.[37] And he particularly rejects the idea that humans behave in the deterministic fashion implied by this theory.[38] Instead of focusing on simple environmental causation, McGee proposes that the pursuit of iron and iron ore drove the Inuit eastwards. The ancestors of the Inuit were the "Old Bering Strait people," who controlled the iron trade across the Bering Straits. When it became obvious that other sources of iron existed to the east they set out to find them. In this way it may even have been the presence of the Norse in Greenland that stimulated Inuit migration toward that island.

The important point, however, is not the teleological debunking of one scientific theory of Inuit origins with another, but to suggest a more complex interplay between myth and history. A scientific approach to the question of origins is in some ways antithetical to the stories told by the indigenous peoples of the Arctic. The modern idea of eastward migration from Asia has been challenged by some Native American scholars as disrespectful to their own creation stories of American origin.[39] But other indigenous communities apparently see little contradiction, and maps of eastward migration feature prominently in the displays of a number of northern museums after consultation with Alaska Native communities.[40] As important components of the stories told about place and identity, scientific theories themselves can be thought of as powerful creation myths, and these too change over time.

An Anti-Arctic

In much the same way that Rasmussen turned to the classical world for the name "Thule" for his northern trading station, European scholars have turned to Greece and Rome to create a prehistory of Antarctica. Writing less than two decades before Rasmussen, the librarian of England's Royal Geographical Society, Hugh Robert Mill, elaborated these ideas in his history of Antarctica titled *Siege of the South Pole*:

> At the dawn of geographical history an Antarctic problem was impossible because the Earth was viewed as a flat disc girdled by the Ocean River and bounded by darkness. Curiously enough the name became possible before the idea. When the early Greek students of the stars, looking out hour after hour and night after night on the wheeling vault overhead, classified the brightest points into groups of constellations they named the most conspicuous of these which never set *Arctos*—the Bear—and the point round which it, in common with the rest of the heavenly host, appeared to turn was called the Arctic pole. The natural antithesis of an Antarctic pole of the heavens, that is a fixed point opposite the Arctic, must have occurred to many minds, for it was easy in imagination to complete the sphere of the celestial vault, traced out in part by the unseen portion of the circuit of the stars, but the flat cake of the habitable world stretched between, separating the domain of light and possible knowledge from that of darkness and the unknowable.[41]

Mill's poetic language functions to set up a creation myth for the Antarctic continent, based on a combination of ancient ideas and geographical speculation. It is interesting to note that in Mill's telling these classical ideas also involved a separation of darkness from light similar to that described by Ivaluardjuk in a very different context.

Building on the notion of an anti-Arctic, Mill sought to "show how the mind of all ages has exercised itself upon this particular problem."[42] The Pythagorean philosophers of early classical Greece world focused their thinking on the idea of balance. They believed that the world was spherical because the sphere was the most perfect form. If the world were round, then "symmetry demanded other worlds breaking up the dreary voids of ocean on which the mind could not otherwise dwell in comfort."[43] The philosopher Aristotle was unsatisfied with speculation based on ideas of perfection, and he sought proofs for the idea that the world was round. These he found in the fact that objects fell towards a common center; there was a circular shadow on the moon during an eclipse; and familiar stars fell out of view when traveling from north to south. With the world established as spherical, the question now became how big the globe was, and was it possible to reach Antarctica? This invoked questions about the nature and extent of the oceans. Mill suggested that the famous world map of the Alexandrian geographer Ptolemy made a significant mistake by assuming a theory of continuous land, labeled as *Terra Incognita*.

Mill was not the first scholar to connect Antarctica to the speculative geography of the ancients, but his book did present a particularly systematic overview of this connection. Since the publication of *The Siege of the South Pole*, almost without exception, general histories of Antarctica begin with a reference to the classical world and to the idea of a balanced "Anti-Arctic."[44] Over time, repetition has created a powerful origin myth for Antarctica, and this story has played an important role in the continent's more recent history.

Two things stand out in the stories told about Antarctica's origin myths. Most obviously, they involve some reference to the Arctic, creating a primordial connection between the two Polar Regions. Early Greek beliefs about the Arctic had focused on the cold boreal winds coming from the north. According to classical myth, these winds came from the Rhipaean Mountains (thought now to be a conflation of the Caucus, Carpathian, and Altai mountain ranges).[45] Beyond the Rhipaean winds was a paradise inhabited by people known as Hyperboreans, who lived unaffected by the boreal winds. The first account we have of travel toward the Arctic north comes from the Greek astronomer and geographer Pytheas from the colony of Massilia (Marseilles). He reported seeing land six days north of Britain, which he labeled Thule. A day further north he came across an impenetrable barrier of sea, earth, and sky, which he labeled Sea Lung. Although it is unlikely that we will ever know the precise location of Pytheas' Thule—speculation focuses on Iceland, the Orkney and Shetland Islands, and the west coast of Norway—the name stuck as a convenient was of referring to land at the far extreme of the world.[46] Centuries later, one of the first places to be named in Antarctica, an island in the South Sandwich Islands, would be given the name Southern Thule by Captain Cook.

A little more subtly, by privileging Greece and Rome in the origins of Antarctica, these stories immediately place the southern continent within the framework of traditional European history. Despite being half a world away from the icy wastes of Antarctica, Europe is placed by the creation myths at the center of Antarctica's history, almost two thousand years before its first recorded sighting. Mill wrote *Siege of the South Pole* with the explicit aim of promoting British efforts within the so-called heroic era of Antarctic exploration. His classical references provided language and structure for accounts of this exploration. In Antarctica, the explorers themselves interpreted their experiences in classical terms. The stories they told upon their return were written in the epic style of the *Iliad* and *Odyssey* as demonstrated by books such as Apsley Cherry-Garrard's *The Worst Journey in the World* (1922) and Frank Hurley's *Argonauts of the South* (1925).[47] The "tragedy" of Captain Scott epitomized these classical references. This was a period where teaching of the classics dominated the curriculum of Britain's elite public schools. Myths and histories from Greece and Rome were seen as an ideal preparation for a career in imperial administration. As a consequence, modern stories from Antarctica had a particular resonance for schoolboys raised on a diet of classical scholarship.[48]

The heroic era was an important stimulus to the imperial carve-up of the Antarctic continent that took place in the years immediately following the publication of Mill's history. In 1908 Britain made a claim to the Peninsula Region of Antarctica directly to the south of South America. This territory became known to the British as the "Falkland Islands Dependencies," and its boundaries—stretching all the way to the South Pole—were clarified in 1917. Britain's claim was followed by assertions of sovereignty over other parts of the continent by New Zealand in 1923, France in 1924, Australia in 1933, and Norway in 1939. In the Peninsula region, Argentina and Chile rejected British sovereignty claims and asserted their own longstanding rights to sovereignty that had been inherited from the Spanish empire. All seven claimant countries could draw upon some connection with the classical past, although this association was made most strongly by Britain and the imperial dominions of New Zealand and Australia. Classical scholarship demonstrated a historical connection to justify this political interest.

Beyond the political bias implicit in Antarctica's classically based creation myths there are a number of other problems with the frequent retellings. These stories are almost the very definition of a teleological, backwards reading of history: we only repeat them because they seem—purely by chance—to have been correct in the belief that there is land in the far south. Mill admits fully to this teleology: "The narrative is not critically exact, for it claims only to afford a basis on which the efforts of modern explorers may be seen in their relation to the gradual unfolding of human knowledge regarding the earth."[49] By focusing only on what we want to see, a teleological reading does little to engage with what these classical scholars were really thinking. In an essay on the origins of the idea of the Antipodes the scholar Avan Judd Stallard argues that the ideas of symmetry or balance leading to a belief in an Antipodes or anti-Arctic simply cannot be found in Greek texts. "Belief that the Antipodes were originally posited either because the Greeks subscribed to a principle of cosmographic symmetry or because they believed the lands in the northern hemisphere must necessarily be balanced by an equal quantity of land in the southern hemisphere," he writes, "is widespread amongst historians and readers alike. These are, however, assumptions of modern scholars, irredeemably at odds with extant evidence."[50]

A focus on classical speculation also privileges learning from the western tradition over the myths and histories told by the people living in closer proximity to the South Pole. As the literary scholar Elizabeth Leane demonstrates, Australian Aborigines, the Maori people of New Zealand, and the indigenous tribes of southern South America told themselves stories of what might lay to the south.[51] Caution is needed when removing these stories from their context, as with their northern counterparts. But in overlooking alternative Antarctic creation myths, we are missing out on a valuable store of cultural knowledge. The Maoris, for example, likely made fairly frequent visits to sub-Antarctic islands such as Campbell Island.[52] Unlike the Greeks and Romans, who could have no way of basing their stories in reality ("the speculations of the Pythagorean philosophers were not restrained by trammels of fact or experience," wrote Mill poetically), the people of the southern hemisphere could see the seas and experience the weather that came from the south. The famous *Sudestada* wind that brought an icy chill to the residents of Buenos Aires was known even to Europeans long before anyone recorded sighting Antarctica.

Such alternative creation stories are themselves not without political implications. There was a brief moment in the early 1970s when Chilean archeologists thought they might have found indigenous remains from Patagonia in the South Shetland Islands.[53] Further investigation, however, revealed that these finds were not authentic and must have been introduced from outside. While the Chilean discovery may have been false, the brief excitement it generated reveals the political power of origin myths, which in turn connects to recent history. Given the contemporary political situation of Antarctica, it should come as no surprise that the dominant narrative privileges an origin myth that reinforces the political status quo. This tends to exclude cultures with more of a direct physical connection to the southern continent.

Norse in Greenland

Another powerful connection between Europe and the Polar Regions comes through the history of the Scandinavian Norse.[54] In contrast to the geographers of Greece and Rome, who generally experienced the Polar Regions from a significant distance, the Norse had a direct connection with the material environment of the Arctic North. From the late eighth century CE, the Norse began a series of maritime expeditions outward from Scandinavia across the Baltic, toward the British Isles and into the Arctic. These expeditions took place on the famous longboats, developed for transportation around the rocky coastlines of Norway, which enabled them to survive long journeys across stormy seas and oceans. Initially, the purpose of these expeditions was to raid towns and monasteries for treasure, earning the name "Vikings," the Norse word for raiders. But over time, the Norse began to make their homes in a number of the regions they came across on their travels. Colonists from the region that is today Norway began to settle the Faeroe Islands shortly after 800 CE, Iceland around 870 CE, Greenland around 980 CE, and even the northwest coast of North America around 1000 CE.[55] Although the American colony at Vinland barely lasted twenty years as a result of conflict with Native Americans, the other settlements became stable communities. The Norse took grazing animals with them and retained fairly extensive trading connections with the Norwegian coast and other parts of the Norse world.

The Norse developed an elaborate set of myths and histories that told the stories of their expansion and colonization. These epic stories of gods and men came to be known as sagas, and constitute a highly sophisticated literary genre. The Norse diaspora was developing into literate cultures, especially after conversion to Christianity, and the written texts provide a fascinating insight into their worldview. The Norse sagas reveal an intimate relationship with the Arctic and sub-Arctic environment. Environmental knowledge was vital for survival, as demonstrated by the need to understand ocean currents and weather for successful navigation. At the same time, the sagas imbued the northern environment with stories that created a sense of shared identity: these were Norse landscapes. In *Iceland Imagined* (2011) Karen Oslund shows how these myths and legends have resonated through history and continue to shape contemporary reality in Iceland, Greenland, and the Faeroe Islands.[56]

Norse expansion into the Arctic and sub-Arctic north unsettles a rigid insider/outsider dichotomy in the history of the region. In Greenland the Norse settled two fjordland regions: the East Settlement on the southern tip of the island, and the West Settlement in the southwest (where the modern capital Nuuk is located). Although the Norse encountered remains of past human occupation, initially at least they did not encounter Inuit. Archeologists suggest that parts of Greenland had first been settled around 2,500 BCE.[57] These settlements lasted for around one thousand years before declining or disappearing. Subsequent human interaction with the island was characterized by the coming and going of different groups of people, which was likely connected to changes in climate and the related availability of animals to hunt for food. The Norse settlements of 980 CE were just the latest of a long series of migrations, and, like others, took place in a period of relatively benign climate. The subsequent longevity of the Norse settlements—they lasted for almost 500 years—created a strong cultural connection between Greenland and Scandinavia and gives an insider status to people of European origins.

As well as offering an important connection between Europe and the Polar Regions, the story of the Norse settlement of Greenland also provides an intriguing mystery that has fascinated historians for generations. After existing for almost half a millennia, the Norse settlements in Greenland ceased to exist sometime in the fifteenth century. When Europeans returned to southern and southwestern Greenland in the centuries that followed, all that remained were ruins. What caused this disappearance, and what form did it take? The American Arctic explorer Isaac Hayes, for example, led an expedition to Greenland in the late 1860s that took an interest in the Norse remains; in 1927, William H. Hobbs, an American polar expert, sought to investigate the disappearance of the Greenland Norse in greater detail (Figure 3). These questions have held particular appeal for scholars who have sought to integrate the environment into human history, since it is often believed that the material environment played an important role in this decline, to the extent that some believe that Norse Greenland suffered an "environmentally triggered collapse."[58] An examination of the attempts to answer these questions suggests that myth and history continue to go hand in hand, even in some of the most recent historiography.

In his book *Collapse: How Societies Choose to Fail or Succeed*, the geographer and ecologically minded historian Jared Diamond uses Norse Greenland as his "most complex case of a prehistoric collapse," adding that it is "the one for which we have the most information."[59] In his extended discussion, Diamond compares Norse Greenland with other Norse colonies that did not experience collapse, such as Iceland and the Faeroe Islands. Although acknowledging that there are not enough examples for a statistically significant "natural experiment in history," he still sees value in a comparative approach. "Differing outcomes," Diamond writes, "are clearly related to environmental difference among the colonies."[60]

Diamond is often accused of placing too much emphasis on the role of the material environment in human history, to the extent of being an environmental determinist.[61] While this is a case that can certainly be made against his earlier book *Guns, Germs, and Steel* (which also contains a discussion of Greenland), the argument he makes in *Collapse* is somewhat more sophisticated. His subtitle—*How Societies Choose to Fail*

Figure 3 and Figure 4 *[Left] Norse remains photographed during Isaac Hayes expedition of 1869. [Right] Norse Ruins in Greenland photographed by Fred Hery, photographer for the William H. Hobbs expedition to Greenland, 1927. (Source: American Geographical Society Library) [47bl) 5501 No.10216 L; (47bl) 5501 No. 14509 S]*

or Succeed—suggests an important role for human agency in response to environmental conditions. In his discussion of Greenland, Diamond expressly rejects the overly simplistic notion that "It got too cold, and they died out."[62] Instead he suggests five ultimate reasons for Norse decline, which in turn relate to the central arguments in his book: Norse impact on the environment, climate change, decline in friendly contact with Norway, increase in hostile contact with Inuit, and the conservative outlook of the Norse. Diamond's list of causal factors emphasizes the environment. Climatic cooling from around 1400 onward, for example, and the corresponding increase of sea ice, was largely responsible for the decline in trade and contact with other parts of the Norse world; the introduction of sheep and other grazing animals exacerbated soil erosion to the detriment of food production. But there is also room for culture in Diamond's analysis, as demonstrated by his discussion of the conservative worldview of the Greenland Norse. It is possible to imagine a scenario, Diamond suggests, where the Norse responded differently and more successfully to a changing environment: they could, for example, have eaten more fish or learned from the Inuit how to hunt ringed seals and whales. In Diamond's view, the Greenland Norse could have survived, and for him this is a cause for optimism despite the fact that they apparently chose not to.[63]

Even though Diamond moves away from an overly deterministic environmental causation in his analysis of societal collapse, his ideas have still come in for sustained criticism. In their book *Questioning Collapse: Human Resilience, Ecological Vulnerability, and the Aftermath of Empire* (2010) editors Patricia McAnany and Norman Yoffee bring together a series of essays that question Diamond's collapse thesis. An argument that runs throughout the collection is the notion that success and failure are inappropriate categories by which to judge human history. "Even examples of societal collapse such as Norse Greenland," the editors write in the introduction, "are also cases of societal resilience when examined carefully."[64] There is a tendency to see abandoned ruins as the mark of societal failure, when in reality moving on and leaving can "be just as accurately viewed as part of a successful strategy of survival."[65] They argue that the notion of "ecocide," and societies choosing to fail, really makes little sense in the face of historical complexity.

In the chapter of *Questioning Collapse* directly addressing Diamond's Greenland case study, Joel Berglund, a former vice-director of the Greenland National Museum and Archives in Nuuk, builds on the argument that the Greenland Norse did not choose to fail.[66] In particular, he presents a range of evidence to counter Diamond's assertion that the Greenland Norse were a conservative society that was unable to adapt to a changing environment. According to Berglund, for example, radio-isotope analysis reveals that the Norse did eat fish and other seafood, undercutting Diamond's accusation about conservatism.[67] Berglund also challenges Diamond's idea of a rapid and traumatic collapse, suggesting that archeological evidence points to a "gradual and leisurely depopulation."[68]

While the arguments against Jared Diamond's collapse thesis have much to commend them, there is also a sense that they evade a central question: what did happen to the Greenland Norse? In the eyes of professional historians, archeologists, and anthropologists, one of Diamond's greatest mistakes is to go too far in his speculation about a fairly rapid and unpleasant societal collapse at some point in the fifteenth century. By going beyond the available evidence Diamond loses some of his academic credibility. But Diamond is careful to say when he is speculating, and by seeking to address the proximate causes of Norse Greenland "collapse" he is asking a question that his popular readership know is important. His critics raise important points about the semantics of words such as "collapse," "decline," "resilience," and "survival," but such an emphasis will never have the same popular appeal as an attempt to address the central question: what actually happened?

A more serious problem with Diamond's analysis than his honest speculation is his tendency to oversimplification. This is revealed by a fondness for lists, and his explanation for the ultimate causes of the decline of the Greenland Norse is reduced to just five factors. The problem with this claim is that it fails to take into consideration the multiple possible factors that might have caused the abandonment of Norse Greenland that are contained with the interactions among human activity, environmental perceptions, and the material environment. There is certainly a need for some degree of simplification in any form of historical analysis, but Diamond arguably goes too far. Did disease play a role in the demise of the Greenland Norse? What about social divisions and unrest? Did fatalism creep into a society cut off for so long from its connections to Europe? These questions, and numerous others like them, fade into the background if the focus is on just five overarching factors. A better approach might be to expand the terms of the debate to show that the abandonment of Norse Greenland and the debates that have followed offer powerful examples of the mixture of myth and history in the environmental history of the Polar Regions.

Terra Australis Incognita

The European Enlightenment of the seventeenth and eighteenth centuries defined itself in direct opposition to myth and superstition. Enlightened thinkers viewed human reason as holding the key to understanding the world and they exhibited a barely restrained hostility toward supposedly more primitive beliefs. Religion—at least in its more traditional forms—was seen as unreasonable and harmful to society, and religious institutions were generally held in disdain. As the historian Richard Drayton showed in *Nature's Government* (2000), a study of European botanic gardens, the idea of improvement was central to Enlightenment thought, and its proponents sought to make the world a better place through observation, categorization, and rational analysis.[69] Although not fully formed, the scientific method offered a powerful tool for understanding and controlling the material world. This notion of control was inextricably connected to the history of European empires, and the claim that knowledge equals power became an unofficial slogan of the age. Where other belief systems embedded humans within nature, the Enlightenment (perhaps building on a Judeo-Christian tradition) tended to create a dichotomy that placed people over and above the rest of the material world.[70]

Within the broader context of Enlightenment, the act of exploration held obvious attractions. Explorers sought to fill in gaps on maps of the world, replacing the unknown with the known. Expeditions introduced scientists to new places, raised interesting questions, and provided data for understanding the natural environment. This knowledge could then be put to work improving the world through activities such as economic botany and geology, laying the foundations for assertions of environmental authority. At the same time as it captured the rational spirit of the age, Enlightenment exploration retained a significant sense of adventure. The risks of sailing into the unknown were very real, and shipwrecks, disease, and hostile contact with local people were common. For at least some of the people who took part in these expeditions—and many more among the interested publics back home—the risks were very much part of the attraction. The combination of rational exploration and adventure created a heady cocktail that proved particularly attractive to European imperial powers of the late seventeenth and eighteenth centuries.[71] Exploration offered a sphere for imperial competition that could substitute, at least some of the time, for armed confrontation.

Toward the end of the eighteenth century, the Polar Regions were two of the largest remaining blank spaces on European maps of the world. In the north, the Arctic was not completely unknown. Since the sixteenth century, European whalers had been making forays into the waters of the Arctic region around Spitsbergen, Greenland, and into the Barents Sea. Along with whale blubber and baleen they brought back geographical information about the environments where they hunted. Some of the coastlines of northeastern Canada had been partially charted by British and French explorers. Britain's Hudson's Bay Company was founded in 1670 to promote the fur trade. While significant gaps remained in the European understanding of the Arctic environment, enough was known by the end of the eighteenth century for naturalists to realize that it was characterized by ice, snow, storms, and intense seasonality.

In contrast to the basic knowledge of parts of the Arctic, Europeans knew almost nothing about Antarctica until the late eighteenth century, and even then major questions remained. Nobody knew for certain whether Antarctica was a continental landmass or just a vast ocean scattered with islands, and nobody really had any idea of exactly what the environment was like. As late as 1819, the Russian explorer Thaddeus Von Bellingshausen could sail southward toward a hypothetical southern continent with detailed instructions about how he should treat the native peoples he encountered.[72] It was no coincidence that the name of this unknown southern land often bore the Latin name Terra Australis Incognita, since it built on the classical speculation about the existence of an unknown southern continent. Implicit in the name was the belief that land would be found in the far south. While Antarctica remained unknown, myth and fantasy could flourish, which in turn motivated exploration.

From the late seventeenth century onward, a number of expeditions sailed southwards in search of Terra Australis Incognita, and other information from the south of the world.[73] Between 1699–1700 the British scientist Edmund Halley sailed into the South Atlantic to make magnetic readings that could help with navigation and expand knowledge about the physics of the earth. His ship, the *Paramour*, reached 52° S, a latitude where the effects of the Antarctic climate could already be felt. In the late 1760s, the French naval captain Louis de Bougainville circumnavigated the world and added speculation about the existence of a southern continent. In the early 1770s, another French explorer, Yves-Joseph de Kerguelen, set out with the explicit goal of proving the existence of a southern continent. He discovered an island in the southern Indian Ocean that today bears his name. But when he made claims that he had discovered a Terra Australis, which went far beyond the actual evidence, he was punished for his mendacity and imprisoned by the French king.

The most famous explorer in the English-speaking world to head southward during the age of enlightened exploration was the British Royal Navy's Captain James Cook.[74] Between 1768 and his death in

Hawaii in 1779, Cook led three major exploring expeditions. Although mostly focused on the Pacific Ocean, these were truly global endeavors, taking Cook toward the Arctic north and the Antarctic south. In Alaska, Cook Inlet bears his name, and he is commemorated by a statue in Anchorage and by the city's famous Captain Cook Hotel. But it is probably for his discoveries in the South Pacific that Cook is best remembered. In Australia, he discovered Botany Bay and charted much of the east coast. In New Zealand he mapped most of the coastline, described the environment, and wrote with a sense of wonder about the dawn chorus of native birds. While these discoveries and extensive surveys revealed potentially valuable lands for European colonization, the fact that both Australia and New Zealand were islands also chipped away at the idea of an extensive southern continent directly balancing the landmasses of Eurasia and North America in the northern hemisphere.

On three occasions during his second expedition (1772–1775), Captain Cook sailed south of the Antarctic Circle. By chance, all three of these crossings took place in areas where continental Antarctica lay further to the south. If Cook had crossed the Antarctic Circle in the Peninsula region, or directly to the south of Australia, it is likely that he would have become the first person to sight the Antarctic continent. Despite initially believing the islands of [South] Georgia and [South] Sandwich to be part of the "Anti-Arctic" continent of classical speculation, Cook did not see any extensive landmass in the far south. He nevertheless hypothesized that land must exist based on the appearance of the icebergs that his ships encountered in the Southern Ocean: "This isle [South Georgia] cannot produce the ten thousand part of what we have seen, either there must be more land or else ice is formed without it ... I still have hopes of discovering a continent."[75] Cook, however, did not think that such land would really be worth discovering.[76] "The inner parts of the Country was not less savage and horrible," he noted of the Isle of Georgia, "the Wild rocks raised their lofty summits till they were lost in the Clouds and the Vallies [sic] laid buried in everlasting snow." The southern coastline, he added, was "doomed by Nature to Frigidity the greatest part of the year."[77]

It would not be for another forty years after the expeditions of Captain Cook that the first recorded sightings of the Antarctic continent would be made. In the event it was the Russian naval officer Captain Thaddeus Von Bellingshausen who was probably the first to sight the Antarctic continent. This expedition followed in the tradition of enlightened exploration, and Cook was a hero of Bellingshausen. In the years that have followed, Cook, Bellingshausen, and other early explorers of Antarctica have been afforded a legendary status in the history of the continent. Their activities and discoveries have an obvious political utility to countries such as Britain and Russia that seek to make a political claim to the Antarctic continent. As a consequence, some of the more difficult questions related to discovery are largely ignored. For example, did the act of seeing land of unknown extent that would only much later prove to be part of the Antarctic continent constitute an act of discovery? In a sense, explorers such as Cook and Bellingshausen have become almost mythical figures, and it is nearly impossible to separate fact from fiction in the early history of Antarctica.

2

SCARCITY AND ABUNDANCE
Marine Exploitation

If a polar landscape is considered in purely aesthetic terms, there is little immediate contrast between the land and the sea. In some places, snow-covered mountains offer a sublime beauty similar to a polar sea littered with icebergs (Figure 5); in other places, the monotony of the open ocean is comparable to a terrestrial ice sheet or a vast expanse of tundra. Considered from a biological perspective, however, there is often a stark contrast between maritime and terrestrial ecosystems in the Polar Regions. The seas and oceans of Antarctica and some parts of the Arctic are sites of high biological abundance; polar lands are often areas of biological scarcity, especially when covered by ice sheets or glaciers. In some parts of the Arctic and in nearly all of Antarctica, so stark is this contrast that much terrestrial life is dependent in one way or another on the productivity of nearby seas and oceans. Seabirds and several species of seals split their lives between water and land, feeding at sea and breeding on shore where their guano provides nutrients for mosses, algae, and occasional vascular plants that inhabit the polar coastline. The reliance on the sea is highlighted in the Arctic by the iconic polar bear, which, although omnivorous, is largely dependent on seals and other marine creatures for much of its subsistence.

Human activities in the Polar Regions have been profoundly shaped by the relative abundance of marine ecosystems and the relative scarcity

Figure 5 *Nordenskiold Glacier, Greenland. Photograph by Louise Boyd. (Source: American Geographical Society Library) [(47b2) 4363 No. 16,713 L]*

of the land.[1] Reflecting the relative bounty of the polar seas, it is no coincidence that Arctic peoples have often lived close to the coast. Many Inuit, for example, have traditionally been a coastal people and lived primarily from the natural resources of the ocean. Whales, seals, fish, and seabirds provide food, fuel, clothing, construction materials, and other necessities for human life. The Inupiat communities of northern Alaska, for example, developed around the hunting of bowhead whales, which provided subsistence and cultural unity. The sea also offers a means of transport, both when frozen and unfrozen, and many Arctic peoples are highly skilled seafarers. "Kayak" is one of the Inuit words that have become part of the English language.

Scarcity and abundance have been familiar themes in the history of Inuit and other Arctic communities. Over the course of a year, there is a clear seasonality to hunting routines. Much of the hunting takes place from spring to autumn. During the darkness of winter, the sea ice thickens, many marine mammals migrate or move to distant ice packs and terrestrial mammals often hibernate. Although some winter hunting is possible, Inuit communities developed strategies for preserving food and stockpiling fuel to last through the winter. In places where salmon or char can be caught, for example, the drying of fish is common. From year to year, fish and animal populations fluctuate, and long periods of scarcity or abundance can occur. In response to this fluctuating supply of food, Inuit communities have developed elaborate planning strategies to prepare for these ups and downs. Perhaps most obvious is the use of as wide a variety of food sources as possible, thus reducing dependence upon the vicissitudes of any single population. As a consequence, Arctic hunting cultures are not the vulnerable, haphazard societies that they have sometimes been portrayed.[2]

In the Arctic, an important change has taken place over the past three or four centuries from subsistence extraction to commercial exploitation, which has usually been associated with the arrival of Europeans and the onset of colonialism in one form or another. This shift has not been absolute: trade has always been an important part of living in the Arctic North, and subsistence hunting remains crucially important to many contemporary Arctic communities. But the broad move from subsistence to commerce has had profound consequences for human relations with the natural world. Jørgensen and Sörlin refer to the process of domesticating nature as "environing."[3] A classic example of this was the Presbyterian minister Sheldon Jackson's attempt to import domesticated reindeer into Alaska from Siberia to replace a reliance on hunting wild caribou, and to encourage conformity to a Jeffersonian yeoman farmer ideal.[4] More often, early commercial hunting in the Arctic simply involved the exploitation of as many natural resources as quickly as possible, with little regard for the future.

The open-access exploitation of many of the living resources in the Arctic and Antarctica evokes what the American scientist Garrett Hardin has called the "tragedy of the commons."[5] Firmly rooted in the Cold War context of the 1960s, Hardin argued that exploitation of open-access resources will inevitably lead to resource depletion and environmental degradation since there is no incentive for individual parties to show any restraint in their extractive activities; in fact, the incentive is to exploit as much as possible as quickly as possible. "Freedom in the commons," he famously wrote, "leads to tragedy for all." While not quite the wholehearted endorsement of private property some have claimed, Hardin's ideas have been much discussed and much criticized.[6] Critics allege that the theory relies on a somewhat myopic way of viewing the world that sees the search for profit above all else, and neglects to take into account the elaborate cultural systems that have developed in many societies in part to regulate the use of natural resources.[7] Despite these criticisms the tragedy of the commons continues to offer a useful starting point for thinking about the history of open-access resources, and the contrasting histories of the Arctic and Antarctica have much to contribute to the debate. In the Arctic, many communities have indeed developed elaborate cultural systems to govern the use of living resources. But in many places these have been challenged by the arrival of profit-seeking outsiders who have little regard for these systems. In Antarctica the lack of an indigenous population offers a case study to test the idea of the tragedy of the commons in possibly its purest form: here, living resource extraction has been commercially driven from the outset.

Underlying any discussion of the tragedy of the commons in the Polar Regions are perceptions of environmental scarcity and abundance. In both the Arctic and Antarctica, the unknown has tended to be filled with perceptions of limitless abundance, especially in the minds of outsiders. The overexploitation of one colony of seals or group of whales matters little if you believe that there are more to exploit just beyond the horizon. In this way, extractive activities such as sealing and whaling have often been at the forefront of polar exploration. The ongoing process of depletion and degradation of resources in one place followed by the search for new places to exploit might be thought of as creating a "resource frontier," in which continual expansion is built into the business model.[8] Abundance, however, has not proved limitless. The filling in of blank spaces on the maps of the Arctic and Antarctica has been accompanied by a dawning awareness that natural resources are not infinite and that scarcity—often caused by humans—is the abiding material reality. In some places, the realization occurred quite quickly, while in others it has taken longer for reality to trump expectation.

Understanding exactly how early sealers and whalers understood and interacted with the Antarctic environment is no easy task. After fur seal pelts and elephant seal blubber, secrecy was the most highly valued commodity among nineteenth-century sealers, and something similar could be said for whalers. Keeping quiet about discoveries of new seal colonies was crucial for making money before competitors could take advantage of the information. "Secrecy ... has been deemed a part, a most important part, of their capital," noted the American adventurer Jeremiah Reynolds in a speech on the history of sealing before the U.S. House of Representatives in 1836.[9] The enigmatic nature of the industry has cast a long shadow over the early history of sealing in both Polar Regions. There are relatively few traditional written documents, and historians are confronted with numerous discrepancies concerning people, places, and dates. As a result of the lack of sources, the historiography of this period remains relatively patchy and underdeveloped.[10] One of the most productive approaches to the unwritten history of natural resource extraction in the Polar Regions is through historical archeology.[11] The Argentine archeologists Andrés Zarankin and María Ximena Sentore, for example, have done extensive research in the South Shetland Islands in an attempt to "voice the silences" of Antarctic history.[12] Their work suggests that archeological evidence from the region diverges significantly from the historical "master narratives," and they suggest that sealers and whalers played a more important and sustained role in the nineteenth-century history of the Polar Regions than is often suggested.[13]

Arctic Sealing

Largely separated from other oceans and often covered in ice, significant parts of the actual Arctic Ocean are relatively biologically unproductive.[14] Much of the energy from sunlight is blocked, nutrients are limited, and primary production is low. Other Arctic waters, however, are among the most biologically productive in the world, with large swarms of krill feeding on microorganisms that graze on the bottom of the sea ice.[15] Northern parts of the Atlantic Ocean, off the coasts of Iceland, Greenland, and Labrador, for example, once teemed with cod and other valuable fish species. The Bering Sea, between Siberia and Alaska, remains one of the world's most valuable fisheries.[16] In contrast to the abundance of these sub-Arctic waters, much of the terrestrial Arctic can be characterized by relative scarcity. The Arctic tundra certainly has a lot more life than the ice sheets of Greenland or

Antarctica, and can often boast large iconic species such as bear, caribou, and wolves. But even in these regions biomass is relatively limited and biodiversity is low. Arctic rivers provide a connection between land and sea, and are often particularly rich breeding sites for species such as salmon and Arctic char. The relative abundance of sub-Arctic marine ecosystems and the relative scarcity of terrestrial life has exerted a significant influence on the human history of the Arctic.

Known by the scientific name "pinnipeds" (a superfamily that includes walruses and sea lions as well), seals provide an interesting group of species for thinking about the relationship between people and the environment in the Arctic north. Varying in size up to the truly massive 4,000 kg of the adult male elephant seal, these marine mammals live most of their lives at sea, but come onto land or sea ice to breed, to rest, and sometimes to moult. Pinnipeds were first classified as a separate taxonomic unit in the early nineteenth century. Today there are twelve species of pinnipeds living in the Arctic or sub-Arctic. Six species of true seals (this designation means they lack external ears) breed on the sea ice and are classified as Arctic ice seals: ringed seals, bearded seals, spotted seals, ribbon seals, hooded seals, and harp seals.[17] Another three species of true seals live in the Arctic or sub-Arctic and breed on land: harbor seals, gray seals, and northern elephant seals. Northern fur seals and Steller sea lions are the two species of eared seals, or Otaridae, which live in the Arctic and sub-Arctic, both centered on the Bering Sea region. And finally, the Walrus constitute a family unto themselves—the Odobenidae—and are characterized by their distinctive ivory tusks.[18] In sub-Arctic Alaska there are also a number of other species that share some similar characteristics to pinnipeds, including sea otters and the now extinct Steller's sea cow.[19]

When they are hunted by people, seals function to transfer energy from marine to terrestrial ecosystems (Figure 5). For many indigenous communities living in the Arctic North, the hunting of seals provides food, clothing, fuel, and construction materials. Seal meat is a staple part of the diet; sealskins provide warm clothing, seal brains are used as a skin softener and preservative, and the sinews provide sewing material; seal blubber fuels the lanterns that provide light and heat through the winter; intestines and windpipes can be used as translucent windows.[20] The bounty provided by seals provides evidence of lives that

Figure 6   *Inuit with dead seal, photographed by Knud Rasmussen (Source: American Geographical Society Library) [(47a)5 No. 12150 M]*

have often been abundant, in contrast to the common framing of Arctic peoples' lives as a response to scarcity. Techniques for hunting seals have changed over time and vary from place to place. They also vary from species to species. The species of seal that breed on land, such as harbor seals and fur seals, tend to be relatively easy to hunt, since they congregate in large numbers in one place. Ice seals are generally much more difficult for humans to kill since they live most of their lives on ice floes and in open water. The Inuit developed sophisticated techniques for killing ice seals that gave them a comparative advantage over earlier peoples of the Arctic North. Jared Diamond attributes the inability of the Greenland Norse to hunt ringed seals as one possible reason for their demise.[21]

As well as providing many of the material necessities of life, the hunting of seals and other animals has been integrated into the spiritual lives of many Arctic communities. Anthropologists and archeologists report elaborate belief systems that have collectively come to be known as sha-manism, following the Siberian word for a religious practitioner. Rather than understanding the successful hunting of an animal as chance or the result of skill, a shamanic view would see the animal offering itself to be killed. If the rituals are followed correctly, the animal is reborn and abundance is maintained. If animal is treated incorrectly, then the result is scarcity. The anthropologist Hugh Brody summarizes this aspect of Inuit beliefs about nature:

> Humans have souls and spirit powers. Humans and animals are equals. It follows that animals must also have a place in the spirit world. It also follows that animals must depend upon the hunt; they must agree to be killed. All northern hunters insist that if animals are not treated with respect, both when alive and dead, they will not allow themselves to be hunted. The hunt is thus a form of contract between partners, in which it is not always clear who is the prey.[22]

Hunted seals, for example, are assumed to be thirsty from living in the salty sea, and the dead carcass is given fresh water.[23] Academic studies of the Inuit and other shamanic northern societies have suggested that such beliefs provide an explanation for fluctuating periods of abundance and scarcity, and offer a semblance of control over a fickle environment. For the practitioners themselves, such attempts to rationalize and explain their beliefs are pointless: this is simply the way things are.

It is easy for outsiders to romanticize the subsistence lifestyle of the Inuit and other indigenous communities of the Arctic. From a distance, it can appear that these societies are living in perfect harmony with the material environment, taking only what they need and showing a profound respect for the lands where they live and the animals that they kill. While there is some truth to these perceptions, caution is also required. Academic debates around the concept of the "ecological Indian" suggest that there can be serious problems with the uncritical belief that indigenous peoples live in harmony with nature.[24] Idealistic perceptions can easily overlook the hardships associated with living with periods of scarcity, focusing instead on times of abundance. It is problematic that the notion of ecological harmony can suggest a static society, and peoples without a history. This has often been used by outsiders to classify indigenous peoples—including Inuit and others in the Arctic—as "noble savages," and to justify paternalistic policies of colonialism. A people without history can quickly become a people in need of assistance, especially in times of material scarcity.[25]

The history of the indigenous communities of the Arctic reveals a much more dynamic relationship with the material world than that implied by an overly simplistic belief in a people living in harmony with nature. Writing about the hunting practices of the Inuit and other Arctic peoples, the archeologist Robert McGee notes:

> The casual and routine overkilling of animals on which people depend for their livelihood belies the romantic view of indigenous hunting peoples as natural conservationists, but it is undeniable that it occurs regularly. Overkilling, with no consideration of the biological consequences, has been consistent among Arctic hunters throughout history.[26]

A great deal of care also needs to be taken with this interpretation, since it too has been used to justify paternalistic politics of colonialism and control in both the Arctic and beyond.[27] But there has certainly been a widespread belief among Inuit that if animals are not hunted their numbers will decline.[28] Such instability connects to what we know about the dynamic history of Arctic communities. Groups of Inuit have moved around the Arctic, communities have traded and fought with their neighbors, and at times groups have been divided by internal conflict. Stories, myths, and social systems have changed to reflect these experiences. The people of the Arctic, in other words, are no different from the people of other parts of the world.

Contact with outsiders has been a part of the history of all Arctic indigenous peoples. Despite what nineteenth- and early twentieth-century explorers and anthropologists tended to report, there is no truth at all in the idea that these were "untainted" communities just waiting to be discovered.[29] There can be little doubt, however, that the scale and impact of contact with outsiders began to increase significantly with the arrival of ever-greater numbers of Europeans into the Arctic. The timing of this arrival occurred differently in different places, but the sixteenth and seventeenth centuries offer a useful point for thinking about when these changes began to accelerate. The reality of the European arrival into the Arctic, at least in the early years, was something akin to Richard White's concept of a "middle ground," a meeting place for the exchange of ideas and goods that did not necessarily favor one group over another.[30]

In 1576 the British explorer Martin Frobisher encountered Inuit on Baffin Island, and became one of the first people to describe their culture for an English-speaking audience.[31] In the years that followed, contact between Inuit and Europeans steadily increased. When, in 1610, the British navigator Henry Hudson sailed into the bay in northern Canada that today bears his name, trade was already taking place between Europeans and Native Americans. Like many of the other European Arctic explorers who followed them, Frobisher and Hudson were seeking a sea route to Asia. But they were also interested in the natural resources that they could find to exploit. Just as with the indigenous communities of the Arctic, seals provided European explorers with food, clothing, and fuel, especially when they got into difficulty, which was far from uncommon.

Alongside their value as supplies for explorers, the natural resources of the Arctic also offered a commercial resource to exploit. The walrus, in particular, offered a potentially valuable commodity. Walrus tusks had been important trading commodities of the Greenland Norse. A religious account from 1327 reported that that 650 kg of walrus tusk was paid in 1327 as a "crusade tax," requiring the killing of 200 animals.[32] The hunting of walrus for their ivory remained an important activity for Early Modern Europeans coming into the Arctic from the sixteenth century onwards. One of the original activities of England's Muscovy Company, founded by royal charter in 1555, was trade in walrus tusk. In 1594, for example, Francis Cherry imported 595 kg of walrus ivory from Arctic Russia.[33] Although walrus ivory was not thought to be as high quality as elephant ivory, it was still a valuable product. Walrus pelts could also be used for making ropes and coverings, and their blubber could be boiled down into oil. Other breeds of Arctic seals had less obvious commercial value, but the blubber could be used as fuel and the meat could be eaten. Arctic fisheries also offered potentially valuable commodities, although most early exploitation took place a little further south.

Despite widespread lack of recognition at the time about what commercial exploitation could do to the living resources of the Arctic, there can be no question that the long-term consequences of the shift from subsistence to commercial exploitation were profound. The impact of the shift certainly varied from place to place and was often not immediate; it was nonetheless pervasive. The environmental historian William Cronon has studied the transition from a system of subsistence to commercial exploitation associated with the arrival of Europeans on the east coast of North America.[34] This shift, founded fundamentally on a move from usufruct rights of common use to private property, had significant consequences for the material environment. While there are obvious differences between the commercial exploitation of maritime mammals in the Arctic north and the terrestrial ecosystems of New England, many of Cronon's insights are applicable to the far north. In many of the places most affected by European trade and hunting practices, the intrusion of commercial exploitation rapidly depleted population stocks and broke down the cultural structures that had governed subsistence resource extraction in the Arctic.

As the environmental historian Ryan Tucker Jones has documented in *Empire of Extinction*, one of the most extreme examples of disruption to indigenous northern communities that occurred as the result of the shift to commercial exploitation took place during the eighteenth century on the Aleutian Islands between Russia and Alaska. Although this region does not fall into the Arctic proper, a strong case can be made for its inclusion in the sub-Arctic, and the Aleut population is linguistically related to the Inuit.[35] The arrival of Russian fur hunters, known as *promyshlenniki*, in the mid-eighteenth century irrevocably changed the lives of Aleut communities and altered both marine and terrestrial ecosystems. Russian expansion from west to east along the Aleutian island chain provides an almost perfect example of a resource frontier in action. As hunters devastated sea otter and fur seal populations on one island they sought new islands to exploit, initially paying little or no attention to conservation.

At the time of the arrival of Russians, Aleut people had been living on the Aleutian island chain for almost 3,000 years. The Aleutian Islanders developed a seafaring culture based on the use of kayaks, and by many measures they were the most maritime people of the northern hemisphere. While much of their food came from the near-shore region, Aleuts relied upon hunting seals and sea lions for fuel, and sea otters for clothing.[36] Like the Inuit, the Aleuts had developed an elaborate belief system that regulated hunting. Rather than stalking skill or other hunting attributes being the determinant of a successful hunt, Aleuts believed that the animals offered themselves to the hunters who had the best moral character as demonstrated by the performance of ritual practice.[37] Just as in much of the rest of the Arctic north, such beliefs did nothing to limit the total number of animals hunted, and ecologists believe that the Aleuts had reduced the number of sea otters prior to the arrival of Russians.[38] There was a belief that sea otters were being "driven away" rather than overhunted.[39]

While Aleut relations with the natural world should not be seen as an Edenic state of harmony with nature, there can be no doubt that the arrival of Russian fur traders radically changed relations between humans and the natural world. After hunting sea otters in the unin-habited Commander Islands in the first half of the eighteenth century, Russian fur traders first arrived in the westernmost Aleutian Islands in 1745. The Near Island islands of Attu and Agattu were the least populated of the Aleutian chain, but the simple fact that they contained human populations completely shifted the dynamic of Russian hunt-ing. The *promyshlenniki* quickly learned that the most efficient means of hunting sea otters was to get the Aleuts to do the hunting for them. There is much debate about precisely how the Russians went about doing this, with opinions ranging from the creation of a system of near slavery to a relatively benign and paternalistic commercial relation-ship.[40] But however it is labeled, Russian dominance ultimately rested on the threat of violence. Although the Aleuts converted to Orthodox Christianity, there was little change in their attitudes toward nature, and they continued to do much of the killing using traditional methods, which often proved the most effective.

By 1760 sea otter populations in the Near Islands closest to Siberia were showing signs of decline. The discovery of the Andrean Islands in that year offered a new lease of life to the sea otter hunters.[41] It was on the more densely populated Andrean and Fox islands that the system of exploiting Aleuts would be fully developed, with examples of women and children being held hostage to force the men to hunt. Once again, commercial exploitation quickly caused a decline in sea otter populations, and this was not helped by the imposition of a tax on the Aleuts that was to be paid in sea otter pelts. In the 1780s the profitability of the Russian Pacific fur trade was restored by the expansion of hunting to the Kodiak Islands, close to mainland Alaska. As the cycle of expansion and extermination continued, the development of a market for fur seal pelts in China relieved a little of the pressure on sea otter populations. Chinese furriers had developed a means of removing the stiff guard hairs on fur seals to create a softer and much more commercially viable product. In 1786 Gavriil Pribylov discovered the Pribylov Islands, to the north of the Aleutian chain. These islands were uninhabited by people, but were the main breeding grounds of the northern fur seals. Exploitation of fur seals followed a pattern similar to the exploitation of sea otters, and Russians moved Aleut hunters to the Pribylov Islands to do the hunting. By the early nineteenth century, fur seal numbers had declined to a point where their future seemed in doubt.[42]

Jones argues that the Russians came to see extinction as a threat to empire. The extinction of Steller's sea cow was in some ways emblematic of this threat, although the reasons for its disappearance were somewhat complex. Concern about extinction led to important scientific developments, not least of which was a challenge to the idea that extinction was impossible. As a consequence of these realizations, Russian imperial authorities sought to put in place conservation measures to alleviate the threat of extinction. One of the primary measures taken was the granting of a monopoly to the Russian American Company in 1799. While the concept of the tragedy of the commons did not apply precisely to the North Pacific fur trade since the region was technically under Russian sovereignty, it was thought the creation of a monopoly would limit indiscriminate slaughter. Within two decades of its creation, the Russian American Company had put in place conservation measures to protect both sea otters and fur seals. "While the measures began in piecemeal fashion," writes Jones, "by the 1840s they were some of the most progressive anywhere in the colonial world."[43] These measures, however, were not enough to preserve the Russian empire in Alaska. In seeking to explain the decline of Russian power in America, the history of sealing on the opposite side of the planet may have played a small role.

Antarctic Sealing

Despite significant chronological overlaps, the history of Antarctic sealing has generally been told separately from the history of sealing in the Arctic.[44] In some ways this makes sense. In the far south there were no indigenous peoples to exploit, and seal hunters had to do the killing of seals themselves. In the Antarctic there were no longstanding social customs in place to regulate the exploitation of nature, however imperfect these may have been. Unlike Russian sealing in the Aleutian Islands and Alaska, where there were at least nominal claims to imperial ownership, no country made any effort to claim ownership of the Antarctic sealing grounds of South Georgia, the South Shetland Islands, or most of the other Antarctic and sub-Antarctic regions where sealing took place. As a consequence of these factors, Antarctic sealing offers something of an idealized case study of the tragedy of the commons. Most of the companies that sailed south during this period were from Britain and the United States, but the crews were thoroughly international and the industry was theoretically open to all.

The obvious differences between Arctic and Antarctic sealing, however, do not mean that there were not important connections between the two Polar Regions. The reason that the hunting of seals began around Antarctica was the fact that there was a market for fur seal pelts, which sealing in the Arctic and sub-Arctic had helped to create. In the early days of the industry this market was predominantly in China, where it was strongly connected to the hunting of sea otters and fur seals in the Aleutian Islands and Alaska. While there was relatively little overlap in the ships and crews involved, environmental ideas were shared between the Arctic and Antarctica. This was demonstrated most clearly by the Russian scientific explorer Thaddeus Von Bellingshausen, who took with him a new environmental sensitivity shaped by the Enlightenment science of Russia's "Empire of Extinction."[45]

The familiar story of the origins of sealing in the waters of the Southern Ocean tends to emphasize the history of exploration over economic history. In this account, the voyages of Captain Cook in the late eighteenth century alerted sealers and businessmen to the economic possibilities of the region. The British naval captain was generally quite scathing about the potential of the lands he saw in the far south. The only redeeming environmental characteristic of the southernmost parts of his journey was the abundance of marine life (Figures 7 and 8). "Seals or Sea Bears [fur seals] were pretty numerous," Cook's report noted of South Georgia, "they were smaller than those at Staten Island [off the southern tip of South America]: perhaps the most of those we saw were females for the Shores swarm'd with young cubs."[46] In more general terms, Johann Forster, the botanist on the expedition, wrote that "the least addition of vegetation enlivens the scene, and even the slow motions of unwieldy and torpid seals and grave pinguins [sic] on the shore, infuse life and cheerfulness into the beholders."[47]

A number of convergent factors led to the creation of a sealing industry on many of the sub-Antarctic islands surrounding the Antarctic continent. There was a degree of scarcity created by the overexploitation of wildlife in the regions directly to the north. At the time of Cook's account, seal hunters were already beginning to work the coastlines of South America and the Falkland Islands, often in association with whaling voyages. British sealing vessels arrived on the island of South Georgia in 1786.[48] These were followed shortly afterward by American and French sealers.[49] This expansion southward from the Falkland Islands and Patagonia was an early example of the development of a resource frontier in the Antarctic Peninsula region. As sealers diminished the populations in one place, they needed to find new seal islands.[50] By the 1810s, South Georgia was established as one of the major centers of Southern Ocean sealing.[51] Between 1815 and 1817, for example, the British sealing vessel *Norfolk* spent a winter at Royal Bay, taking 5,000 fur seal pelts and 3,500 barrels of elephant seal oil.[52]

As sealers killed seals, they learned about their biology and breeding habits. In the early years of sealing on South Georgia, the most sought-after prey were fur seals. In late October and early November, adult male fur seals came on land, and competed with each other to establish territories.[53] Females arrived shortly afterwards to pup and to breed with the dominant males. The fur seals then remained until April on a ten-day cycle of feeding and nursing.[54] Combined with the fact that they had never faced terrestrial predators, these reproductive habits left fur seals vulnerable to sealers. Entire colonies could be slaughtered in a matter of days. Fur seals were killed with a blow to the nose and then skinned with a knife at a rate of up to sixty an hour.[55] The sealers then

Figure 7 and Figure 8 *Young male fur seal (left) and adult male elephant seals (right). Photo Credits: Adrian Howkins and Nigel Milius.*

soaked the skins in brine for preservation before packing them on their ships. Sealers were aware that a beach could be exploited in this manner for one or two seasons before being "almost entirely abandoned by the animals."[56] While such an explanation appears euphemistic today, it seemed to make sense to early sealers that seals simply avoided the beaches on which hunting occurred. This corresponded with similar ideas in the northern hemisphere.

The other species of importance to the early Southern Ocean sealing industry were elephant seals, which were hunted for their blubber rather than their pelts.[57] Sealers encountered tremendous differences in size between male and female elephant seals, with four-ton adult males up to six times larger than adult females (which would prove to be the biggest sexual dimorphism of any mammal). Sealers killed large male elephant seals with guns and smaller seals with clubs and lances. The blubber was then boiled in large caldrons known as try pots to render the fat. Elephant seal oil was very similar to high-quality whale oil, and the two were often mixed. Just like whale oil, elephant seal oil was used for lighting, lubrication of machinery, paint manufacture, and other processes connected to the world's developing industrial economies.

The nature of the sealers' work and the way that they engaged with the environment perpetuated the industry's lack of sustainability.[58] Known as "nomads of the sea," early nineteenth-century sealers ranked at the very bottom of the maritime hierarchy and their work was both unpleasant and dangerous. Life aboard ship was cramped, temperatures were often bitingly cold, and the work was brutal and filthy. Many sealers drowned in the icy Antarctic seas, or died of starvation or exposure after being stranded on desolate beaches.[59] Rather than working for a fixed wage, sealers usually worked for a share of the profits.[60] This "lay system" provided a clear incentive to kill as many seals as possible, regardless of the future. Many sealers wanted to make money quickly before quitting the industry and turning to less hostile and dangerous environments to earn a living.[61] Even those who saw sealing as a vocation had little incentive to hunt sustainably, since it was unlikely that their competitors would do the same. In contrast to the many places where there was an established history of common property resource use, the novelty and geographical isolation of the rapacious Antarctic sealing industry helped to prevent the development of sustainable hunting practices.[62] For most of the people involved, Antarctic sealing was an industry without much of a history and without much of a future: the unregulated, competitive nature of this Antarctic "workscape" fostered a distinctly short-term vision.[63] This problem was exacerbated by the belief in limitless abundance, which was the result of a paucity of environmental knowledge and the confidence that new seal colonies could always be found.

By the mid 1810s, seal populations on South Georgia were becoming seriously diminished by excessive hunting, and sealers were beginning to look even further afield for new beaches to exploit.[64] Between 1818 and 1820, for example, two British sealing vessels explored the potential of the South Sandwich Islands for sealing operations, but found them unsuitable.[65] During this period, it is very likely that sealers made a number of unrecorded discoveries in the South Shetland Islands and Antarctic Peninsula region, possibly including the first sighting of the Antarctic continent. Given the multinational labor force involved in sealing, it is therefore possible that any one of a number of nationalities may have been the first to sight the continent, including sealers from South America.[66] But as a consequence of the secretive nature of their industry, almost nothing is known of the discoveries that sealers may have made before the first recorded sightings of the Antarctic continent were made in 1820. Given the nature of the sealing industry's resource frontier, it is no coincidence that one of these first "official" sightings of continental Antarctica was made by the young American sealing captain Nathaniel Palmer.

Initially, concerns over the decline of seal populations did not seem to bother Antarctic sealers such as Nathaniel Palmer, who simply believed that they would find new locations in which to hunt, as they always had done. The 1821–22 season saw around forty sealing ships working in the South Shetland Islands. Unlike in previous years, however, it was a poor season and few discoveries were made of any commercial value. In December 1821, Nathaniel Palmer and the British sealer George Powell sighted the South Orkney Islands, several hundred miles to the east of the South Shetlands. But although the two archipelagos were quite similar in appearance, the South Orkneys proved to contain relatively few seals. At the end of the season, the Fanning Company with which Palmer was associated was dissolved as a result of poor returns.[67] Combined with its unsustainable hunting practices, the closing of the Antarctic Peninsula's resource frontier threatened to destroy the sealing industry.

One of the few sealers who did seem to understand the problem of declining seal populations was the British sealing captain James Weddell. He estimated that 320,000 fur seals had been killed in the South Shetland Islands in the first two seasons of hunting, adding that the killing of adults had also resulted in the deaths of around 100,000 fur seal pups.[68] His response, however, like others, was to look for new seal colonies to exploit. As a former British naval officer and an excellent navigator, Weddell had a particular affinity for charting and surveying work.[69] Shortly after Palmer and Powell had discovered the South Orkney Islands, Weddell also sighted land in this vicinity.[70] Although he also found the archipelago to be of little value for seal hunting, he decided to return to the area in the 1822–23 season to expand his search for land. He spent a few weeks sailing around the islands before making a sustained push to the south. In mid-February 1823, Weddell's ships, the *Jane* and the *Beaufoy*, reached a new farthest south of 74° 15'S and 34° 16'W.[71] But despite sailing a considerable distance south of the Antarctic Circle, Weddell did not find land, and the ships returned to South Georgia without a cargo of fur seal pelts. Although he had no success in his commercial objectives, Weddell did encounter an entirely new species of seal that came to be known as the Weddell seal, and the sea he sailed into was later named the Weddell Sea in his honor.[72]

One of the people who was most aware of the problem of declining seal populations in the south was the Russian naval captain Thaddeus Von Bellingshausen. As early as January 1821, Von Bellingshausen wrote that the number of fur seals in the South Shetland Islands was perceptibly diminishing. "As other sealers also were competing in the destruction of the [fur] seals," he noted, "there could be no doubt that round the South Shetland Islands just as at South Georgia ... the number of these sea animals will rapidly decrease."[73] He added that once numerous elephant seals "had already moved from these shores further out to sea."[74] Such attitudes make sense when they are placed alongside the intellectual innovations taking place in imperial Russia, as discussed by Jones' *Empire of Extinction*.[75]

Although difficult to prove, it is likely that the development of southern sealing had an impact on Russian political and economic interests in Alaska. In 1799 the Russian American Company instituted a monopoly on the fur trade with China. Although profits remained relatively high for some years, it is likely that the development of Antarctic sealing may have reduced the effectiveness of the monopoly. By the middle of the nineteenth century, the Russian American Company had become largely unprofitable, and Russia was rapidly losing interest in its territories in North America. There were many reasons for this decline, including distance from centers of power, inefficiencies within the system, and a general lack of interest. In 1867, Russia sold Alaska to the United States for a price of $7.2 million. While it is unlikely that competition from southern seal pelts played a decisive role in the decline of the Russian American Company, it is not unreasonable to speculate that the development of Antarctic sealing played at least a minor role in what would turn out to be a major geopolitical transition in the Arctic.

Arctic Whaling

The weakness of the Russian American Company in the mid-nineteenth century was highlighted by the fact that American whalers began hunting in Alaskan waters while Russia remained the nominal sovereign. From 1848 onwards, American whaling vessels began to make the perilous journey northward through the Bering Strait into the largely ice-covered Chukchi Sea and east to the Beaufort Sea in pursuit of bowhead whales. Driven largely by the scarcity of whales in other more accessible parts of the world, this was the latest—and in many ways the final—stage in a resource frontier of Arctic commercial whaling.

For Inupiat communities on the north coast of Alaska and the tip of Siberia, bowhead whales rather than seals have long been the most important prey species. These massive creatures could reach sizes of up to 100 tons, and they are the only large species of whale endemic to the Arctic.[76] Techniques for hunting these large animals on their annual migration to the Chukchi and Beaufort Seas developed over hundreds of years. Despite their size, bowhead whales were relatively easy to kill, owing to their slow speeds and propensity to float after being killed. While the theory that the eastward migration of Inuit from Alaska to Greenland was driven almost entirely by the bowhead whale has been challenged, the hunting of whales undoubtedly played a role in decisions about where Inuit villages were located. The successful killing of a whale could provide a community with abundant resources. As a consequence, the communities that hunted whales could support relatively large populations. Whale meat provided ample food supplies, including the delicacy of muktuk, a layer of fat taken from close to the skin. Whalebones were used for tools and construction materials. Blubber supplied fuel for the lanterns that supplied heat through the winter. Baleen served a number of purposes; it was used for killing polar bears, coiled in seal meat which was then frozen. The bear would take this bait and as the meat thawed in the bear's gut the baleen would spring open, a deadly surprise. Just as with the hunting of seals, elaborate rituals accompanied the hunting of whales by Inupiat communities. The whale hunt was a community event that required the participation of almost all the members of a village to hunt and process the animal. While Inupiat communities certainly traded some of the products provided by the annual whale hunt, whaling took place largely for subsistence. In contrast, when whalers from the United States began to arrive in northern Alaska in the middle of the nineteenth century, their motivations for killing whales were almost entirely commercial.

By the time American whalers began arriving in the Bering Sea, Europeans and Americans had been hunting whales in other parts of the Arctic for over 250 years. Commercial whaling in the Arctic had begun off the coasts of Spitsbergen (which the Dutch had discovered in 1596), and northern Russia in the late sixteenth century. In 1611, England's Muscovy Company began whaling operations around Spitsbergen, although initial results were not positive as both its whaling ships sank. The Dutch made a claim to the discovery of Jan Mayen Island in 1614 (although it had probably already been sighted), and this proved to be a valuable whaling ground. As the number of bowhead whales declined in this region, whalers moved on to the seas around Iceland and the east coast of Greenland, as well as off the north coast of Russia. By 1720 whaling was common in western Greenland and the bays and channels of what is today the eastern Canadian Arctic.[77] The historian of the Arctic Richard Vaughan estimates that between 1661 and 1800 Dutch whalers alone killed over 65,000 whales in the waters between Spitsbergen and Greenland.[78] As competition intensified, it became common practice to leave parties to overwinter in the Arctic, so that they would be ready to start hunting whales as soon as the summer season began. Many of these overwintering parties suffered horribly, and scurvy was a particular problem as a result of lack of vitamin C.[79]

Commercial whaling in the Arctic was driven by the market for whale oil, and this in turn was driven by the incipient industrial revolution in Europe. When whaling began in the Arctic, there were three main uses for whale oil. It was used in the manufacture of soap, especially by merchants in England and Holland; it was used in the leather and textile industries; and it was used for lighting.[80] In the early years of whaling, whale oil in relative terms was never the most valuable commodity, but prices were good enough to sustain the industry. Baleen, or whalebone, served a variety of functions, perhaps most famously being used as the boning in women's corsets. As the industrial revolution continued, whale oil was increasingly used in place of tallow as a lubricant for machines. This new demand helped to increase commercial interest in the whaling industry. From the mid-eighteenth century onwards, the British reentered the Arctic whaling industry, largely from the port of Hull, and became the dominant European whaling nation in the years following the Napoleonic Wars.[81] Another major whaling nation at this time was the newly independent United States, and there was significant rivalry between Britain and America.[82]

In the 1849 summer season, forty-six American vessels went north through the Bering Strait, and this number rose in the years that immediately followed.[83] While the commercial exploitation of bow-head whales off the coast of Alaska was inextricably connected to the expanding industrial economy of the nineteenth century, hunting continued to follow largely traditional methods. Commercial whalers killed bowhead whales with a thrown harpoon, and then flensed them on shore or alongside the ship. Just as with the sealing industries of the Arctic and Antarctic, working conditions were fairly miserable for northern whalers. They had to endure long periods away from family living in cramped, unsanitary conditions. Pay was generally low and usually tied to a percentage of the profit, leaving little incentive for good conservation practice.

Some Inupiat benefited from the new opportunities offered by Arctic whaling, especially through trade with winter whaling stations.[84] For most Inupiat communities, however, the impact of nineteenth-century commercial whaling was almost universally negative. The most significant consequence was the decline in whale and other marine mammal populations. Vaughan estimates that over 18,500 whales were killed in the Beaufort Sea whale fishery between 1848 and 1914.[85] In addition, an estimated 100,000 walrus had been killed by the mid 1870s, massively reducing an important food supply.[86] The whaling industry brought large numbers of whites into contact with the Inupiat communities of northern Alaska, where they introduced European diseases and cultural habits into the Arctic. In a particularly extreme example, starvation and smallpox killed an estimated 1,000 people of a total population of 1,500 on St. Lawrence Island in the Bering Strait between 1878–81.[87] Along with other trappings of modernity, whalers brought firearms and alcohol into the Arctic, both of which created new social problems.

Over time, declining whale populations off the coast of northern Alaska also had a major impact on the whaling industry, which was already suffering as a result of the increasing shift to mineral oil. Following the disastrous season of 1871, when thirty-two American whaling ships got stuck in the ice and had to be abandoned, the American whaling industry shifted from New Bedford to San Francisco: much closer to the Beaufort Sea fishery.[88] But this move proved to be a temporary reprieve, and the Arctic whaling industry was in terminal decline. The industry was hit hard by the collapse of the market for baleen in 1907. At the turn of the twentieth century, commercial whaling off the coast of Alaska was largely restricted to a handful of shore stations, which began to adopt modern whaling techniques. By this stage, commercial Arctic whaling was being completely eclipsed by the development of a modern whaling industry around the continent of Antarctica.

Antarctic Whaling

While American whalers pushed the logic of the northern hemisphere's resource frontier to its geographic conclusion in the Bering Sea and the Arctic Ocean, whalers in Norway adopted a different strategy.[89] Over the second half of the nineteenth century, Norwegian whaling entrepreneurs sought a technological solution to the problem of scarcity. Whales that could be caught by traditional means had indeed been hunted to the point of extinction in much of the northern hemisphere. But there still appeared to be abundant sightings of the larger, faster rorqual whales that could not easily be caught by traditional methods on account of their large size, speed, and tendency to sink when killed. Norwegian whalers began to experiment with ways to hunt blue whales, fin whales, and other species of rorqual whales, the largest living creatures anywhere on the planet. Such innovation would shift the balance of power in global whaling away from the United States and Britain toward Norway, and would have major implications for the history of both Polar Regions, especially Antarctica.

The most important whaling innovator in the nineteenth century was the Norwegian Sven Foyn. He began his career hunting seals in Greenland and Svalbard in the 1830s. Aware of the abundance of rorqual whales in seas around Norway, Foyn recognized a commercial opportunity and dedicated much of the rest of his career to developing technologies to kill these massive animals. The most dramatic innovation was the attachment of a grenade to the harpoon that would explode on impact, killing or maiming the whale and reducing the struggle. Rather than being thrown by hand, these grenade harpoons were fired by gunpowder, increasingly their range and effectiveness. Foyn added motors to the catcher vessels to improve their speed and reduce the reliance on whaling crews. Air pumps were developed to inflate the

carcasses of dead whales before they sank. Foyn was applying the technologies and methods of the factory system to the industrial slaughter
of whales.

The era of modern whaling brought about by Foyn's technological
innovations created something of a resource frontier within a resource
frontier. Norwegian whalers found themselves able to hunt species of
whale that had previously escaped exploitation, and this reset the geographical frontiers of the whaling industry. For several decades at the
end of the nineteenth century, whales and whale oil were once again
plentiful to the point of overproduction. But it did not take long before
modern whaling techniques reduced rorqual whale populations around
the coasts of Norway and in other relatively accessible locations in the
Arctic. While Foyn's innovations undoubtedly added to the complexity of the whaling industry, the logic of the resource frontier appeared
to remain inexorable and hunting-induced scarcity in the northern
hemisphere helped to cause expansion into the southern hemisphere.

Northern whalers had pursued their prey in the waters of the
southern hemisphere from at least the second half of the eighteenth
century, and these expeditions continued into the nineteenth century,
as famously described by Herman Melville in *Moby Dick*. But these
expeditions were largely confined to the hunting of sperm whales, right
whales, and sometimes humpback whales in the warmer waters of the
Atlantic, Pacific, and Indian Oceans. It was not until the late nineteenth
century that whalers began to take an active interest in the waters of
the Antarctic Ocean around the coasts of the Antarctic Peninsula. In
the early 1870s, the German Eduard Dallmann sailed southwards and
explored the waters of the Antarctic Peninsula region to prospect for
whales. In the southern summer of 1892–93 a Scottish expedition from
Dundee explored a similar area.[90] Both of these expeditions were looking for right whales, which had been reported abundant by James Clark
Ross in the 1840s. But although they both encountered large numbers
of rorqual whales, they did not find the easy-to-hunt right whales that
they were looking for.

At around the same time as the Scottish expedition, the Norwegian
Carl Anton Larsen led a third exploratory whaling expedition to the
Antarctic Peninsula region. Larsen was also interested in finding right
whales, but unlike the expeditions from Germany and Scotland, he did

not immediately dismiss the possibility of exploiting the larger, faster rorqual whales that he found around the Antarctic Peninsula. His own experiences of whaling in the northern hemisphere off the coasts of Norway had alerted Larsen to the probability that northern whaling stocks would soon be depleted. This experience also familiarized Larsen with the technological innovations that were making possible the hunting of rorqual whales. Although other Norwegian whaling entrepreneurs were skeptical of the logistical challenges of southern whaling and wary of overproduction, Larsen took a long-term view and remained persistent.[91]

Between 1901 and 1903 Larsen played a role in the Swedish Nordenskjold expedition to the Antarctic Peninsula region.[92] His participation was largely motivated by the possibilities that this involvement would offer for further developing his ideas for southern whaling. In early 1903, Larsen got more than he bargained for when his ship, the *Antarctic*, sank as he sailed toward Snow Hill Island to pick up Nordenskjold and his five-man party. The sinking of the *Antarctic* precipitated one of the most remarkable stories of survival and rescue of the so-called heroic era of Antarctic exploration. Larsen and his crew were forced to spend a winter in Antarctica, separated from Nordenskjold, and from three of their own party who had been sent to communicate with the Swedish explorer. Despite the difficult circumstances, only one crewmember of the *Antarctic* perished during the winter. Larsen and his men along with the two other separated parties were rescued by the *Uruguay* from Argentina, and they were taken to Buenos Aires in December 1903 where they received a hero's welcome.

Ever the opportunist, Larsen used the publicity generated by his safe return to Buenos Aires to drum up financial support for his plans for an Antarctic whaling industry.[93] Early twentieth-century Argentina was booming as a result of its abundant agricultural exports, and Larsen successfully raised money for the founding of the PESCA whaling company. Larsen returned to Norway to purchase equipment and to hire Norwegian whalers and PESCA began whaling operations from the island of South Georgia in 1904. They established a shore station in Grytviken Harbor on the northern shore of the island. Although the total catch of 173 whales was not quite as high as Larsen expected, it was enough to keep the company operating beyond its first season.

The years that followed the establishment of PESCA's whaling station at Grytviken Harbor on South Georgia saw a rapid expansion of Antarctic whaling. Larsen had shown it was possible to overcome the logistical challenges of whaling in Antarctica, and other whaling entrepreneurs were now willing to give it a go. Much of the capital for Antarctic whaling and nearly all the labor came from Norway, although Britain and Chile were also involved, along with Argentina. One shore station was built at Deception Island in the South Shetlands, but most whaling companies set up their stations on the northern coast of South Georgia. Perhaps surprisingly, given its vast interests in Arctic whaling in the nineteenth century, as well as in the Antarctic sealing industry, companies from the United States showed very little interest in joining the nascent Antarctic whaling bonanza, probably as a result of other economic opportunities and the increased competition from mineral oil.

The development of a modern whaling industry on the island of South Georgia radically changed perceptions of the Antarctic environment, and increased interest in the question of sovereignty. In the early days of Antarctic whaling, whalers relied on shore stations and sheltered harbors to process their catch. The processing of whale blubber required large quantities of fresh water as well as boiling vats at high temperatures: much easier to accomplish on shore rather than on a ship at sea. Ownership of these territories therefore held out the possibility of taxing and regulating the whaling industry. This turned a region that that had no commercial attraction into a potentially valuable colony.

The British government had asserted a nominal claim over the island of South Georgia since Captain Cook had taken possession of the island in the late eighteenth century. But the British government had done little during the nineteenth century to demonstrate its sovereignty over this uninhabited island, and by the early twentieth century there was some confusion about ownership. In 1908 the British sought to end this confusion by making a formal sovereignty claim to a vast expanse of territory south of the Crown Colony of the Falkland Islands in the Atlantic Ocean. The territory was named the Falkland Islands Dependencies, and initially consisted of "the groups of islands known as South Georgia, the South Orkneys, the South Shetlands, and the Sandwich Islands, and the territory known as Graham's Land, situated in the

South Atlantic Ocean to the south of the 50th parallel of south latitude, and lying between the 20th and the 80th degrees of west longitude."[94] An amendment in 1917 clarified that the Dependencies were not meant to include Patagonia, and formally extended the claim all the way to the South Pole. The British claim effectively applied this longitude-derived "sector principle" to Antarctic sovereignty, borrowing an idea that was being developed in the Arctic.

As historians Peder Roberts and D. Graham Burnett have shown in recent works on the history of Antarctic whaling, the British government established a scientific research project known as the Discovery Expeditions to assert its environmental authority through the creation of useful knowledge about Antarctic whales.[95] In a neat circularity, the British used taxes from the whaling industry to pay for science, which then provided useful information for the regulation of whaling, and supported sovereignty. Where before an international free-for-all had created a tragedy-of-the-commons situation in the case of sealing, British government officials and whale scientists hoped to prevent this from happening again by creating the conditions for a sustainable

Figure 9 *Deception Island Whaling Station showing feeding sea birds, photograph by Hubert Wilkins. (Source: American Geographical Society Library) [(48al) 53156 No. 5290 L]*

whaling industry in the Southern Ocean. It was a highly ambitious project, but one very much in keeping with wider plans for developing the Polar Regions in the first half of the twentieth century.

On a local scale, the whaling industry and the associated attempts to "improve" South Georgia and other sub-Antarctic Islands such as Deception Island had a significant impact on the environment.[96] Construction of buildings, the production of waste, and the use of fossil fuels produced industrial pollution where none had existed before. The presence of hundreds of rotting whale carcasses on the beaches and waters around the whaling stations created an appalling stench. Photographs suggest that these carcasses attracted seabirds to scavenge on the dead flesh, undoubtedly with some impact on bird populations (Figure 9). On the island of South Georgia, some of the most significant environmental impacts were associated with the introduction of invasive species.[97] Rats had been inadvertently introduced to the island, probably by sealers in the early nineteenth century. They wreaked havoc with local bird populations, which had not known terrestrial predation. The deliberate introduction of reindeer as food and sport for the whalers exacerbated the environmental problems associated with invasive species.

On a broader scale, the British government's dreams of creating a sustainable whaling industry in the Southern Ocean came up against environmental and technological realities. Within a few years of Britain's sovereignty claims to the Falkland Islands Dependencies, another technological innovation massively reduced the viability of British intentions to tax and regulate the Antarctic whaling industry. In 1929 the *Lancing* became the first "pelagic" whaling ship—all operations could be conducted in the open sea—to operate in Antarctic waters. The development of pelagic whaling very quickly took away from the British government the ability to control the whaling industry. With no effective regulation, the Antarctic whaling industry was thrown back into the tragedy of the commons.[98] In the years that followed there was a massive expansion of whaling in the Southern Ocean that reduced whale populations to near extinction. In the middle of the twentieth century this would be exacerbated by the Cold War.

3

NATURE CONQUERED, NATURE UNCONQUERED

Polar Exploration

"Adventure," the Norwegian polar explorer Roald Amundsen is supposed to have said, "is just bad planning." This famous quote has often been interpreted as a not-so-subtle dig at Captain Robert Falcon Scott, Amundsen's deceased British rival in the race to the South Pole, and in many ways it was. But it also sums up something of the paradox of exploration, especially in the Polar Regions. On the one hand, it was possible to make some preparations for what the conditions might be like by piecing together previous experience and scraps of geographical knowledge. Amundsen had extensive experience of living and working in both the Arctic and Antarctica, and he put this to use on his relatively trouble-free arrival at and safe return from the South Pole in the 1911–12 southern summer. On the other hand, exploration was by definition a journey into the unknown, and it was impossible to plan perfectly for what you did not know. Without going there, nobody could have any idea, for example, of how low temperatures on the polar plateau might fall, or how many crevasses might be encountered. Adventure could never be entirely separated from the act of exploration, and that was part of its great attraction. The irony of the quote is that Amundsen was almost certainly the most accomplished polar adventurer of the early twentieth century.

It would be no exaggeration to suggest that most of the historical writing on the Polar Regions has focused in one way or another on the themes of exploration and adventure. In the Arctic, European exploration began over two thousand years ago with the expeditions of Pytheus to an unknown northern land. In Antarctica, European exploration only really began to get going a little over two hundred years ago in the eighteenth century with the voyages of Captain Cook and others. By the nineteenth century, however, the level of European exploration increased exponentially in both Polar Regions, and would continue well into the twentieth century. Building on the mentalities of the European Enlightenment, polar explorers fed off a popular fascination with adventure and with the filling in of blank spaces on maps of the world. Newspaper readers would wait eagerly for scraps of information about the success or failure of expeditions to the Arctic or Antarctica, and exploration was very much a reciprocal relationship between explorers and their publics.[1] It is hardly surprising, therefore, that later generations of readers have also been attracted to tales of adventure, survival, and death from the Arctic and Antarctica, and that histories of exploration dominate the "Polar Regions" shelves of most popular bookstores.

In contrast to cultural historians of the Polar Regions, environmental historians have been relatively slow to embrace the theme of exploration as an activity.[2] Exploration does not fit readily into three of the central themes of environmental history: how humans have degraded the environment, how people have sought to "save" the environment, and how scholars have understood the environment through natural history and the developing science of ecology.[3] Although exploratory expeditions have certainly had some impact on the environment they travel through—as demonstrated by a photograph taken during Isaac Hayes'1868 Arctic expedition, titled "The game. Six polar bears captured before breakfast" (Figure 10)—these "declensionist narratives" of environmental degradation generally pale in comparison to the environmental consequences of settlement and systematic resource extraction. By definition, explorers are seeing places for the first time, supposedly in an "untouched" state, so there is little immediate need for an environmentalist consciousness. And while many polar explorers, such as the Australian geologist Douglas Mawson, were trained scientists, much of the "real science" was done by the people who received

Figure 10   *Photograph from Isaac Hayes 1869 Arctic Expedition titled "The game. Six bears captured before breakfast." (Source: American Geographical Society Library) [(47b3) 531456 No. 10247 L]*

and processed this new information or by those who followed and had time to investigate properly.[4]

The Polar Regions offer good locations for environmental historians to embrace the theme of exploration.[5] At a macro level, environmental histories of exploration in the Polar Regions connect to the theme of imperialism through ideas of discovery and the "conquest of nature." Under international law, the act of being first to sight and record a new place conveys certain rights to the country that makes the "discovery." This has given exploration a strong political emphasis, especially since the eighteenth century. More profoundly, exploration has often been presented as the first stage in a multistep process of conquering the natural world: explorers venture into the unknown and their act of seeing new places is followed by mapping, claiming, extracting, and administering.[6] In the Polar Regions, as in many other parts of the world, these initial acts of geographical discovery helped to lay the foundations for the imperial appropriation that followed. In the Arctic and Antarctica, the ability to conquer nature had the added advantage of demonstrating imperial power far beyond the place being conquered. As the most inhospitable places on the planet, the Polar Regions offered an ideal sphere for the conquest of nature *in extremis*: if the environmental hostility of the extreme high and low latitudes could be overcome, there was no part of the world where nature could not be subdued.[7] It is perhaps no coincidence that almost all the major imperial powers of the nineteenth and early twentieth century sent expeditions to the Polar Regions. Exploration offered another sphere for imperial competition, as well as a distraction from some of the less savory aspects of imperialism.[8] Accounts of polar exploration were widely distributed to enthusiastic publics, and these stories functioned as affirmations of racial hierarchies and imperial vitality.[9]

On a micro level, histories of exploration focus on the importance of human bodies in environmental history. The bodies of explorers became cold and hungry, lacked vitamins, and broke down. Bodies moving through the Polar Regions responded to the external reality of the environment being explored, whether through frostbite, malnutrition, or a hardening to the rigors of constant exercise. In his biography of the American explorer Zebulon Pike, the environmental historian Jared Orsi examines how bodily discomfort became central to a certain sense of nationalist virtue in the early Republican United States.[10] A very similar case could be made for the connections between polar explorers and the imperial powers they came from. The deaths of Britain's Captain Scott and his companions, for example, have often been portrayed as tragic martyrdoms for the empire, and the popular fascination with the minutia of how they died played a central role in this mythmaking.[11] A focus on individual bodies also helps to demonstrate the multiple connections between the history of exploration in the Arctic and Antarctica, which are more obvious in the history of exploration than in almost any other theme.[12] The same men often explored both north and south, very often using the same ships and airplanes; fingers that had become frostbitten in the Arctic could hurt again on Antarctic expeditions, and vice versa. Following Britain's Captain James Cook, among the most famous "bi-polar" explorers were James Clark Ross, Roald Amundsen, Hubert Wilkins, and Richard E. Byrd. These men brought experiences gained in one Polar Region with them when they traveled into the other, and this profoundly shaped the way they understood the new environments that they encountered.

A little more subtly, the history of exploration in the Arctic and Antarctica provides useful case studies for thinking about the broad range of interactions among human activity, environmental perception, and the material environment that are the subjects of environmental history. Although these interactions are difficult to untangle, there is often a relative simplicity to the histories of Arctic and Antarctic exploration that allows for specific interactions to be pulled out and analyzed. The recurrent belief in an "Open Polar Sea" during the nineteenth-century exploration of the Arctic, for example, offers an opportunity for thinking about the relationship between human actions and environmental perceptions. The idea that there would be ice-free water in high northern latitudes motivated explorers to undertake risky expeditions to find a northwest sea route from the Atlantic to the Pacific. Only after a long history of recurrent failure did the actual experience of traveling in the Arctic convince explorers and geographers that no such Open Polar Sea existed. Similarly, in the early twentieth century, Scott and Amundsen's race to the South Pole offers a number of insights into the relationship between the material environment and environmental perception. Despite seeking to conquer polar nature on behalf of the British Empire, Captain Scott (like all other polar explorers) found his experience of Antarctic exploration profoundly shaped by the material reality of the polar environment: "My God, this is a terrible place," he wrote in his diary at the South Pole. Scott's never-completed return journey from the bottom of the world offers an example of how human perception can shape the material environment, as growing despondency and despair added to the destructive power of the Antarctic. While polar explorers rarely had a significant impact on the material environment they traveled through—at least in comparison to the changes that would often follow—they did learn to modify their immediate environments through an increased use of technology. Technological developments in polar exploration, especially an increasing use of airplanes in the third and fourth decades of the twentieth century, offer examples of the relationship between human actions and the material environment. The act of bringing technologies such as airplanes to the Arctic and Antarctica brought about relatively minor modifications to the physical environment that would have major implications for what explorers could do in those places.

Despite the recurring attempts to "conquer" polar nature during this period, and despite the numerous human bodies that were sacrificed to this cause, the Arctic and Antarctica in many ways remained distinctly unconquered. Into the 1950s, for example, large blank spaces continued to exist on maps of Antarctica. The history of exploration was nevertheless a fundamental part of the broader histories of economic development, political rivalry, and contests over the environment in the Polar Regions, which are more often looked at through the lens of environmental history. At the same time, an environmental history approach can offer a new perspective on the history of exploration and present a new way of thinking about what has often become an overly familiar subject. Despite a recurrent tendency to look at the history of polar exploration as being separate from wider historical events, it is important to see these expeditions as a fundamental part of the environmental histories of the Arctic and Antarctica.

Open Polar Sea

Between 1903 and 1906 the Norwegian Roald Amundsen on board the *Gjøa* became the leader of the first expedition to sail from the Atlantic Ocean to the Pacific Ocean through the archipelagos of Arctic Canada.[13] The journey helped to establish Amundsen as one of the preeminent polar explorers of his age. He combined experience in the Arctic with experience in Antarctica, having been a member of Adrien de Gerlache's *Belgica* expedition of 1897–99, which became the first group to spend a winter south of the Antarctic Circle.[14] The *Gjøa* voyage demonstrated that a northern sea route from Europe to Asia— the fabled Northwest Passage—did exist, and could be navigated. But the difficulties faced by Amundsen and his crew made a mockery of longstanding beliefs in an "Open Polar Sea." Between September 1903 and August 1905, the ship was stuck in sea ice in a natural harbor on King William Island. When the ship was finally able to get free, it was only two months before it again got stuck in the sea ice, this time near Hershel Island, and had to spend another winter in the Arctic. Although Amundsen and his crew were able to put these delays to productive use, the difficulty of the voyage hardly suggested that this could be a commercially viable shipping route.

The search for a northern sea route from Europe to Asia illustrates the utility of viewing a history of exploration through the lens of environmental history.[15] The history of European attempts to find a Northwest Passage to Asia fits neatly into an imperial history of attempts to conquer nature and control the environment: the discovery of a northern sea route held out the possibility of gaining a major geopolitical advantage, and this was a major motivating factor. The significant death toll that accompanied this quest attests to the suffering endured by human minds and bodies as a result of the hostility of the polar environment. The search for a Northwest Passage also offers an excellent case study of the relationship between environmental perception and human activity within the history of exploration. During the nineteenth century in particular, the idea of an ice-free Open Polar Sea led to explorers recurrently risking their ships and their lives in the erroneous belief that conditions would improve just a little further to the north. In retrospect, the search for the Northwest Passage might be seen as a classic example of the triumph of optimism over observation. Explorers, geographers, businessmen, and politicians wanted to believe in the existence of an open Polar Sea, and this belief repeatedly trumped the significant evidence that was gathering to the contrary. In reality, sea-ice conditions tended to get worse with latitude. The belief in an Open Polar Sea caused sailors to get into greater difficulty as they sailed northward. It was only toward the end of the nineteenth century that collective experience began to win out over wishful thinking as human activity shaped environmental perceptions. For a long time in the exploration of the Arctic, what explorers believed about the northern environment was at least as important as the material reality in shaping what they attempted to do.

In many ways Amundsen's voyage through the Northwest Passage represented the culmination of at least two millennia of speculation, exploration, and the accumulation of geographical knowledge. Beginning with the first Greek ideas about the Arctic and Antarctica, geographers and cartographers have debated the nature of the Polar Regions. Were there oceans or continents at the top and bottom of the world? And if they were oceans were they open water or covered in ice? John Cabot had begun the quest for Northwest Passage in 1497, but there was little initial success.[16] In his famous world map of 1569 the Flemish cartographer Gerardus Mercator portrayed the Arctic as an open polar sea, while he placed a continent at the bottom of the southern hemisphere.[17] Other early British expeditions, such as those of Frobisher and Hudson, took a lead in searching for a route through the Canadian Arctic. Belief in an Open Polar Sea was reflected in the instructions given to Captain Cook in 1776 that he should return to Britain from the Pacific via the Northwest Passage (an instruction he was unable to follow).[18]

Despite some evidence to the contrary, at the beginning of the nineteenth century there was a widespread belief in an Open Polar Sea in the Arctic. Explorers had noted the tendency for good weather to predominate during summer in high northern latitudes. Sea ice would surely melt in the near-constant summer sunlight, believed geographers and explorers such as Louis Antoine de Bougainville, Samuel Engel, and David Barrington, not altogether unreasonably.[19] The American John Cleve Symmes added a more metaphysical dimension to the Open Polar Sea thesis, with his belief in a hollow Earth with openings at the Poles.[20] He believed that it would be possible to enter the center of the earth by traveling to the top or bottom of the world, and that these openings might warm the Polar Regions. Although today this would be regarded as the very definition of pseudo science, at the time it was treated by more than a handful of explorers and geographers with some seriousness.[21]

In the Polar Regions, human bodies are organisms that have to interact with the environment in order to stay alive, every bit as much as polar bears, penguins, or other creatures of "nature." The greatest direct threat faced by Arctic expeditions during the nineteenth century was not the cold or the sea ice, but scurvy: a hidden killer. Before the discovery of vitamins, little was known about the causes of this deadly malady. It was understood that scurvy could be prevented by eating fresh fruit and vegetables, and by the nineteenth century, most maritime voyages were able to stock up on sufficient fresh supplies to get them through; lime juice was seen as particularly effective. For expeditions attempting to explore the Polar Regions, however, this was not such an easy task, especially when ships became trapped in ice. Edible fruit and vegetables were scarce in the Arctic, and it was not uncommon for stranded expeditions to eat mosses and lichens in an often vain attempt to ward off scurvy. It was certainly possible to obtain sufficient vitamins from eating fresh animal flesh—especially whale skin and seal liver—but this required quantities not always available.[22] Although the science of vitamins would develop rapidly toward the end of the nineteenth century, it would not be until the middle decades of the twentieth century that biochemists would be able to isolate and manufacture vitamin supplements, which would make life for polar explorers much safer.

In the aftermath of the Napoleonic Wars, it was the British Royal Navy that once again took a lead in the search for the Northwest Passage. Understanding the commercial advantages that the discovery of a shortened route to Asia would bring, the British Parliament offered a series of rewards for any expedition making progress toward sailing through the Arctic. Between 1818 and 1828, the British Royal Navy sent no fewer than twelve expeditions to the Arctic, with the central aim of searching for a sea route to Asia.[23] The mastermind behind these voyages was the senior naval officer John Barrow, who made it his life's work to find the Northwest Passage.[24] Despite the publicity generated by these voyages, they made little progress toward their intended goal, and by the late 1820s, the naval hierarchy was rapidly losing interest.

In 1829, when Captain John Ross of the British Royal Navy, accompanied by his nephew James Clark Ross, made another attempt to find the Northwest Passage, they had to do so on board a private expedition with no official backing from the Navy. This expedition had little more success in achieving its central goal than its predecessors, but was interesting for a number of reasons. Despite losing its ship, the *Victory*, nineteen of the twenty-two members survived the expedition and were rescued by a whaling vessel after over three years in the Arctic. The crew was able to overcome the threat posed by scurvy because the Netsilik Inuit supplied fresh meat to the British explorers, in an act of charity.[25] This dependent relationship highlights fundamental differences between the abilities of the Inuit and the British to survive in the polar environment. The traditional environmental knowledge of the indigenous inhabitants of the Arctic allowed them to meet their own material needs and still have a surplus with which to aid struggling strangers. Ross and his men lacked the knowledge of the Arctic environment to survive unaided, and would likely have perished without the assistance they were given. The British, however, were aided by the fact that, unlike most of the naval expeditions of the time, there were not too many of them for the available supply of fresh food. This was a lesson that other Arctic expeditions would be slow to learn, as the British Royal Navy's "proper way to do things" repeatedly trumped actual experiences of traveling through the Arctic.

In one of its most publicized achievements, members of the Ross expedition became the first people knowingly to reach the North Magnetic Pole, or at least to get very close to it.[26] Shortly after returning from the Arctic, James Clark Ross set about organizing an expedition to Antarctica with the aim of locating the South Magnetic Pole. In the rational and utilitarian spirit of the times, he believed that finding this point in the southern hemisphere would aid British navigation and facilitate an extension of British naval power. Unlike his uncle's Arctic expedition, James Clark Ross's Antarctica expedition enjoyed the full support of the Royal Navy, with additional backing from the scientific establishment. Ross also highlighted that a journey to Antarctica would add to British maritime prestige by sailing across some of the most hostile and unknown seas in the world. The fact that the United States and France were also participating in the so-called magnetic crusade of the late 1830s, with the respective expeditions of Charles Wilkes and Dumont D'Urville, only added to the urgency for Great Britain. In heading south after gaining experience in the north, James Clark Ross followed Captain Cook's lead in building a naval career that combined the two Polar Regions. Lessons learned in the Arctic benefited Ross in Antarctica: he knew, for example, that a supply of fresh meat could help to keep his men free from scurvy. An approach that combined exploration in the Arctic and Antarctica would become increasingly common in the century following Ross's return.

James Clark Ross's Antarctic expedition was an incredible success.[27] The *Erebus* and *Terror* sailed further south than any other expedition had previously achieved, into the sea that today bears his name. The ships sighted the trans-Antarctic mountains, named Victoria Land after the Queen, and made a vague sovereignty claim to the region on behalf of the British Empire. They also encountered Ross Island and a barrier of ice today known as the Ross Ice Shelf. In an example of human activity narrowing the gap between imaginations of nature and encounters with the real thing, the expedition came to realize that the south magnetic pole was almost certainly located inland, and therefore inaccessible to a naval voyage. On his way back to England, Ross made several important discoveries around the Antarctic Peninsula region on the opposite side of the continent. In terms of both areas explored and scientific findings, this was among the most successful expeditions to the Polar Regions.

James Clark Ross spent part of his expedition docked at Hobart in Van Diemen's Land (now Tasmania). While there he spent time with Governor John Franklin and his wife Jane. John Franklin was a naval officer who had previously led three of the British Royal Navy's expeditions to the Arctic in the late 1810s and 1820s. Meeting with Ross helped to rekindle Franklin's passion for polar exploration, and demonstrates the importance of connections between the Arctic and Antarctica. Upon his return to Britain Franklin was chosen to lead another British naval expedition after John Ross had turned down the opportunity.

Franklin's would become the most infamous Arctic expedition of the nineteenth century. It set off in May 1845 with high hopes of finding the Northwest Passage from Europe to Asia. The expedition's two ships were the *Erebus* and the *Terror*, which had been the ships used by James Clark Ross on his recent expedition to Antarctica. Buoyed by Ross's successes in the south, this was a period of tremendous geographic optimism, and Franklin and his backers in the British Admiralty believed that enough knowledge had now been accumulated to make it possible to find a route through the Canadian Arctic. Under the continued influence of the now-octogenarian John Barrow, however, Franklin's expedition would see little innovation in the practice of Arctic exploration. In particular, the expedition remained very large, thereby ignoring the insights gained by John Ross and James Clark Ross that smaller expeditions had a higher chance of survival if they were to get into trouble.

After the Franklin expedition failed to return by the end of 1846, some polar experts began to worry. John Ross offered to lead a rescue expedition in February 1847, but the Admiralty rejected his offer. By 1848, there was still no news of Franklin's expedition, and the Admiralty sent a ship to look for the lost party. Franklin's fate became a *cause célèbre* of mid-nineteenth–century Britain, and the search for the missing explorer became a media sensation. Jane Franklin made passionate appeals on behalf of her disappeared husband, offering a reward of £5,000 for his rescue.[28] By the time the British government offered an additional £20,000 in March 1850, it was looking increasingly unlikely that any members of the Franklin expedition would be found alive.

In total, there were at least sixteen attempted rescue expeditions that could be described as serious, and several others that were more frivolous or amateur in their composition (in the hope of collecting a reward).[29] In August 1850 remains were found of Franklin's 1845–46 winter quarters on Beechey Island, off the southwest coast of Devon Island. The graves of three men were discovered, but no message had been left concerning which direction the expedition was taking. Four years later in October 1854, John Rae, an employee of the Hudson's Bay Company, arrived in London to report that local Inuit had seen white men fitting the description of Franklin and his crew. It would not be until 1859 that Francis Leopold M'Clintock found the remains of the Franklin Expedition scattered along the shores of King William Island. Diaries reported that Franklin had died on June 11, 1847, after his ships had become jammed in the ice. Early in the summer season of 1848, the 105 men who had survived the winter made an attempt to get to a region where game might be found. But weather conditions, sea ice, and a lack of food prevented anyone from achieving this goal. The hostility of the Arctic environment proved too much for the minds and bodies of the British polar explorers.

The causes of the Franklin tragedy have been much debated. In 1938, for example, Vilhjalmur Stefansson included the Franklin expedition in his *Unsolved Mysteries of the Arctic*.[30] As with the Greenland Norse, who Stefansson also discussed, it is unlikely that there will ever be a definitive answer to the question of what happened to the Franklin expedition. Lead poisoning from tinned foods, pneumonia, and even social breakdown and cannibalism have been mooted as potential factors. A more prosaic but likely explanation is that the crews of the *Erebus* and *Terror* succumbed to scurvy and malnutrition. There were too many people for the available food supplies, and that proved to be a fatal equation.

Although unsuccessful in the rescue of a single member of Franklin's unfortunate crew, the search helped to stimulate further interest in Arctic exploration, especially in the United States.[31] The belief in an Open Polar Sea continued to shape the exploration of the Arctic into the second half of the nineteenth century, as explorers stubbornly refused to learn from their collective experiences. After spending the winter of 1860–61 stuck in the sea ice north of Smith Sound, for example, the American explorer Isaac Israel Hayes remained convinced that he had seen an Open Polar Sea.[32] In the summer of 1879, an expedition sponsored by Gordon Bennett and led by George W. DeLong on board the *Jeannette* made an attempt to reach the Open Polar Sea by a different route through the Bering Strait. This also ended in disaster when the ship became stuck in the sea ice in the Chukchi Sea, with the deaths of twenty out of the thirty-three crew, including DeLong. Combined with the loss of life on the Greely expedition during the First International Polar Year (1882–83), the tragedy of the *Jeannette* expedition did much to put an end to speculation about an Open Polar Sea. From the mid 1880s onwards, all serious attempts to travel in high northern latitudes would plan on crossing the Arctic sea ice in one fashion or another.

Another consequence of the accumulated experiences of Arctic travel was a growing willingness to learn from the Inuit. On an extended sledging expedition during his expedition of 1878–80, for example, Lieutenant Frederick Schwatka of the U.S. Cavalry sought to live by eating an Inuit diet of fresh meat. In general, most of the expeditions of this period got on reasonably well with the local inhabitants they encountered, as demonstrated by a sketch from the Schwatka expedition (Figure 11). Despite the persistence of clear racial hierarchies, there was an acknowledgment that western expeditions could learn valuable skills from the Inuit for living and traveling in the Arctic. Some of these lessons would also prove useful for expeditions in Antarctica.

By the time Amundsen sailed through the Northwest Passage between 1903 and 1906, virtually every part of the route had been sailed by at least one previous expedition. Amundsen and his five companions were simply the first people to make the voyage as a single journey. Explorers and geographers already knew that the Northwest Passage would have little commercial value as a result of the difficulty of the journey and the inherent dangers posed by polar navigation.

Figure 11 *Schwatka Expedition Sketch (Source: American Geographical Society Library) [From Archive]*

The voyage of the *Gjøa* was nevertheless a remarkable achievement. The small size of the expedition revealed that Amundsen had learned important lessons from the numerous failed attempts to cross from the Atlantic to the Pacific over the course of the nineteenth century. The journey cemented Amundsen's reputation as one of the preeminent polar explorers of his age, and the experiences he gained stood him in good stead to continue his adventurous career on the other side of the planet. Along with his mentor Fridtjof Nansen, he was a passionate Norwegian nationalist and realized the important role that polar exploration could play in constructing a sense of national identity at a time when Norway was gaining its political independence from Sweden.

Looking back at the nineteenth-century expeditions to the Arctic that culminated in Amundsen's traverse of the Northwest Passage between 1903–06, one thing that stands out is the tremendous loss of life. Several hundred European and North American sailors and explorers died in the search for a northern sea route from the Atlantic to the Pacific. These figures are even more incredible when compared to the death toll from the so-called heroic era of Antarctic exploration, which took place roughly from 1895–1917. On the Franklin expedition alone,

129 men lost their lives, almost exactly ten times more than the number of people killed as a direct result of Antarctic exploration during the entire twenty-year "heroic age" at the turn of the twentieth century.[33] A number of factors account for this high mortality rate in the Arctic. The first is simply that many more expeditions headed to the north than went to the south, and the expeditions were often much larger. Another is the relative chronology, with Antarctic exploration generally taking place at a later date and being able to learn from earlier failures in the Arctic. An insistence on continuing to take large expeditions to the Arctic that exceeded available food supply suggested an inability to learn. Simple bad luck was also a factor in several of the disasters. But the recurrent beliefs in an Open Polar Sea undoubtedly played a role in the Arctic death toll by encouraging ships to sail further north and take greater risks than they likely would have done if such an idea had not existed. It is impossible to say exactly how many deaths can be attributed to an environmental perception that would prove erroneous, but the persistence of the idea of an Open Polar Sea in the history of Arctic exploration clearly reveals the importance of the relationship between human activities and ways of understanding of the Arctic environment within environmental history.

Race for the Poles

In 1877 John Oldfield Chadwick, a fellow of Britain's Royal Geographical Society published a pamphlet with the somewhat convoluted titled "Perseverance in Arctic Exploration: An enquiry whether the advantages which may be expected to result from a successful Expedition to the North Pole are sufficient to justify further efforts in the attempt." In it he made a sustained argument that the British should be the first to reach the North Pole:

> The foremost advantage I would hope for and claim is, that the Pole should be first reached by our own countrymen. The spirit of enterprise and adventure, which in the past has contributed so materially to the universal ascendancy of the British race, is still in abounding vigor; and it must be held to be an object of laudable national pride that the long-standing problem, if ever solved, should be solved by Britons.

The effort will be great, the strain gigantic—but its subsequence good influence will be proportionate.[34]

Oldfield's case explicitly combined science and exploration with an unashamed sense of racial supremacy, all tied together by the idea of conquering polar nature. Such patriotic calls for continued polar exploration were not unique to Britain, and similar nationalistic pleas could be heard in the United States and a number of European countries.

In some ways the race to the North and South Poles that culminated in the early twentieth century might be seen as an extension of the search for an Open Polar Sea. There were similar elements of excitement and adventure to the story and there was definitely a degree of blurring in the two histories: the Norwegian Roald Amundsen would once again play a starring role. But in other ways the race to the geographical poles was quite different. Unlike the search for a northern sea route, the act of getting to the top or bottom of the world had little practical advantage, especially after the idea of an Open Polar Sea was dismissed. The poles were geographical abstractions, points on the map with little obvious significance beyond being the places with most winter darkness and most summer light. The first explorers who attempted to get to the poles tended to plan a simple out-and-back journey, leaving extensive scientific investigation for another time. There was little expectation that anything worthwhile would be found. The race to the poles was very much about getting to specific places, but these places were far less important for what they were than for what they said about the men, nations, and empires that proved they could reach them.

In both the scale of the challenge and its abstract nature, the geographical poles were fitting goals for the high modernist imperial powers of the early twentieth century.[35] As implied by Oldfield, the more hostile the environment, the more the supposed conquest was believed to reflect back on the power and prestige of the country doing the conquering. Human bodies were the sites where these imperial ideologies of environmental conquest played out. The race, gender, and social class of these bodies were believed to be determinants of how well they could withstand the hostility of the polar environment: white male bodies were thought to be uniquely capable of surviving the worst conditions of the Arctic and Antarctica (and although white male working-class bodies were deemed physically capable, their abilities to cope mentally were sometimes questioned). A focus on human bodies also helps to reveal the importance of the relationship between the material reality and environmental perceptions within environmental history. For all the imperial rhetoric that underlay the attempts to get to the North and South Poles, polar exploration brought explorers face to face with the material reality of the Arctic and Antarctic environments. Snow and ice, hunger and malnutrition, intense cold, and incessant winds became powerful determinants of environmental perception. At the same time, human understanding continued to shape the reality of the material environment. A powerful sense of national or imperial honor and a will to survive could, at times, overcome some of the worst environmental conditions. At other times, despair and despondency could exacerbate the threat posed by the environment.

Despite the urging of John Oldfield Chadwick, it was the United States rather than Great Britain that took the lead in the final stages of the quest for the North Pole. Between 1893 and 1909, eight American expeditions attempted to get to the top of the world, in comparison to one expedition from Norway, one from Italy, and one from Sweden.[36] The so-called "American Route" between Ellesmere Island in the Canadian Arctic and Greenland appeared to offer the easiest route through the polar ice to get as close as possible to the North Pole. The race appeared to reach its climax in the summers of 1908 and 1909. In April 1908 the American doctor and polar explorer Frederick Cook claimed to have reached the North Pole as leader of a small party of Inuit on April 21, 1908. One year later, the American naval officer Robert Peary made an identical claim, saying that he had reached the North Pole on April 6, 1909 at the head of a party of explorers that included the African American Matthew Henson and four Inuit. There seems to have been a sense that the presence of nonwhites on both of these expeditions diminished a little of their achievements, and Matthew Henson, in particular, found that his contributions were marginalized in the celebrations of Peary's expedition.[37] In the years that followed, both Cook and Peary continued to assert that they had reached the Pole first and an acrimonious debate has raged.[38] As a geographical abstraction located on constantly moving sea ice, navigation was difficult and proof of arriving at the right place was almost impossible to demonstrate. In general the political and military establishment in the United States tended to support Peary's claim and dismiss Frederick Cook as an imposter who lied about his position. In recent years, however, it has become common to challenge the claims of both men and leave the title of first to the North Pole for a slightly later generation.

One reason that the British did not play an active role in the climax of the race to the North Pole was that their attention had already turned southward. The first serious attempt to get to the South Pole was made by Britain's Captain Robert Falcon Scott during the *Discovery* expedition of 1901–03. With his companions Edward Wilson and Ernest Shackleton, he crossed a little over 400 miles of the Ross Ice Shelf, but could not make it onto the Polar Plateau of the East Antarctic Ice Sheet. Just as it had in the history of northern exploration, scurvy took its toll on the polar party, and Shackleton was particularly affected. Undeterred, however, Shackleton returned to Antarctica in 1907 as leader of his own expedition to make a second attempt to get to the bottom of the world. He made it to within ninety miles of the Pole before deciding that the conditions and the available food would make it suicidal to continue. "Better a living donkey than a dead lion," he wrote despondently to his wife. Despite its failure, Shackleton's expedition suggested that getting to the South Pole was a realistic possibility. In another achievement, three of Shackleton's expedition members reached the South Magnetic Pole, belatedly achieving the goal of the nineteenth-century "magnetic crusade."[39]

Late in 1910, Captain Scott returned to Antarctica to make his second attempt to get to the South Pole. As a result of weather conditions and sea ice, it was necessary to arrive at least a year early in order to be in place to set out for the pole early in the following season. By this stage, as demonstrated by the tone of Hugh Robert Mill's *Siege of the South Pole* (1905), the British had come to believe that it was their right to be the first to get to the bottom of the world, and an element of entitlement had crept into the planning process.[40] During the voyage south, therefore, Scott was surprised to learn that he would have competition in his attempt to get to the South Pole from Roald Amundsen. The Norwegian explorer had previously been planning an expedition to the North Pole, but was deterred by the news that two American expeditions were claiming to have reached the top of the world.

Amundsen decided instead to make an attempt to get to the South Pole, and he turned his ship the *Fram* southward. Members of Captain Scott's expedition treated the news as something akin to treachery on the part of their Norwegian rival, and this reflected the real fear that the Norwegians would be successful in their goal to be first to get to the South Pole.

In his controversial joint biography of Scott and Amundsen, the British historian Roland Huntford sought to debunk the myth of Captain Scott by highlighting a number of differences between the two polar explorers.[41] Many of Huntford's criticisms of the British explorer stemmed from what he perceived as his lack of polar experience. In contrast to his Norwegian rival, Britain's Captain Scott had not spent a significant amount of time living and working in the Arctic. Scott's insistence on using horses to pull his sledges contrasted with Amundsen's use of dogs, which was the far more efficient Inuit method of travel. While Amundsen utilized a number of Inuit-style tools and clothing, Scott mostly used British manufactured provisions. And perhaps most significantly, Scott's leadership style came directly from the rigidly hierarchical style of the British Royal Navy, while Amundsen employed a much more flexible and to some degree more egalitarian approach, which had worked for him in the Arctic. Although the differences between the two explorers were perhaps not quite as stark as Huntford portrayed, Scott's lack of polar experience certainly worked against him on a number of occasions.

The race to the South Pole reached its denouement in the austral summer of 1911–12. Starting from further away and trying an unknown route, Amundsen got an earlier start than his British rival. Utilizing dog sleds to their fullest potential, Amundsen's four-man polar party made good progress across the ice and reached the South Pole on December 14, 1911. Here they erected the flag of the newly independent State of Norway and left a triumphant note proclaiming their pride in being the first to get to the bottom of the world. Then they turned around and headed back to the *Fram*. Man-hauling their sledges after the horses had died, Captain Scott and his four companions arrived at the South Pole on January 17, 1912, over a month later than their Norwegian rivals. They were devastated to see the flag of Norway already flying, and the disappointment of losing a race they had expected to win undoubtedly took its toll on their morale and shaped the way they perceived the environment. Unlike in the Arctic, where the hope of support from indigenous peoples always existed, Scott and his companions were very conscious that they were completely on their own. Edgar Evans died on February 17; Titus Oates followed on March 16 with the famous statement "I'm going outside, I may be some time"; the three remaining explorers died in their tents sometime at the very end of March as they waited for a storm to subside. The following season, the bodies of Scott, Wilson, and Bowers would be found along with diaries and photographs explaining what had happened.[42]

It was perhaps Amundsen's great bad luck to have beaten one of history's most famous losers. As the British public sought to process the tragedy of Captain Scott, the nineteenth-century death of John Franklin in the Arctic provided something of a model, thereby creating a connection between Scott and the Arctic in death if not in life. The legend of Captain Scott enabled the British to rescue something of the spirit of conquering nature from the failure to be first to the South Pole. Scott and his companions may have been beaten both by Roald Amundsen *and* the Antarctic environment, but according to the retelling they had died like gentlemen. The apparently stoic manner of their deaths suggested that they were never completely defeated, and it kept the focus of the story on the heroism of British bodies. Over the course of the twentieth century, Scott's story would be an important narrative as the British extended their attempts to assert their imperial control over the Antarctic environment.

Aerial Exploration

In 1897 the Swedish Andrée expedition made an attempt to use a hot air balloon to get to the North Pole from the north of Spitsbergen. The expedition ended in tragedy with the deaths of Andrée and his two companions, although their bodies wouldn't be found for over thirty years.[43] Despite this failure, aviation would play a major role in the future of polar exploration. With the assumption that both poles had been reached overland by the early twentieth century, attention turned to flying to the top and bottom of the world. In both Polar Regions it is possible to identify a second "race for the Pole" with airplanes replacing dog sleds and man-hauling as the transport of choice. This technological transition was fostered quite blatantly by media magnates wanting to sell newspapers. Like the competition to be first overland, there was a significant overlap between the two Polar Regions, both in chronology and personnel. Men such as Richard E. Byrd, Hubert Wilkins, and Lincoln Ellsworth flew over both the Arctic and Antarctica, and Roald Amundsen also turned his attention toward flying over the North Pole after his triumph in the south.

As the scholar Marionne Cronin has pointed out in a recent discussion of the Arctic exploits of Richard Byrd, the introduction of modern technology into the field of polar exploration presented a number of challenges to imperial ideas of conquering nature.[44] By coming between human bodies and the natural environment, technologies such as the airplane broke a direct link between perceptions of racial fitness and masculine superiority and the act of exploration. Despite claims to the contrary, however, the use of airplanes for the exploration of the Polar Regions represented an evolution of attempts to conquer polar nature rather than a radical break from the recent past; technology had never really been absent from the history of polar exploration.[45] Polar aviation continued to put human bodies in situations of risk (sometimes more so, as demonstrated by the deaths of Andrée and his companions), and technological innovation itself became a sphere for imperial competition. This allowed for what Cronin refers to as "complex sometimes ambivalent re-imaginings of the polar environment that sought to preserve a space for masculine heroism within a technologically advanced modern world."[46] A related way of looking at the introduction of modern technology into the field of polar exploration is to see it as part of the changing relationship between the material environment and human activities. Although exploration did little to change polar environments as a whole, airplanes and other technological innovations modified the immediate environment as experienced by explorers. The polar environment seemed very different from the seat of a heated airplane, for example, than when man-hauling a sled across the Polar Plateau. At the same time, these innovations expanded what explorers could do in the Polar Regions: flying, in particular, made possible a far wider range of exploration. While technology would never be a panacea for all the difficulties that humans faced in the Polar Regions, it has been an integral part of the environmental histories of both the Arctic and Antarctica.

The relatively rapid attainment of both poles by aircraft contributed to the fact that this second race to the poles never generated quite the same popular enthusiasm as the first. Coupled with the fact that a second race was always likely to have an element of repetition and anticlimax, there was not enough drama, and arguably not enough tragedy to sustain this sequel. While attention often focuses on Amundsen and Byrd, the exploits of one of the less-heralded polar aviators from the 1920s offer insights into the environmental-history dimensions of early polar aviation. Labeled the "Last Explorer" by his biographer Simon Nasht, the Australian-born Hubert Wilkins lived a boys-own life of near constant adventure.[47] After experiencing at first hand the consequences of drought on his family farm in South Australia, Wilkins built a career based on the embrace of technology, especially cinema and aviation. He moved to Europe and reported on the war between Turkey and Bulgaria in 1912. Wilkins was then invited to participate in Viljhalmur Stefansson's ill-fated Canadian Arctic Expedition of 1913–16. Despite the many problems of the expedition, Wilkins developed a good relationship with Stefansson, and fairly quickly moved from being the photographer to playing a leadership role. After returning from the Arctic, Wilkins was plunged into the horrors of the First World War as an official photographer (initially alongside his fellow Australian polar photographer Frank Hurley, who had been to Antarctica with Ernest Shackleton). In the aftermath of the war, Wilkins turned his attention to Antarctica as part of relatively small and forgettable expeditions. In the early 1920s, he also found time to report on the drought and famine in the Soviet Union before turning his attention back to the Polar Regions, and to the challenges of aviation.

In 1926, Wilkins won funding from the Detroit Air Club for a plan to fly over the North Pole from Alaska, exploring in the process one of the largest unknown spaces anywhere on the planet.[48] Several earlier Arctic explorers had believed they had seen land in this region, and this had been one of Stefansson's goals for the Canadian Arctic Expedition. Wilkins set out to use modern technology to prove the existence of a large Arctic landmass one way or the other. In emphasizing science, technology, and geographical exploration, Wilkins was giving his sponsors in the Detroit Air Club exactly what they wanted to hear. The city of Detroit was trying to sell itself as the city of the future based on its established automobile industry and its up-and-coming aviation industry, and an association with the aerial exploration of the Polar Regions seemed to offer an ideal opportunity.[49]

In the event, Wilkins's attempts to fly over the North Pole were largely anticlimactic. As Byrd and Amundsen raced to the top of the world from the north of Spitsbergen, Wilkins suffered a series of technical problems that put two of his planes out of action. On May 13, 1926, Wilkins watched the arrival of Amundsen's airship, the *Norge*, at Point Barrow, on its way from becoming the second—although in retrospect probably the first—expedition to fly over the top of the world. Four days earlier, on May 9, Byrd claimed to have made an out-and-back flight over the North Pole from Spitsbergen, although major doubts have been raised over the veracity of this claim. Wilkins's disappointment at apparently not even being the runner-up in the aerial race to the North Pole was tempered by the fact that Amundsen's expedition had done little to explore the region north of Alaska where land might be found. True to his indomitable spirit, Wilkins continued with his attempts to fly across the Arctic, and returned for two further seasons in Alaska. He finally made the successful flight in 1928. No major new landmass was sighted.[50]

Fresh from his success in flying across the Arctic, Wilkins turned immediately to Antarctica. While neither of his two previous expeditions to the far south had been great successes, they had given him first-hand experiences of the Antarctic Peninsula region directly to the south of South America. Wilkins was convinced that aerial exploration could modernize exploration in Antarctica in much the same way as it had already done for the Arctic. Unfortunately for Wilkins, Richard Byrd also had the same idea. For a brief moment, it looked as if the drama of the earlier race for the South Pole might be repeated and newspapers were keen to get in on the action. Wilkins received funding from the newspaper magnate William Randolph Hearst, and Byrd had support from the *New York Times*. The competition was another anticlimax. Although Wilkins made the first motorized flight in the Antarctic continent on November 16, 1928, he never made a proper attempt to get to the South Pole. Byrd achieved that goal on November 28, 1929.

Wilkins and another American aviator, Lincoln Ellsworth, would continue flying exploits in Antarctica for the next decade, but the public largely lost interest.[51]

The historian Stephen Bocking argues that an aerial perspective can be a powerful tool for controlling polar landscapes.[52] This is certainly true. On their flights across the Arctic and Antarctic the early polar aviators reported seeing thousands of square miles of territory, often for the first time. If land was to be found north of Alaska, for example, Wilkins was correct in thinking that it would be an aviator who would discover it. But at the same time, the benefits of aerial survey for exploration and cartography were not immediate, and they would take several decades to perfect. When Wilkins made his longest flight in the Antarctic Peninsula region on December 20, 1928, he reported that the Peninsula was not in fact connected to the continent of Antarctica, so was therefore an island. On his published map of the expedition he named the strait of water that separated Grahamland from Antarctica after his explorer friend Stefansson (Figure 12). A photo of the Detroit Aviation Society Plateau (named in honor of his earlier sponsor in the Arctic) taken during the same flight, however, gives a clue as to the difficulties of aerial surveying and cartography. With the image distorted both by clouds and the movement of the plane it is difficult to make out what is land and what is sea ice. A few years later, Wilkins' claim that the Antarctica Peninsula was not a peninsula would be proved false by the British Grahamland expedition. This mistake was held to count against his reputation as a polar explorer. The problem was not so much the understandable error he made, but the fact that he was so insistent that the Peninsula was disconnected from the continent. Wilkins was not helped by the fact that his next high-profile polar expedition was a somewhat farcical failed attempt to navigate under the South Pole in a submarine.

In June 1928 Roald Amundsen lost his life in an air accident while looking for the Italian crew of Nobile's *Italia* airship. As well as ending a quite extraordinary life, his death might be seen as marking a transition in the history of polar aviation away from adventure and the quest for polar firsts toward air travel for transportation and economic exploitation. In an article published in *The Polar Times* in 1936 the Australian Antarctic explorer Douglas Mawson was quoted as saying the "advent

Figure 12 and Figure 13   *[Top] Wilkins' map of the Antarctic "Peninsula."*
[Bottom] Wilkins' view of the Detroit Aviation Society Plateau during the flight
when he made the map. (Source: American Geographical Society Library) [(48al) 43
No. 5234 M]

of airplane [in Antarctica] will give access to mineral deposits and help
in development of other industries."[53] In the short term, it would be
aviators from the Soviet Union rather than Norway, the United States,
or the British Empire that would make some of the most important
contributions to the regularization of polar air travel.[54] By the second
half of the twentieth century flying would become a way of life in the
Polar Regions, and it played a major role in economic development
efforts.[55] In making this transition, polar aviation retained an element of
"conquering nature" from the great age of exploration in the Arctic and
Antarctica. But from now on, interest in the Polar Regions was much
more permanent, and the impact on the material environment would
be significantly greater.

4

DREAMS AND REALITIES
Economic Development

In 1927, shortly before his death in an Arctic air accident, the Norwegian Roald Amundsen published an English translation of his biography titled *My Life as an Explorer*.[1] Alongside an extended account of his accomplishments, Amundsen reserved space for a blistering attack on Vilhjalmur Stefansson, another famous polar explorer of the early twentieth century. While Amundsen saw Stefansson's belief in "blond Eskimos" simply as a far-fetched idea, he viewed his ideas about a "Friendly Arctic" as reckless:

> It is entirely possible that some adventurous spirits, seeking a fresh thrill in the North, may be misled by this talk about the "friendliness" of the Arctic and will actually attempt to take advantage of this "friend-liness," and venture into those regions equipped only with a gun and some ammunition. If they do, certain death awaits them. In my opinion, based on long experience and careful study, even a good marksman cannot "live off the country" in the Arctic.[2]

In the Norwegian version of his biography, Amundsen was even more scathing. He wrote that he would wager everything he owned that if Stefansson were ever to try living off the land on drifting sea ice he would not survive "more than eight days counted from the day of starting."[3] For Amundsen, not only was Stefansson not telling the truth but he was propagating a highly dangerous idea.

Amundsen's criticism raised the ire of Stefansson and his friends and supporters who shared the idea of a "Friendly Arctic." A letter likely written by Isaiah Bowman, the President of the American Geographical Society, described Amundsen's discussion of Stefansson as the "vitriolic, ill-timed, and bad-spirited comment of a jealous and narrow minded man."[4] The polar aviator Hubert Wilkins defended Stefansson and his methods of polar exploration. "It has been my pleasure and privilege," wrote Wilkins, "to find in Stefansson a careful and accurate scientific observer, whose statements of fact have at times been misquoted and misrepresented in newspapers but whose books, when carefully read, impart reliable information and tend in no way to mislead the public or adventurous spirits seeking knowledge of Arctic conditions." In a draft review of *My Life as an Explorer*, Wilkins repeated a familiar criticism of Amundsen's own methods of polar travel: "In all his polar travels Amundsen has shown little personal desire to kill anything for food more difficult to hunt than the dogs hitched to his sled."[5]

The dispute between Amundsen and Stefansson might be dismissed as a storm in a teacup resulting from a clash between two inflated egos. But at stake in this argument were two visions of the Polar Regions that were in some ways fundamentally different. Amundsen was the preeminent polar explorer of the early twentieth century; Stefansson was the preeminent Arctic booster. It suited Amundsen and his reputation to present the Polar Regions as the most hostile environments imaginable, since this enhanced his reputation as a conqueror of polar nature. His ideas were supported by certain environmental determinist geographers such as Ellsworth Huntington, who believed that civilization in the Arctic would never flourish as a result of the hostile climate and barren landscape.[6] Stefansson, on the other hand, sought to build his career by challenging the notion that the Arctic was an inhospitable wasteland, and replacing it with the idea that it was ripe for development. "When the world was once known to be round," he wrote, "there was no difficulty in finding many navigators to sail around it. When the Polar Regions are once understood to be friendly and fruitful, men will quickly and easily penetrate their deepest recesses."[7]

Over the course of the twentieth century history of both Polar Regions it is possible to see the respective visions of Amundsen and Stefansson jostling for supremacy, in popular imagination, policy discussions, and in academic debates.[8] Amundsen's vision of hostility sought to retain the Polar Regions as places apart from the rest of the rest of the world: forboding, dangerous, and retaining an inherent sense of excitement. At the same time—building on Stefansson's boosterism—dreams of economic and social development in both the Arctic and Antarctica were increasingly common. These dreams were often caught up with utopian ideas of creating a new society. At times these visions were relatively mundane, developing, for example, the ideas contained within Frederick Jackson Turner's frontier thesis of the North American West.[9] At other times, dreams of development in the Polar Regions often read more like science fiction than reality. As some of the last perceived "empty spaces" in the world, the Polar Regions offered fascinating spaces for fantasy to flourish, and these fantasies often had a "last chance on earth" quality. Writing in the late 1970s, the Canadian judge Thomas Berger noted: "Remember, the North really is our last frontier: after we have passed this frontier there is no other frontier beyond."[10] As a consequence, both the Arctic and Antarctica have fascinating "histories of the future," which examine the ways in which the futures of the Polar Regions have been imagined at different times in the past.[11]

At the turn of the twentieth century, some parts of the Arctic and Antarctica had already been locations of economic activity through sealing, whaling, and other extractive activities. But these resource frontiers generally came with little sense of sustainable economic development. In contrast, over the course of the twentieth century, numerous attempts were made to bring about long-term and large-scale development in the Polar Regions.[12] In the Arctic, Stefansson spent his career in dogged pursuit of various development schemes, undeterred by spectacular failures such as a disastrous attempt to settle Wrangel Island north of Siberia. In Antarctica, the American explorer Richard E. Byrd built a station called Little America on the Ross Ice Shelf, which he hoped would be a center for Antarctic development and American renewal. On the island of Spitsbergen, at least for a while, coal mining offered a very real opportunity to make a profit out of the

Arctic environment. In the Antarctic Peninsula region, Argentina and Chile contested British claims and put forward very different visions of polar development. In Greenland, Danish colonialism attempted a radical shake-up of Inuit society in an attempt to turn mobile hunting cultures into settled, controllable communities. In all of these cases, and in a number of others, dreams of sustained development brought their promoters face to face with the material reality of the polar environment, often with undesired and undesirable consequences.

The distinctive visions of Amundsen and Stefansson were not altogether in opposition. Many of the plans for economic development in the Arctic and Antarctica over the course of the twentieth century had more than a small element of "conquering nature" built into them. The circumstances and scale were different from Amundsen's achievements as an explorer, but the underlying principle was the same. Dreams of economic development were often premised on ideas of the racial and gender superiority of white European males and development schemes in the north almost always involved the process of assimilating economically unproductive indigenous peoples.[13] Building on the aerial exploration of the early twentieth century, there were also technological and scientific dimensions to these development schemes, posited on the idea that human ingenuity could overcome the worst conditions that nature could offer. Taken together, such attitudes often led to an arrogant and confrontational approach, mirroring similar trends in other parts of the world.[14]

The history of economic development in the Arctic and Antarctica once again shows the power of ideas in environmental history. But unlike exploration, which had a limited immediate impact on the material environment, economic development often brought about significant changes to polar landscapes. These were particularly pronounced in the case of the Arctic, where economic efforts were more widespread and more sustained. But they were also evident in Antarctica in places of intense human activity, such as the island of South Georgia, which for a while was the center of Southern Ocean whaling. In the Arctic, economic development has frequently been presented as beneficial to local communities, and sometimes it has been. But the "conquest of nature" mentality implicit in many of these schemes has often proved detrimental to the very people who were supposed to benefit most. The anthropologist Hugh Brody writes: "Profound misunderstandings arise when representatives of settled, acquisitive cultures seek to help or to change mobile hunting cultures."[15] While environmental historians have challenged overly simplistic declensionist narratives, it cannot be denied that much social and environmental damage was done by economic development schemes in both the far north and the far south.

The (Un-)Friendly Arctic

Vilhjalmur Stefansson is one of the most colorful and controversial figures in the history of the Polar Regions. Born in Manitoba, Canada, in 1879 to Icelandic immigrants, he grew up in the United States and spent most of his life there. His exploits in exploring the Arctic were substantial, but unlike his rival Roald Amundsen they were nothing spectacular. Instead of achieving fame through the achievement of a string of polar firsts, Stefansson instead built his career on an idea: the notion of a "friendly Arctic."[16] He sought to turn upside down what people thought they knew about the far north.[17] Rather than being cold, miserable, and hostile to human occupation, he believed that with the right mindset and a little preparation the Arctic could be perfectly habitable and productive. Since so much of Stefansson's career rested on the belief in a friendly Arctic, it is sometimes difficult to know how many of his own ideas he actually believed. But Stefansson proved to be in the right place at the right time and his ideas were tremendously influential, not least as a result of his charismatic personality. The notion of a friendly Arctic helped to lay the foundations for economic development in the Polar Regions to such an extent that it is difficult to begin any discussion about twentieth-century economic development in the Arctic without some reference to this highly idiosyncratic explorer and writer.[18]

Stefansson's upbringing in the U.S. West would profoundly shape his later thinking about frontiers, and about the transformation of wilderness into productive land. Largely as a result of his Icelandic heritage he developed a passionate interest in the Arctic. After studying for a while at the State University of North Dakota he graduated from the State University of Iowa (now the University of Iowa) before beginning graduate studies at Harvard. As a student of anthropology at Harvard he made two trips to Iceland in 1904 and 1905, the first visit taking place in the year that the country attained home rule from Denmark.

In 1906 the American Polar Expedition led by Einar Mikkelsen and Ernest de Koven Leffingwell offered Stefansson the opportunity to conduct anthropological fieldwork around Hershel Island in the west Canadian Arctic.[19] After failing to meet up with the main body of the expedition as a result of a delayed ship, Stefansson began to live with the Inupiat people to learn more about their culture and language. This was starting to become standard practice for ethnographic research of the early twentieth century, but was still something of a rarity in the Arctic. Although Stefansson was arguably a little less systematic in his methods, there were clear parallels here with the approach taken by his Danish contemporary Knud Rasmussen. In total Stefansson's first trip to the Arctic lasted for sixteen months, and it whetted his appetite for a return. In particular, the young anthropologist heard rumors about a group of "blond Eskimos" living on Victoria Island, and he believed that these people might be descendants of Norse settlers from almost one thousand years ago.

Stefansson's second expedition to the Arctic, from 1908–12, set out with the intention of finding the blond Eskimos. This time he was in joint command of the expedition with Rudolf Anderson, although the two men would not enjoy the best of relationships (a theme that would become quite common with Stefansson's expedition partners). Stefansson successfully located the group of people he had heard about, known as the Copper Eskimos, living on Victoria Island. He lived with the Copper Eskimos for a year, and it was on this expedition that he fathered a child with an Inuit woman named Pannigabluk, although he kept this a secret.[20] Stefansson believed that through the Copper Eskimo he had found a connection with the early Norse explorers of North America, and he followed then-contemporary anthropological practices of skull measurements and other biometric indicators to help prove this. Upon his return to the United States, a headline in the *Seattle Times* proclaimed: "American explorer discovers lost white tribe, descendants of Leif Ericsson."[21] Although Stefansson and his supporters would later claim that such sensationalist reporting misrepresented his findings, he was more than happy to bask in the publicity these stories generated. He wrote a book about his experiences titled *My Life*

Among the Eskimo (1913).[22] In retrospect, using modern techniques for genetic history, Stefansson's beliefs would prove to be little more than wishful thinking.[23] But at the time his claims helped to build his reputation as a polar expert.

Stefansson's third expedition to the Arctic, from 1913–16, was by far his most ambitious. Stefansson won financial support for the expedition from the Canadian government by appealing directly to the threat that Canada might lose out on lands in the western Canadian Arctic as a result of rivalry from the United States. Given Stefansson's dual nationality, such a geopolitical motivation seemed a little suspicious to some at the time. But it is testimony to Stefansson's growing status as an Arctic booster that he was able to pull this off. Stefansson proved himself equal to anyone in combining politics and fundraising with exploration. His Canadian Arctic Expedition would be the largest expedition sponsored by the Canadian government, and had the explicit goal of claiming new lands in the Arctic for Canada.

Not everything went to plan for Stefansson and the Canadian Arctic Expedition.[24] On the journey along the north coast of Alaska, the *Karluk* (on which Stefansson was sailing) became separated from the other ships and became stuck in the sea ice. After a number of forays forward and back to the shore to communicate the ship's predicament and hunt for fresh food, Stefansson became separated from the ship when a storm swept it northward. Under the command of Captain Bartlett, the *Karluk* drifted to the northwest and broke up and sank in the sea ice about eighty miles from Wrangel Island, north of Siberia. The crew crossed the sea ice to get to the island, losing eight men on the journey. The dead included the Scotsman John Murray, who had sailed south to Antarctica with Shackleton on the *Nimrod* expedition and collected important biological samples at Cape Royds.[25] Wrangel Island provided little relief to the survivors, since food was scarce. Bartlett and an Inuk named Kataktovik crossed to Siberia and Alaska to seek relief, but sea ice conditions were bad. When a relief expedition did arrive in September 1914, three more men had died.

Stefansson's separation from the *Karluk* led to accusations that he had abandoned his duty to command the expedition. It is difficult to know whether or not these accusations are true. But what is certain is that as the crew on board the *Karluk* faced a desperate struggle for survival, Stefansson continued his exploration and anthropological research in the North American Arctic. Following his return Stefansson gave up active Arctic exploration for a career of writing, lecturing, and generally promoting his ideas about the great potential of the far north. He was a prolific writer, and over the course of his life he published over four hundred articles and twenty-four books.[26]

Stefansson's third expedition provided material for his second book, *The Friendly Arctic* (1921). In it, he set out his theory that it was perfectly possible to "live off the land" throughout the year in the Arctic North. He attacked the notion that the Arctic was a barren, inhospitable wilderness, claiming that even the Eskimo were not to be trusted with some of their descriptions of the region. "'Barren Ground' is a libelous name by which the open land of the north is commonly described," he wrote. "This name is better adapted for creating the impression that those who travel in the North are intrepid adventurers than it is for conveying to the reader a true picture of the country."[27] Stefansson systematically sought to debunk what he saw as an erroneous image of the Arctic that only survived as a result of a lack of knowledge. He saw his recent expedition as a successful attempt to demonstrate what he called the "fourth stage" of polar exploration, in which "food suitable for men and dogs could be obtained anywhere on the polar sea."[28]

Shortly after completing *The Friendly Arctic* Stefansson set about writing a more expansive book to elaborate his ideas. If explorers could survive in the Arctic North by living off the land with just a gun and ammunition, then the region was not as hostile as it might appear, and was—by a certain leap of logic—ripe for economic development. In *The Northward Course of Empire* (1922) Stefansson drew explicitly on his upbringing on the North American frontier to posit the Arctic as an extension of westward expansion and manifest destiny.[29] This allowed Stefansson to transfer the myth of the frontier into the Arctic North: "There is no northern boundary beyond which productive enterprise cannot go till North meets North on the opposite shores of the Arctic Ocean as East has met West on the Pacific."[30] In chapters with titles such as "The Fruitful Arctic, ""The Livable North," and "The Established Arctic Industries" he sought to present a series of case studies to make his point. In correspondence with Richard Byrd's Antarctic Expedition several years later, he elaborated on one of his connections with the U.S. West: "flights in the Arctic are of a pioneer nature in the sense that many will follow eventually where the leaders show the way, just as railways now follow the Oregon trail."[31] In making these connections with the westward expansion of the United States there was a similar sense of manifest destiny in Stefansson's writings about the North.

At the same time as writing *The Northward Course of Empire* Stefansson was involved in organizing another expedition to the Arctic, but this time one he would not participate in directly. The main aim of the expedition in Stefansson's mind was to prove his ideas about living off the land in the far north, but it also had a geopolitical motivation. He won (tentative) support from Canadian government to send an expedition to Wrangel Island north of Siberia in an attempt to demonstrate Canadian sovereignty. This was the island where the *Karluk* had been marooned for nine months in 1914 during the Canadian Arctic Expedition. The aim of the expedition was for a small party of settlers to live off the land on Wrangel Island, making money from the hunting of Arctic fox pelts. The expedition consisted of five members: Allan Crawford from Canada, Fred Maurer, Lorne Knight, and Milton Galle from the United States, and the Inupiat seamstress Ida Blackjack. Fred Maurer had been on the *Karluk*, Lorne Knight had traveled with Stefansson in Arctic North America and all four men on the expedition were passionate disciples of the idea of a friendly Arctic. The role of Ida Blackjack on the expedition as a seamstress offered a fascinating insight into gender relations in Arctic exploration.

As described in detail by the author Jennifer Niven in *Ida Blackjack: A True Story of Survival in the Arctic*, the Wrangel Island expedition did not go according to plan.[32] All four non-Inuit members of the expedition died as a result of poor decision-making and malnutrition, and only Ida Blackjack survived. In his diary Lorne Knight left a chilling description of what it was like to die from scurvy. Thinking that his experiences might be of use to someone who had not had a chance to experience the condition at first hand, Knight compared his symptoms to an entry on "Scurvy" from their copy of *Spoffards New Cabinet Cyclopedia*:

RESPIRATION IS HURRIED ON THE LEAST MOTION. Very much so.

THE TEETH BECOME LOOSE. Only two old snags on the upper jaw.

THE GUMS ARE SPONGY. Just around the two loose snags. The lower jaw is OK.

THE BREATH IS OFFENSIVE. No more so than bad teeth would made it.

LIVID SPOTS APPEAR ON DIFFERENT PARTS OF THE BODY. Only on the back of my left leg between the knee and the lower part of the fleshy part of the rump. These spots are not livid, however, but like a "black and blue" bruise in color. The leg is considerably swollen, and is quite hard to the touch, but not very painful to the touch. The right leg is also swollen a little, but is not near as bad as the left, and yet lacks the dark spots. I can find no other spots on my body.

OLD WOUNDS, WHICH HAVE LONG BEEN HEALED UP, BREAK OUT AFRESH. Not yet.

SEVERE WANDERING PAINS ARE FELT, ESPECIALLY AT NIGHT. These pains do not bother me much now, but a month or so they were quite painful, at night.

THE SKIN IS DRY. No.

THE URINE SMALL IN QUANTITY. Yes, a little less than usual, but not small.

THE PULSE IS SMALL, AND FREQUENT. Yes, a little weak, and 72 per minute.

THE INTELLECT, FOR THE MOST PART, CLEAR AND DISTINCT. Perfectly so.[33]

This was one of Knight's last diary entries, and two months later he died. As he mentioned in his diary, this was the second time in his short life that he had experienced scurvy. The first was when he was on an "ice trip" with his hero Stefansson in 1917. Reading his description of his slow death from insufficient vitamins, it is difficult to retain the optimistic idea of a "friendly Arctic."

Knight's three companions were never seen again after they made an attempt to cross the sea ice to Siberia. The rescue of Ida Blackjack in 1923 brought to light the fiasco of Stefansson's Wrangel Island scheme. Stefansson faced numerous recriminations, not least the criticism he received from Roald Amundsen. Wrangel Island was formally taken by the Soviet Union in 1924. Despite this tragic setback, Stefansson continued to promote the idea of Arctic development as if nothing had gone wrong. Many of his ideas today sound a little odd: he believed, for example, that Arctic musk oxen were related to Scottish Highland cattle.[34] Until 1928 Stefansson promoted the benefits of an all-meat diet in order to show that living off the land in the Arctic was not only possible, but preferable for good health. Perhaps the most remarkable thing about Stefansson is that his ideas were not dismissed as completely crazy. In fact he remained tremendously influential throughout his life and his idea of a "friendly Arctic" provided the intellectual foundations for many development schemes in the North. Even the Soviet Union would take up many of Stefansson's ideas in support of their own attempts to colonize the Arctic.[35]

Little America

Although quite different in background and temperament to Viljalmur Stefansson, the American polar adventurer Richard E. Byrd was part of the same generation of polar explorers and the two men had many similar ideas. If Stefansson can be thought of as the preeminent Arctic booster of the first half of the twentieth century, a strong case could be made for Byrd being the equivalent for Antarctica (although the Australian Douglas Mawson could perhaps make a similar claim).[36] Stefansson and Byrd were not close friends, and they were occasionally rivals. Byrd's publicity team, for example, reacted with annoyance when Stefansson gave a talk in 1929 that appeared to challenge the utility of Byrd's Antarctic flights.[37] But their correspondence suggests that their relationship was generally cordial and supportive. While Byrd never made the case for a "friendly Antarctic" to match Stefansson's claims for the Arctic, the careers of both men were built on the idea of development in the Polar Regions.

Richard Byrd had been born into a patrician family of politicians in the state of Virginia and enjoyed a privileged upbringing.[38] After breaking his leg at the U.S. Naval Academy in Annapolis, he decided that aviation offered him the best opportunity for career advancement and adventure. It is not altogether clear whether Byrd actually enjoyed flying, and he certainly did not share the live-or-let-die mentality of Hubert Wilkins. But he became a proficient navigator and he was able to make himself one of the most famous aviators of the interwar period. In 1926 he claimed to be the first man to fly to the North Pole, although this claim has subsequently been challenged. In 1927 he participated in the race to become the first person to fly nonstop across the Atlantic, only narrowly losing to Charles Lindbergh. And in 1929 he rapidly won the race to be first to fly over the South Pole. This latter achievement is widely accepted, and in many ways it represented the highlight of Byrd's career as a polar explorer.

Byrd, however, was much more than an explorer. He was a talented fundraiser, and used his extensive contacts and connections to win financial support for his expeditions from everyone from John D. Rockefeller to the young readers of *Boy's Own Magazine*. He displayed an exceptional talent for publicity, and he showed an ability to master the media that today seems remarkably ahead of its time. While for most polar explorers, publicity was a means to the end of winning funding for their expeditions, Byrd seems to have been attracted to publicity for its own sake, and it is difficult to separate his motivations. He embraced radio, film, popular magazines, and even board games to get his message across.[39] He was helped by the fact that he was a much better writer than many of his fellow polar explorers, and his books are among the most interesting discussions of Antarctica published in the first half of the twentieth century. Simon Nasht, the biographer of Hubert Wilkins, somewhat pejoratively refers to Byrd as being in "the hero business."[40] For Byrd, this would probably have been a compliment.

Along with his talents for fundraising and publicity, Byrd was also a true Antarctic visionary. He saw Antarctica as playing an important role in the future of the United States and he argued repeatedly for the U.S. government to take a lead in exploring and developing the southern continent. His vision was not quite as explicitly commercial as the case made by Stefansson for the Arctic, but he certainly did not reject the idea that activity in Antarctica could be profitable. Like Stefansson, Byrd's polar vision can usefully be thought of as a continuation of Frederick Jackson Turner's frontier thesis, with all the tensions and contradictions that this implies.[41] For Byrd, Antarctica was vital for American civilization because it offered an opportunity to escape from the pitfalls of civilized life. In making this case, the Antarctic could not be presented as being too friendly, since it relied on a narrative of man against nature. But in much the same way as Turner's frontier thesis entailed the taming of the U.S. West, Byrd's Antarctic vision contained the implicit belief that with the right people and the right attitudes the southern continent could be subdued and made productive.

Many of Byrd's visionary ideas about Antarctica can be found in the book he wrote in 1930 about his first Antarctic expedition, in which he flew to the South Pole. The book was titled *Little America*, the same name he gave to the temporary station that he established on the Ross Ice Shelf. It sold over 13,000 copies in its first week of publication, and immediately became one of the best-selling books about exploration up to that time.[42] The name "Little America" conjured up a sense that the United States was taking possession of the continent, and this sense of colonization was picked up on by his readers and admirers. A song he received from Clara A. Hanson honoring his expedition, for example, began its chorus: "Hail, Hail to you, Little America / We welcome you a part of our dear land."[43] Upon the publication of *Little America*, the publishers Putnam's Sons included an insert advertising a competition with a prize for the best letter (not to exceed 250 words) received on the theme of "The value, to the civilized world, of the Byrd Antarctic Expedition."[44] In Byrd's mind, exploration was not peripheral to the affairs of state, but central to the future of the United States.

An explicit statement of Byrd's Antarctic vision can be found in his description of the first winter at Little America:

> In a word, we are trying to get away from the false standards by which men live under more civilized conditions. The Antarctic is a new world for all of us which requires its own standards, and these are materially different from those set up in civilization, whereby we venerate prestige, influence and associated characteristics and ignore the inconspicuous, but equally valid properties. Now that vital operations have ceased for the winter, the hand is quite as important as the brain, and the digging out of house entrances and windows after a storm, the care of fires, etc. are prime factors in keeping alive. *They* are the essential things. This fact I have tried to drive home, not always with success.[45]

The Antarctic environment had a vital role to play in restoring the balance of American culture, moving it away from social prestige and entitlement and toward a more egalitarian culture based on physical labor and shared values in the face of a hostile environment. As the last sentence of the quotation implies, not everyone was fully on board with Byrd's vision of a new world in Antarctica, and the expedition certainly endured some difficult moments. But the resonance with Turner's thesis was there for all to see, and Byrd's Antarctic vision of a new American frontier attracted tremendous popular support.

Byrd's vision for Antarctica was developed on his second Antarctic expedition, when he attempted to become the first person to spend a winter alone on the southern continent. The "Advance Camp" meteorological station was located 200 miles from the rebuilt Little America. Byrd sought to justify his decision to winter alone through a combination of scientific reasoning and pop psychology. The meteorological readings needed to be taken to give an idea of the conditions in the interior of the continent, where nobody knew how cold it could get in the middle of winter. There was not enough room in the advance camp for three people, Byrd argued, and having just two people could lead to a risk of social breakdown if they did not get along. To an even greater extent than his first expedition, Byrd's attempt to winter alone perhaps represents the apogee of his ambition to prove himself as the conqueror of polar nature.

Unfortunately for Byrd the heater at Advance Camp malfunctioned, and he found himself being slowly poisoned by carbon monoxide. Each day presented a choice between enduring the cold or inhaling noxious gas. As his radio communications became more erratic, the men at Little America decided that they would have to risk a winter journey across the Ross Ice Shelf in order to save his life. Byrd was rescued in August, thereby thwarting his ambition of becoming the first person to spend an entire winter alone on the Antarctic continent. But he refused to become too dispirited by his failure. He wrote a book about his experiences at Advance Camp titled *Alone*.[46] Drawing upon his carbon monoxide–fueled diary entries, this book rapidly became a classic of Antarctic literature. Alongside an account of the day-to-day struggle for survival, the book expanded on the ideas for Antarctic civilization set out in *Little America*.

In the late 1930s, Byrd returned to Antarctica with a two-pronged expedition.[47] Whereas his previous two expeditions had been privately funded, the U.S. Antarctic Service Expedition would be his first to receive its backing from the government. The aim of this expedition was to establish two continually occupied stations on the Antarctic continent: one at Little America and one on the Antarctic Peninsula at Marguerite Bay. Byrd was given instructions to prospect for mineral wealth and make sovereignty claims on behalf of the United States. In testimony to the Senate Committee on appropriations given in 1940, Byrd reported finding 147 different minerals in Antarctica.[48] While such a claim made no mention of the quantities of these finds and completely ignored the logistical difficulties of extractive activities in such a harsh environment, it does show that both Byrd and his backers were thinking of how to make money from the Antarctic continent.

In the event, the outbreak of the Second World War interrupted Byrd's plans for the permanent occupation of the Antarctic continent as American priorities shifted to other parts of the world. Byrd's two Antarctic stations were hastily evacuated, and most of his men returned directly to service in the war. Byrd himself served with distinction as an admiral in the Pacific. Despite two major Antarctic expeditions that took place in the immediate postwar period, the Second World War set back U.S. plans for permanent occupation of Antarctica almost twenty years. It would not be until the preparations for the International Geophysical Year of 1957–58 that Americans began to live year-round in stations on the southern continent. Once again, Byrd was at the center of these Antarctic activities. By the time of his death in 1957, the Antarctic visionary had been involved in five major expeditions to the southern continent, including three flights over the South Pole.

A case could be made that Byrd's visionary ideas for Antarctic development had little immediate impact on the environment. But his career functioned as an important transition from an age of temporary expeditions to the era of permanent occupation, and this would have major implications for the physical environment, at least on a local scale. In 1961 a bust of Captain Byrd was unveiled at McMurdo Station to honor the life of America's most important Antarctic pioneer. Since then the station has continued to grow, to the point where its summer population sometimes approaches 2,000 people. In the 1970s and 1980s, McMurdo came in for sustained criticism from groups such as Greenpeace and the Antarctica and Southern Ocean Coalition for its lax environmental practices. Rubbish was frequently burned or left on the sea ice to melt through into the South Ocean. As the bust of Byrd continues to survey McMurdo Station, it is easy to imagine him feeling

a tinge of regret underlying a general sense of pride in the fulfillment
of many of his ideas.

Spitsbergen / Svalbard

While the visionary ideas of Stefansson and Byrd were setting the intellectual stage for the development of the Polar Regions in the first half
of the twentieth century, economic activities on the unpopulated Arctic
island of Spitsbergen—or Svalbard by its Norwegian name—were
already underway and having a very real environmental impact. As one
of the most northerly islands on the planet, Spitsbergen had long been
a center for commercial sealing and whaling. In the early twentieth century it had been an important location for the race to the North Pole,
and several of the most famous Arctic expeditions, including Andrée's
balloon expedition and the polar flights of Amundsen and Byrd, began
or ended on the island.

Since the origins of commercial whaling and sealing around
Spitsbergen in the early seventeenth century, coal had been gathered
to supplement fuel supplies. In 1906 the American industrialist John
Munroe Longyear founded the Arctic Coal Company to begin the
commercial extraction of coal from the island. The company established a town called Longyear City (the name changed in 1925 to
Longyearbyen), and by 1910 two hundred mostly Norwegian miners
were working on the island. In the years that followed, other companies
from Britain, Sweden, the Netherlands, and Norway arrived. In 1927,
the Soviet Union gained a foothold on Spitsbergen with the purchase
of the Pyramiden mine from Sweden followed by the purchase of the
Branentsburg mine from the Netherlands in 1932.

In a recent book on British mining interests in Spitsbergen titled
Frozen Assets, the historical archeologist Frigga Kruse has shown how
mining on Spitsbergen was connected to global networks of imperial
politics and industrial economics.[49] In particular, coal from Spitsbergen
was used by British factories and transportation companies.[50] Kruse
also reveals how the Arctic environment played an important role in
this history. On a global scale, the need for Arctic coal revealed an
increasing fossil fuel dependency faced by Britain and other industrial
countries. On a local scale, the nature of the environment shaped the

economic development of Spitsbergen. At a very basic level, if coal had not been present, the history would have been very different. But the quality of the coal, its depth under the ground, and its proximity to the coast were also important determinants of the success and failure of mining operations.

Most of the workers employed in the early Spitsbergen coal mining industry came from Norway. In much the same way that sealing and whaling in the Polar Regions were generally quite unpleasant industries in which to work, there was little that was attractive about the labor involved in extracting coal from Spitsbergen's frozen rocks and tundra. This was a truly bleak place to earn a living. Historical archeology reveals something about the Spitsbergen "workscape." Unlike sealers and whalers, who generally returned home during the Arctic winter, many of the miners on Spitsbergen worked year round, enduring intense cold and darkness. It was nothing unusual for early twentieth century mining companies to pay little attention to their impact on the environment, but in the hostile working conditions of Spitsbergen this tendency was exacerbated.

Despite the inhospitable nature of the landscape, for a short period of time in the early twentieth century, the nascent coal mining industry on Spitsbergen radically changed perceptions of the Arctic environment, at least in this particular location. A place that had been dismissed as a barren wasteland, as a place to fish and hunt and then to leave, came to be seen as a potentially valuable possession. These changed environmental perceptions led a number of countries to take an interest in the question of sovereignty. Uncertainty surrounded the history of discovery of Spitsbergen, with Norwegians, Dutch, and Russians all claiming the first sighting. This complicated the question of sovereignty.[51] In the early twentieth century the island was nominally claimed by Norway, which used the Norse name Svalbard to demonstrate a longstanding interest. But the international nature of the island's coal mining industry meant that the United States, Britain, Sweden, the Netherlands, and Russia all had a stake in the question of ownership. Not all of these countries wanted to formally possess Spitsbergen, but they all showed an interest in keeping the island open for trade and extractive activities on the best possible terms.

In 1920, nine countries signed the Spitsbergen Treaty in connection with the Paris Peace Conference at the end of First World War. The treaty stated that the island belonged to Norway, but with two important concessions. Spitsbergen was to remain a free economic zone and it was not to be used for "warlike purposes." These concessions put limitations on the normal exercise of sovereignty, creating a space that was largely national but partially international. Given the nature of the environment, and its former status as effectively *res communis*, it is perhaps no coincidence that this experiment in sovereignty took place in the Polar Regions. For the mining companies working in Spitsbergen at the end of the First World War, the Spitsbergen Treaty had little direct impact: business continued in much the same way as it had before the outbreak of hostilities. But the Spitsbergen Treaty would have a significant influence on legal thinking about the Polar Regions, both in other parts of the Arctic and in Antarctica. Some legal historians, for example, have seen it as an important part of the background for the Antarctic Treaty of 1959.[52]

With a couple of important exceptions, the coal mining industry on Spitsbergen was not particularly successful or long-lasting, and by the mid-twentieth century it was in decline. Many locations in other parts of the world offered coal that could be extracted for a fraction of the cost and human effort. The same global networks that had helped to stimulate the industry also contributed to its demise. The Norwegian Store Norske Company continues to mine coal at two locations on the archipelago, and the Russian Arktikugol Company maintains limited operations at Barentsburg.[53] But these mining operations are motivated as much by the respective political interests of Norway and Russia in the archipelago as by the profitability of the industries.

In its relatively short lifespan, the Spitsbergen mining industry had a significant impact on the physical environment of the high-Arctic environment. Since the island was unpopulated, mining in Spitsbergen did not set off the chain of radical social and environmental repercussions that it would in many other parts of the Arctic. But as historical archeologists have helped to show, the direct impacts of mining activities were substantial. The mining industry increased the number of people living and working in the island's fragile tundra ecosystems. In their spare time many miners would hunt and fish, helping to deplete populations. Coal was blasted out of the ground using dynamite and other invasive techniques, leaving scars across the landscape. Tailings and other potentially toxic waste products were left on site owing to the prohibitive cost of removal. And when mining operations ceased, rarely were any efforts made to remove buildings or equipment because of the high costs involved.

Despite its lack of long-term success, early twentieth century coal mining on Spitsbergen helped to demonstrate that extractive industries were possible, even in the high Arctic. Alongside ideas such as Stefansson's "friendly Arctic," this practical demonstration of the viability of economic activity helped to change thinking about both Polar Regions. Over the course of the twentieth century numerous other mining and drilling operations were founded across the Arctic in places like Norilsk in Russia, Nanisivik in Canada, and Prudhoe Bay in Alaska. There were often strong connections among mining operations in different parts of the Arctic in terms of technology transfer and shared expertise. The environmental impact of coal mining in Spitsbergen would be repeated in these other parts of the Arctic, and in places where there were indigenous communities, environmental change would often be accompanied by social dislocation.

South American Antarctica

Just as in the Arctic, nationalism was a powerful force in attempts to develop Antarctica over the course of the twentieth century.[54] In the century's middle decades, Antarctica provided a stage for Australians and New Zealanders to perform their increasing sense of independence from Great Britain. For members of the white elite in apartheid South Africa, Antarctica offered an ideal space for demonstrating their supposed racial supremacy (and in later years would be one of the few international spheres from which they were not expelled). But few countries can match Argentina and Chile in their strong sense of nationalist attachment to the southern continent. For the governments of Buenos Aires and Santiago, overlapping claims to the Antarctic Peninsula offered important statements of national prestige and independence, and over the course of the twentieth century large parts of the population came in both countries to believe that Antártida Argentina or Antártica Chilena were fundamental parts of their national territories.

As a demonstration of this "environmental nationalism," President
Perón was fond of proclaiming that Argentina's territory stretched from
the city of Salta in the north to the South Pole in the south.[55]

The motivations for South American claims to the Antarctic
Peninsula region were complex.[56] On one level, the belief existed in
both Argentina and Chile that sovereignty rights to the Peninsula
region had been inherited upon independence from Spain, and that
these in turn went back to the Treaty of Tordesillas of 1494, which had
divided the world between Spanish and Portuguese spheres of influence "from Pole to Pole." On this reading the Antarctic Peninsula
region belonged to Argentina and Chile simply because it did. But the
Antarctic continent had not been discovered until after Argentine and
Chilean independence in the early nineteenth century, and very little
was done by either country to acknowledge their Antarctic claims until
the first decades of the twentieth century. In Argentina, British claims to
the "Falkland Islands Dependencies" functioned as a powerful motivation for asserting a counterclaim to Antártida Argentina. The Falkland
Islands, or Islas Malvinas, as they were known in Argentina, had long
been a cause of nationalist ire since they had been taken in 1833 by
Great Britain from a handful of settlers from the Rio de la Plata region,
and the dependencies were an egregious extension of this "theft." In
Chile, nationalist preoccupations focused on the threat that Argentina
would take territory that was rightfully Chilean, as they believed had
happened in Patagonia at the end of the nineteenth century. But shared
legal arguments with Argentina and the global anticolonial sentiments
of the nineteenth century made it expedient for Chileans also to focus
their sovereignty campaign against British claims.

The overlapping sovereignty claims of Argentina and Chile and their
shared rejection of British claims to the Falkland Islands Dependencies
helped to create an uneasy alliance around the idea of a "South
American Antarctica."[57] The two countries could not agree on which
of them owned what parts of the Antarctic Peninsula region, but they
could agree that the territory belonged to them and not to a distant
colonial power. In making the case for a South American Antarctica,
Argentine and Chilean lawyers and politicians drew upon the nature of
the Antarctic environment. They argued, for example, that the Andes
Mountains continued underneath the Drake Passage to reemerge as the

Antartandes in the Antarctic Peninsula, and this geological connection gave them special rights to ownership of this southern land.

When the first official Chilean expedition to Antarctica sailed in 1947, Chilean Minister for Foreign Relations Raúl Juliet proclaimed that the region belonged to Chile however valuable or not its economic resources might prove to be.[58] In a sense, the nationalist motivations for South American sovereignty claims in Antarctica made the question of economic gains irrelevant. Unlike Great Britain, where interest in Antarctic sovereignty had an obvious commercial dimension through the promotion of a sustainable whaling industry, Antarctica belonged to Chile and Argentina simply because it did. But notions of development were not entirely absent from the South American Antarctic vision. In the early days of their active interest in Antarctic sovereignty, proponents of sovereignty claims in both Argentina and Chile faced a tough task convincing the population that such claims were a worthwhile activity. In the early 1940s, for example, Enrique Cordovez, a member of the Chilean Antarctic Commission, wrote a series of articles and policy papers describing the economic benefits that would follow from ownership of the Antarctic Peninsula region.[59]

In other ways, however, especially in the 1940s and 1950s, South American ideas about Antarctic development had more of a spiritual than a material dimension. In much the same way that Admiral Byrd promoted U.S. interests in Antarctica to renew American civilization through the shared challenge of the Antarctic environment, writers in Argentina and Chile stressed the potential of Antarctic sovereignty to bring about social unity and regeneration. In 1948, for example, the Argentine poet Luis Ortiz Behety published a book of poetry titled *Antártida Argentina: Poemas de las Tierras Procelares*, which mixed sacred imagery with nationalist fervor.[60] In a similar spirit, the extreme right-wing Chilean writer Miguel Serrano lauded the opportunities that the Antarctic environment offered for Chileans to prove themselves equal to any nation.[61] For both Argentines and Chileans, Antarctica offered a stage for performing South American national identity both to themselves and to the world. This entailed a degree of development, although this was initially very different from that put forward by Britain through its claims to the Falkland Islands Dependencies.

Both Argentina and Chile produced Antarctic visionaries comparable in their ideas, if never quite their fame, to America's Admiral Byrd. In Chile, the army officer Ramón Cañas Montalva promoted a geopolitical vision of Chilean sovereignty in the Antarctic Peninsula region that proved tremendously influential in shaping government policy in the late 1940s and throughout the 1950s. He saw the Antarctic Peninsula as holding the strategic key to the Drake Passage, and it was vital for Chile's national security that they protect their rights to this region.[62] General Cañas was also instrumental in organizing the first visit to Antarctica by a head of state when President González Videla visited in February 1948.[63] In Argentina, another army officer, Hernán Pujato, came to play a prominent rule in the Antarctic policy of President Juan Domingo Perón.[64] Pujato's Antarctic vision had a clear developmentalist agenda, outlined in a five-point plan for exploring and colonizing the continent. Both Perón and Pujato wanted Argentina to beat the British in producing scientific information about the Antarctic environment that could be put to use in managing the region in a productive manner. In order to prepare for these scientific expeditions Pujato went on an army-training course in Alaska and purchased Arctic husky dogs to pull Argentine Antarctic sledges.

In another connection to the Arctic, Argentine armed forces working in Antarctica adopted the motto: "Our North is in the South."[65] In the years following the military overthrow of President Perón in 1955, official interest in Antarctica remained strong, although it mostly came through the military. In 1978 Emilio Palma became the first child to be born in Antarctica, after the seven-months-pregnant wife of an Argentine army officer was flown to Esperanza Base to give birth. In the 1970s and 1980s, Chile's military dictator Augusto Pinochet was a strong proponent of Chilean interests in Antarctica, and he made a visit to the continent in 1984. Although the two South American countries continued to compete with each other, they often took a common position during international political discussions of the southern continent. Over time, the Argentine and Chilean positions on Antarctica became closer to mainstream thinking, with a focus on science. But much of the distinctiveness of the South American vision of Antarctic development remains in place up to the present.

Danish Greenland

In 1921 an exhibition was held in Copenhagen to celebrate the 200th anniversary of the arrival of the Norwegian clergyman and trader Hans Egede in Greenland. Since Norway had been ruled from Denmark at the time of Egede's arrival, the event was also commemorated as marking the anniversary of Danish colonial rule over the world's largest island.[66] Many writers, both at the time and since, have characterized Danish colonial rule in Greenland as a form of benevolent paternalism.[67] "The Danish government of Greenland has long been a model of disinterested colonial administration," wrote Trevor Lloyd, Canadian consul to Greenland from 1944–45. "The welfare of the native people has been the sole criterion of success."[68] The Royal Danish Trade Monopoly for Greenland had been created in 1775 to control all trade with the island, and since then the colony had remained almost completely closed to the outside world.[69] This policy was justified as a means of protecting Greenlanders from the supposedly corrupting influences of civilization, and fits with a paternalistic view of a static society.[70] All trade and almost all industrial activities were controlled directly by the Danish State.

The realities of Danish colonialism in Greenland, however, were not completely benign. At the time of the Egede anniversary, around 15,000 Greenlanders were living under Danish rule, and their lives had been significantly changed by the experience of colonialism.[71] In some ways Danish colonialism reversed the dependent relationship that had seen John Ross saved by the generosity of Netsilik Inuit in the early 1830s. "Primitive conditions may still be met with in Greenland," wrote V. Borum, the Superintendent of Cultural Affairs in Greenland in 1948, "but the 200-year-old European influence has left many distinct traces, and in several fields has totally changed the original conditions."[72] Conversion to Christianity changed Inuit relations with the natural world, as shamanism and traditional beliefs came to be frowned upon. New opportunities to trade with Denmark encouraged a commodification of nature, or at least the parts of nature that were seen as profitable. And although colonial administration was often quite weak, Danish rule created new power dynamics that disrupted traditional hierarchies. One of the most egregious abuses of power took place in the 1920s.

Responding to the threat that Norway might challenge Danish sovereignty to Eastern Greenland, Danish colonial authorities moved an entire Inuit village to demonstrate that Danish subjects were occupying the entire habitable coastline.[73] This move came at considerable social cost, and revealed a profound lack of understanding among Danish administrators for the connection between Greenlanders and their local environment.[74]

During the 1920s and 1930s, an important shift took place in the economic basis of Greenlandic society, away from largely subsistence seal hunting and toward commercial cod fishing. Official accounts tend to attribute this change to purely environmental factors, as demonstrated by a 1951 report from Finn Nielsen of the Greenland Department:

> As is well known climatic changes have occurred all over the world since the 1920s. In Greenland the climate is becoming constantly milder with the result that the abundance of seal known in former days has almost disappeared. The seal have drawn north, away from the inhabited regions and in their stead great quantities of codfish have appeared in the waters round Greenland.[75]

It is estimated that the annual number of seals caught per person in Greenland declined from eight in 1910 to five in 1935. While changing environmental conditions undoubtedly had an impact on this economic change, a deterministic reading takes away agency from the Greenlanders and maintains them in a "traditional" state. The extensive use of motorboats for fishing, for example, suggests that Greenlanders were very capable of making informed economic decisions about how best to respond to new economic opportunities by utilizing modern technology.[76] An important result of this economic shift was the continued movement of people into larger settlements.

On July 10, 1931, the government of Norway declared that it was bringing a large part of East Greenland just north of Scoresbysound under Norwegian sovereignty.[77] This move was the culmination of several years of legal wrangling between Norway and Denmark.[78] Norwegian sealers had been working in the region since 1847, and hunters had been trapping blue and white arctic foxes and other animals since 1908 (Figure 14).[79] During the 1920s, Danish moves to extend their trading monopoly from the west coast to the whole of Greenland, raised concern among the Norwegians working in this part of the island. Despite several attempts at compromise, discussions between the two countries broke down, and in June 1831 a handful of private Norwegian whalers and sealers unilaterally announced the occupation of "Eirik Raudes Land," named after the Viking who had supposedly discovered Greenland.[80] With significant public support, this move forced the Norwegian government to move away from its traditional claim that East Greenland was legal *terra nullius* and to make a claim. The Danish government responded by calling on the Norwegians to take the case to the International Court of Justice in The Hague, which was accepted.[81] Two years later, in April 1933, the Court ruled in Denmark's favor, declaring that requirements for demonstrating legal "effective occupation" were less stringent in Greenland's Arctic environment. In a similar fashion to the Spitsbergen ruling thirteen years earlier, this ruling would have important repercussions for questions of sovereignty throughout the Polar Regions, especially in Antarctica.

Figure 14 *Hut "Bakkehuset" belonging to More-Gronlands Expedition – from Aalesund, Norway and occupied winter of 1930–31 by two Norwegian hunters, photograph by Louise Boyd (Source: American Geographical Society Library) [(47b2)22 No. 9820 M]*

While the threat from Norway functioned as a catalyst to a more active Danish colonial rule in Greenland, changing environmental perceptions played an important role in this change. Stefansson's idea of a friendly Arctic resonated with what colonial administrators wanted to hear. For much of the colonial period, taxpayers in Denmark were effectively subsidizing Danish rule in Greenland, and anything that could be done to make the colony pay for itself was welcome. In 1878 the Danish government had created a Commission for the Direction of Geographical Research in Greenland, with the aim of creating a better understanding of the resources of the colony.[82] Economic surveys such as Sydney Ball's *The Mineral Resources of Greenland* (1922) suggested that there were some valuable minerals to be found, even if these were not abundant: "The continental island Greenland," he wrote, "although not a large producer of minerals, is of interest to economic geologists, because of the character of its ore deposits, and to mining engineers, because the greater portion of its revenue is derived from royalties levied upon an ore of aluminum."[83] By the late 1930s, profitable cryolite mining was taking place around the town of Ivigtut in the south of the island, and there was also some mining of graphite, coal, and copper. In the south of the island, the Danes also had some success in promoting settled agriculture, although even by 1929 stock numbers were limited to 700 goats, 2,500 to 3,000 sheep, and 70 horned cattle.[84] There was also a nascent canning industry around the town of Holsteinborg.[85]

As in so many other colonial situations around the world, activist Danish rule in Greenland focused on creating settled communities out of highly mobile hunting societies.[86] When people lived in one place it was much easier for them to be counted, taxed, and controlled, which were central goals of the "high modern" colonial state.[87] A settled population could also be put to work in mines, processing plants, and factories, where they would usefully contribute to the economic productivity of the colony. This resettlement program came at tremendous social cost to many Greenlandic communities who found themselves caught in the classic dilemma of Arctic indigenous peoples of being stuck between tradition and modernity.[88] Greenlanders seemed to face a choice between abandoning their traditional lifestyles and embracing the modern world, or rejecting modernity and clinging to their cultural identity. This was a false dichotomy, but proved an effective tool of colonial hegemony.

Another important stimulus to the development of Greenland came from the Second World War. The military occupation of Denmark by Nazi Germany in April 1940 left Greenland cut off from colonial rule and isolated. Although there was some talk in the United States about purchasing Greenland from Denmark, this came to nothing, and the main concern from both Americans and Canadians was to put the island to use in the war effort.[89] As the war progressed, the Greenland cod fisheries provided an important source of food to the Allied war effort, and the island's cryolite mines were vital for the manufacture of aluminum in the United States and Canada.[90] As in many other parts of the world, Greenland's wartime experience gave its people a taste of freedom from colonial rule. This was particularly intense in the case of Greenland, which had been cut off from the world for so long.

With Danish rule in Greenland restored by the defeat of Nazi Germany, the aftermath of the Second World War saw considerable pressure to modernize. Following a visit of the Danish Prime Minister to Greenland, a Royal Commission was created in 1948 to investigate the future of the colony. This commission reported in 1951, and two years later, Greenland become fully integrated into the Danish State. In theory this change marked the end of Greenland's colonial status, but in reality major economic, cultural, and political disparities remained. The 1950s and 1960s witnessed renewed efforts to accelerate the trends that had been taking place under Danish colonialism and modernize the island. Government development schemes included the construction of social housing around the country to encourage urbanization. These housing schemes included the construction of the infamous "Blok P" in the capital Nuuk. Stories are told of congealed blood clogging the drains as Greenlanders butchered seals in the bathtubs as they sought to adapt to their new urban existence. Until its demolition in 2012, Blok P functioned as a potent symbol of the failures of Danish attempts to develop Greenland and the arrogance of a colonial system that paid little attention to the relationship between people and the environment.

5

WAR AND PEACE
The Cold War

From the mid 1940s into the 1990s, the Polar Regions played important roles in the Cold War, and were profoundly shaped by east-west hostilities. Although the most threatening conflict in history never became a "hot war" on a global scale, tensions between the Soviet Union and the United States were the dominant geostrategic realities in both the Arctic and Antarctica throughout this period. Through the lens of environmental history, the Cold War might be seen as a competition between two very different socioeconomic systems to demonstrate environmental authority.[1] As two of the most environmentally hostile regions on the planet, the Arctic and Antarctica offered an ideal stage for demonstrating mastery over nature. Despite the sometimes radically different methods employed by the two sides, the shared goal of conquering nature through a form of high modernism often led to quite similar social and environmental consequences on both sides of the ideological divide.[2] Socially, indigenous peoples in both communist and capitalist regions of the Arctic often suffered from the results of increasing development and from the military escalation taking place in their homelands.[3] The Cold War saw a significant increase in the scale and extent of environmental change, often dwarfing the impact of the development projects of the early twentieth century.

Despite this shared experience of superpower rivalry, the Cold

War played out very differently in the two Polar Regions. The confrontation between the Soviet Union and the United States created a "Nuclear Arctic," bristling with atomic weapons and massively changed by associated development projects. As the front line between the two superpowers, almost no part of the Arctic escaped completely from the consequences of military buildup.[4] In the far south, in contrast, superpower rivalry contributed to the creation of a "nuclear-free Antarctica" through the signing of the Antarctic Treaty of 1959. This treaty established the world's first nuclear test ban, indefinitely suspended sovereignty claims and established a "continent dedicated to peace and science." As a consequence of these divergent histories, changes to the physical environment were often quite different in the Arctic than in Antarctica.

Recent years have seen a significant growth in historical studies of the Cold War in the Polar Regions.[5] Many of these studies have focused on similarities and differences between capitalist and communist experiences, especially in the Arctic.[6] A comparative polar perspective further complicates this history. Why did the Cold War play out so differently in the two Polar Regions? Any answer to this question relies upon a careful examination of the interactions among politics, science, and the environment in the far north and far south. On the one hand, the geographic location of the Arctic as a border zone between the Soviet Union and the United States goes a long way to explaining why the North Polar Region became a highly militarized region. It made sense that such a strategically important location would get sucked into the conflict. On the other hand, the distance of Antarctica from the centers of conflict in the northern hemisphere did not guarantee that the southern continent would escape military conflict. Studies have suggested that there was nothing inevitable about the signing of the Antarctic Treaty, and it is easy to imagine a slightly different combination of events that might have seen Cold War hostilities extending to the bottom of the world. An extension of this logic back to the Arctic might also suggest that if just a few things had been different, its Cold War history may have developed in another direction as well.

Something of the unpredictability of Cold War environmental history can be seen in the history of whaling in the second half of the twentieth century. By the mid 1950s, global whale populations—by now concentrated in the Polar Regions, especially Antarctica—were becoming precariously low as a result of overfishing. Helicopter spotters, radar, and ever more efficient processing techniques created a modern version of the tragedy of the commons, in which individual operators had little incentive to protect an open-access resource.[7] Beneath this overarching explanation, several authors have identified ideological dimensions to the decline of whale populations.[8] American diplomats insisted on an open-access "first come first served" quota system that encouraged competition; the Soviet Union was able to continue whaling even after it became unprofitable for other countries as a result of its very difficult economic system. Rather than being a simple story of environmentalists against whalers, the history of the whaling moratorium of the 1980s was immersed in the politics of the Cold War, with the United States taking a lead in the campaign to prohibit global whaling.[9]

Taken alongside the unpredictable Cold War history of whaling, the fact that the superpower rivalry played out so differently in the Arctic and Antarctica over the second half of the twentieth century is a powerful argument against any form of determinism, whether political or environmental. The environmental histories of the Polar Regions serve as warnings against sweeping statements about the impact of the Cold War on the environment, or about the environmental consequences of capitalist or communist economic systems. The nature of environmental change was dependent upon multiple factors and could be radically different in different places. At the same time, the history of the Cold War reveals that the nature of the environment alone does not determine political or military histories. The Arctic became a battleground in a way that few would have predicted in the early twentieth century; Antarctica became a "continent for peace and science" partly, but not only, as a result of its environment and perceptions of that environment. A comparative polar perspective suggests that a deterministic reading of Arctic and Antarctic history simply cannot be sustained.

The Nuclear Arctic

In the years that followed the Russian Revolution of 1917, the newly created Soviet Union made a sustained effort to develop the Arctic in order to extract resources and bring Marxism to the people of the north. Despite a handful of expeditions dating back to the eighteenth century, much of Arctic Russia remained largely unexplored and almost entirely economically undeveloped into the early twentieth century. This would change rapidly with the growing interest of the Soviet Union in conquering Arctic nature. The ideas of Vilhjalmur Stefansson proved popular in the Soviet Union, and communist development schemes shared much with those of other parts of the Arctic.[10] In both systems there were uneasy tensions between the notion of a friendly Arctic and the realities of a hostile environment. But the imposition of a Marxian ideology on top of these projects meant that there were also significant differences. A centralized command-and-control economy could attempt to do things in the Arctic north that would be much more difficult in the more free-market systems of Arctic Scandinavia or North America. Political and ideological imperatives would mean that development would take place extremely rapidly, with very little concern for local communities or the environment. Most important, Soviet planners wanted to show that their political system was better than the capitalist alternative, and the Arctic offered an ideal stage for doing this.

The historian Paul Josephson examines the history of Soviet Arctic development in *The Conquest of the Russian Arctic* (2014).[11] He suggests that Soviet attempts to change the north changed over time, but that there were a number of constant themes and tensions, such as the fact that the Soviet system was in no way supremely rational.[12] Development efforts focused on the Arctic northwest, and the cities of Arkhangelsk and Murmansk were two of the most important centers. As a result of these development projects, the population of the Soviet Arctic almost doubled between 1926 and 1935, increasing from 656,000 to 1,176,000.[13]

One of the first projects was the construction of a canal between the White Sea and the Baltic Sea, which made the resources of the Russian Arctic much more accessible. The successful completion of the canal in 1933, after only eighteen months of construction, created an appetite for large-scale geo-engineering projects that tended to characterize the Soviet "conquest" mentality towards the north.[14] The naming of the canal after Joseph Stalin reflected the leader's enthusiasm for Arctic development.[15] Communist efforts to develop the Arctic were premised on the idea that the Soviet model was superior in its ability to harness both nature and people to its cause.[16]

By the mid 1930s, a central goal of Soviet Arctic policy was also to extract natural resources to facilitate national industrialization and economic self-sufficiency. Nickel mines were developed at Norilsk, coal mines at Vorkuta, and gold mines at Kolyma.[17] An elaborate system of slave labor camps known as gulags was created in the Russian north to provide workers for these mines and development projects. Gulag labor played a valuable role in substituting for technology as the Soviet Union industrialized. Gulags also served propaganda purposes: as they created fear in the population at large, they also sought to reeducate political prisoners toward thinking like a collective. These were brutal places to work and life expectancy among the prisoners was tragically short. The writer Aleksandr Solzhenitsyn described an "archipelago of gulags" across the Arctic and sub-Arctic and wrote about their horrors.[18] Work on Joseph Stalin's White Sea Canal, for example, was estimated to have cost the lives of around 25,000 gulag workers.[19]

The combination of massive inputs and massive outputs caused unprecedented environmental change in the Soviet Arctic. Despite the belief that socialism created harmony with nature, the mining cities of the Soviet North became some of the most polluted places on the planet.[20] According to the environmental historian J. R. McNeill, the pollution generated by the nickel mining town of Norilsk damaged an area of boreal forest the size of Connecticut, the men had the highest lung cancer rate in the world, and during the 1980s the town generated more sulfur dioxide than the country of Italy.[21] The Soviet Arctic city was, in some ways, a very different "workscape" to the sealing beach, the whaling ship, or even the Spitsbergen mine, but all were largely unpleasant places in which to work.[22] As in other parts of the Polar Regions, the nature of the working conditions—especially for those in the gulags—contributed to a spiral of environmental decline, where there was little incentive to create a sustainable future.

Although the northwest was central to Soviet development, no part of the Arctic escaped completely. Soviet officials referred to indigenous northern communities by the generic term "little peoples of the north," overlooking significant differences among them.[23] In eastern Siberia, for example, close to the Bering Sea, Chukchi reindeer herders presented a dilemma to Soviet planners.[24] In some ways, these herding communities were already living in a state of primitive communism, where there were few possessions and everything was shared. But Soviet officials also realized that the ideology of Marxism was completely alien to these herders, and consequently they needed educating. A system of collectivization was instituted, which represented a radical change in the lives of the herders. Somewhat ironically, in pushing a Marxist ideology, Soviet planners found themselves pursuing policies that were not so very different from those being practiced toward nomadic peoples in many parts of the noncommunist world.

In the 1930s, there was a major push for science and exploration in the Soviet Arctic. A central figure in this quest was the scientist, adventurer, and administrator Otto Schmidt, who became known as the "Commissar of Ice." Schmidt proved adept at combining a career in scientific administration and publishing with climbing through the ranks of Communist Party politics. By the early 1930s Schmidt was head of the Glavsevmorput, the bureaucratic institution that oversaw Arctic affairs. "Our goal," he wrote, "is to study the North in order to settle it economically ... for the good of the entire USSR."[25] Soviet Arctic research focused on the physical sciences, including meteorology, oceanography, and geology.[26] This scientific research brought practical benefits in the form of improved weather forecasts, ocean charts, and geological maps. But Arctic science also gave the Soviet Union an important sphere for demonstrating the superiority of the communist system.

Soviet Arctic research produced scientific achievements but also had geopolitical goals. Science and exploration helped to demonstrate political occupation of the Arctic, and in the early years of the Soviet Union, a number of Arctic territories were brought under direct Soviet sovereignty. Wrangel Island, for example, which had been the location of Stefansson's ill-fated attempt at Arctic colonization in the early 1920s, was definitively brought under Soviet rule by a group of explorers in 1926. As part of the International Polar Year of 1932–33, Russian scientists asserted their sovereignty over Victoria Island, east of Spitsbergen (Figure 15). In its use of science and exploration to assert sovereignty, the Soviet Union was continuing a long tradition that was particularly strong in the Polar Regions.

Figure 15   *Three Russians hoisting the flag of USSR in Victoria Land, c.1933.*
(Source: American Geographical Society Library) [(47c2)54 No. 8399 M]

In a similar way that the Northwest Passage became a major geopolitical goal of the nineteenth century, a central ambition of Soviet Arctic policy was to make the Northern Sea Route north of Siberia a viable route for commercial shipping. In order to facilitate this aim, the Soviet Union constructed a number of state-of-the-art icebreakers, adding to the existing Arctic fleet.[27] In 1932, Otto Schmidt led the first expedition to navigate the Northern Sea Route in a single year on board the icebreaker *Sibiryakov*.[28] This expedition helped to make Schmidt's reputation as a hero of the Soviet Union. Pictures of icebreakers plowing through the Arctic sea ice provided an ideal image to illustrate communist attitudes toward the conquest of nature. But the Soviet obsession with the Northern Sea Route was far more than simply rhetorical. The practical benefits conferred by the ability to navigate through the Arctic ice would prove invaluable in keeping Russia supplied during the Second World War. Interest in Arctic shipping would continue throughout the Soviet period, and in 1977 the nuclear-powered icebreaker *Arktika* would become the first surface vessel to reach the North Pole.[29]

In the late 1930s, Soviet scientists instituted a series of North Pole "Ice-Stations" in which camps were built on the floating sea ice (known by the initials SP for *Severny Polus* meaning North Pole). As they drifted, the scientists kept a range of meteorological and oceanographic measurements, which filled in important gaps in knowledge about the Arctic environment. A better understanding of the Arctic Ocean basin, in particular, had utility not only for shipping and submarines but also for questions of sovereignty, as would later be demonstrated by the importance of the Lomonosov Ridge for extending Russian sovereignty claims to the North Pole. Living on the ice stations was dangerous work, since the sea ice could easily break up and melt. Over the years, Soviet scientists perfected this method of research, and by the early 1970s, SP 22 would set a record of 3,120 days of drifting covering a distance of 17,069 km.[30]

During the 1930s Soviet aviators took a definitive lead in polar flying. In May 1937 Valerii Chkalov became the first pilot to land at the North Pole in a flight that included Otto Schmidt among the crew.[31] Soviet aviators worked closely with the floating ice stations to provide supplies and relief. Most important, Soviet aviators made a number of flights across the Arctic Ocean, demonstrating the feasibility of a trans-Arctic air route. While westerners such as Hubert Wilkins had done much to pioneer a trans-Arctic air route, it was these far more extensive Soviet flights that would turn the dream of polar air routes into a reality.[32] Flying across the Arctic had the potential to significantly cut journey times from Europe to America and Asia.

In the United States, polar experts looked on with a mixture of admiration and fear of what the Soviet Union was achieving in the Arctic. In the late 1930s, for example, *The Polar Times* gave extensive coverage to the Russian ice stations and feats of polar aviation. Under the headline "Fliers Alight at North Pole and Establish Soviet Air Base" much of the October 1937 edition of the magazine was dedicated to coverage of Chkalov and Schmidt's achievements.[33] The tone of the reporting was mostly fascinated admiration for what the Soviet Union was achieving, but there was a slight undertone of concern that it was Russian communists rather than American capitalists who were taking a lead in Arctic aviation. During the Second World War, the United States and Soviet Union fought together as unlikely allies in the war against Nazism. In the Arctic, the war diminished exploration, but the sea routes and air routes that had been pioneered in the 1920s and 1930s took on a new strategic significance for the supply of armaments and provisions to the besieged Soviet Union. For example, aviators flew American-made planes from Alaska to Russia to supply the Soviet Air Force.

On August 6, 1945, the dropping of an American nuclear bomb on the Japanese city of Hiroshima radically changed relations between the United States and the Soviet Union. The bomb threatened to give the United States a tremendous military advantage over the Soviet Union, and two countries that had so recently been allies in the war against Hitler rapidly entered a nuclear standoff. In this new conflict, the trans-Arctic air routes pioneered by men like Schmidt suddenly gained a new geopolitical importance. The Arctic Ocean offered the shortest distance for planes—and by the late 1950s missiles and nuclear submarines—to cross from one superpower to the other.

The Soviet Union tested its first nuclear bomb in August 1949. This event stimulated a rapid arms race between the two superpowers. One of the results of this arms race was the creation of a highly militarized, nuclear Arctic. Approximately one-fifth of all Russian nuclear tests took place in the far north, mostly on the island of Novaya Zemlya.[34] These tests included the largest yield nuclear explosion of all time in 1961 (nicknamed *Tsar Bomba*).[35] It also made sense to position nuclear weapons and nuclear powered ships and submarines close to the front line, so that they could respond as quickly as possible to a strike—or threat of a strike—from the other side. By the 1980s the Arctic Ocean had become, in the words of writer Charles Emmerson, a "Soviet Nuclear Bastion," with almost fifty nuclear submarines attached to the Soviet Northern Fleet.[36]

As a result of the nuclear weapons testing and buildup, some regions of the Soviet Arctic added to the dubious distinction of being among the most polluted places in the world the title of "among the most radioactive." In this way the policy of mutually assured destruction came to have a major impact on the people and environment of the Arctic north. In addition to its military uses, nuclear power also provided additional energy for ongoing Arctic development schemes. Fallout from nuclear testing at Novaya Zemlya contaminated the landscape; nuclear waste was dumped into the Arctic Ocean in large quantities;

nuclear submarines were often scuttled at sea; and more nuclear reactor accidents took place among the ships of the Northern Fleet based in the city of Arkhangel than in the rest of the world put together.[37]

The United States responded to the buildup of nuclear weapons in the Soviet Arctic by creating their own nuclear arsenal in the Arctic north. The logic for nuclear buildup in the capitalist Arctic was identical to that in the communist Arctic: weapons located in this region had the best chance of making a strike against the Soviet Union in the event of a nuclear confrontation. The environmental and social consequences of military buildup and the associated development project were often very similar. In order to learn more about the Arctic environment, the U.S. Army established the Cold Regions Research and Engineering Laboratory (CRREL) in Hanover, New Hampshire, in 1961. The location of this research center built on the polar expertise that had developed at Dartmouth College through its association with Vilhjalmur Stefansson. Along with several other similar civilian and military research institutions, CRREL served both rhetorical and practical functions in demonstrating U.S. mastery of the polar landscape.

Among the most high-profile locations of U.S. military presence was the Thule airbase in northern Greenland.[38] Construction of the base began in 1951 in the same region that Knud Rasmussen had built his famous trading station. In the early years of the Cold War, the Thule airbase developed into an elaborate base for long-range bombers that could theoretically fly forward and back to the Soviet Union in the event of hostilities. Fighter planes stationed at Thule could also be used to intercept Soviet bombers. The establishment and development of the airbase had major consequences for local Inuit communities. In contrast to the Danish policy of paternalism that was pursued across much of the island, the Thule airbase brought local Inuit into sustained contact with the outside world. One of the most remote communities in Greenland suddenly became one of the most cosmopolitan.

In a project associated with the Thule airbase, U.S. military planners sought to create an elaborate nuclear arsenal under the ice sheet in northern Greenland.[39] Known as Project Iceworm, or "the city under the ice," and located at Camp Century, this endeavor was one of the most ambitious attempts to demonstrate a mastery of polar nature. The United States sought to construct an entire city under the ice.

Unfortunately for U.S. military planners, the project failed as a result of structural weaknesses in the ice, which made it unsuitable for extensive construction. The project would nevertheless make an important contribution to the study of climate and climate change as a result of a study of the ice-cores drilled there.[40]

The logic of mutually assured destruction required knowledge of a nuclear attack as soon as possible so that an immediate response could be launched. As a result, U.S. and Canadian policymakers sought to construct a string of early warning systems that would detect an attempted Soviet strike. The most well known was the Defense Early Warning (DEW) Line that was built between 1954 and 1957 and stretched from Alaska to Baffin Island in Canada.[41] The General Electric Corporation played a key role in building the DEW Line, and a promotional brochure presented the work as a triumph of free market ingenuity and a classic example of President Eisenhower's "military industrial complex." As the anthropologist Stacy Fritz has shown, the DEW Line had a number of significant social and environmental consequences for the Inuit communities living close to it:

> Study findings revealed that the short life cycle of a very small arctic radar base can literally and figuratively permeate and shape the land and the lives of several generations of people around it. While the sites are a largely normalized part of everyone's lives along the arctic coast, each community has its own particular history with the DEW Line and each individual has their own opinions on militarization in the Arctic.[42]

While social and environmental change was not always welcomed by Arctic communities, they adapted to it and life kept going. This was in keeping with broader changes to Arctic culture and the environment that resulted from Cold War militarization.

The historian Ronald Doel has written of the Pentagon's "fascination with the Arctic" during the early Cold War.[43] Although this interest spanned the Arctic, the State of Alaska was an obvious focal point.[44] A lot of the military buildup and many of the economic development projects were fairly traditional. Military bases, for example, were built and expanded in various regions. But there were also several high-profile development schemes. One of the most extraordinary projects was a plan from the late 1950s to geo-engineer the Arctic landscape using a nuclear explosion.[45] With the code-name Project Chariot, physicists at the U.S. Atomic Energy Commission led by Edward Teller sought to demonstrate a potential peaceful use of nuclear power to create a deep-water harbor at the Point Hope region of Alaska. While ostensibly peaceful in its purpose, this project might be seen as another attempt to demonstrate the superiority of the capitalist system over communism in the conquest of nature. In the event, the plan was never put into practice as a result of significant opposition from Inupiat communities and environmentalist groups. Resistance to Project Chariot in fact served as an important stimulus to Inupiat political consciousness through the founding of the *Tundra Times*.[46]

Cold War tensions remained a defining feature of the history of the Arctic into the late 1980s. But as a central location for superpower conflict, it was perhaps fitting that the region should play an important role in the diminution of Cold War hostilities. On October 1, 1987, Secretary General of the Communist Party Mikhail Gorbachev gave a famous speech at Murmansk calling for a reduction in the militarization of the Arctic and the beginning of greater cooperation among Arctic states.[47] He wanted a nuclear-free zone to be declared in Northern Europe and suggested that the Arctic should become a "Zone of Peace." Science and the environment were central to Gorbachev's vision of a demilitarized Arctic. The Murmansk Speech is often cited not only as an important milestone in the end of the Cold War but also as a stimulus to the modern politics of the Arctic. In making a call for Arctic cooperation, Gorbachev could draw upon a successful model of international agreement from the other end of the planet, where the Antarctic Treaty had been promoting peace and science for more than quarter of a century.

Nuclear-Free Antarctica

At the outbreak of Cold War hostilities in the second half of the 1940s, the United States already had quite an extensive recent history of Antarctic exploration through the expeditions of Admiral Byrd and Lincoln Ellsworth in the 1920s and 1930s, and through Hearst's sponsorship of Wilkins. In the aftermath of the Second World War the

United States sent two official expeditions to Antarctica, Operation Highjump and Operation Windmill, with the purposes of training troops in polar conditions, charting the still largely unknown Antarctic territory, and reducing the social burden of a rapid decommissioning of troops. At the same time, a private U.S. expedition under the command of Finn Ronne ventured into the contested Antarctica Peninsula region where the dispute between Britain, Argentina, and Chile was rapidly intensifying.[48] The extensive use of aircraft on these expeditions, while practical for the purpose of exploration, was also meant to demonstrate U.S. technological superiority (Figure 16). While these expeditions continued to lay claims for a possible U.S. sovereignty claim to Antarctica, official policy remained that the United States reserved its rights to any part of the continent and refused to recognize any sovereignty claims.

In the second half of the 1940s, the Soviet Union began sending whaling expeditions to the Southern Ocean, which became known

Figure 16 *Finn Ronne Expedition: The cargo-carrying Norseman, Nana, being made ready, September 29, 1948 (Source: American Geographical Society Library) [(48al) 53332 No.32,229 S].*

as the Slava whaling fleet. Russian oceanographers took advantage of these voyages to conduct research into the nature of the Southern Ocean. Unlike the United States, the Soviet Union could not boast a recent history of involvement with the southern continent, in large part because their energies had been almost entirely focused on the north. But politicians and geographers were fairly quick to embrace the early nineteenth-century expedition of Thaddeus Von Bellingshausen, which was likely the first expedition to sight the Antarctic continent.[49] In June 1950, the government issued a statement saying that the Soviet Union should be consulted about any international consideration concerning the Antarctic continent. This was taken as a statement of intent that the Soviet Union intended a greater involvement with Antarctica, and Soviet policy developed into a reservation of rights to the whole of the Antarctic continent that was similar to the United States.

The real stimulus for large-scale superpower involvement in Antarctica came from plans for a massive scientific research project known as the International Geophysical Year (IGY) that would take place from 1957–58.[50] The idea for the IGY came mostly from the scientists in the United States and Britain. While the scope of the IGY was truly global, its particular focus was to be outer space, the Arctic, and Antarctica. The launch of the Sputnik satellite by the Soviet Union took place under the auspices of the IGY, and much valuable research took place in the Arctic. But it was Antarctic science that caught much of the world's attention during the IGY, largely because of a continued lack of knowledge about the southern continent. Twelve countries participated directly in IGY Antarctic research, including the United States, the Soviet Union, Britain, Argentina, and Chile. The quest to learn more about the Antarctic environment offered the two superpowers a sphere in which to compete without the immediate threat of military conflict. During the IGY, the scientific contributions of the United States and the Soviet Union would by far eclipse the research of the other ten participants.[51]

For a while there was some doubt as to whether the Soviet Union would take part in the Antarctic section of the IGY. A deliberate attempt was made to exclude Soviet delegates from a meeting that was held in Paris in 1955 to discuss plans for IGY Antarctic research. Three days into the meeting, however, a Soviet delegation under the leadership of the geophysicist Vladimir Belousov showed up.[52] After apologizing for being late, Belousov announced that the Soviet Union was looking forward to conducting science in Antarctica and was planning on building a research station at the South Pole. This location had the advantage of being a physical demonstration of the rejection of sovereignty claims, since six of the seven national claims to Antarctica converged at the bottom of the world as a consequence of the sector principle. The Soviet announcement caused quite a stir among delegates, since the United States had already announced that it was intending to construct a station at the Pole. For a moment it looked like Cold War tensions might extend to the very bottom of the world. In what appeared to have been a remarkable example of quick thinking, however, Belousov rapidly announced a change of plans: if the South Pole was already taken, then the Soviet Union would construct a station at the so-called "Pole of Relative Inaccessibility"—the place in Antarctica furthest from any coastline. This goal made a lot of sense to the Soviet Union since great fanfare had accompanied Cherivichney's achievement of the North Pole of Relative Inaccessibility in the middle of the Arctic Ocean in May 1941.[53]

Following Belousov's announcement, international planning for the IGY continued apace, now with the Soviet Union fully involved. The competition to build a research station in the most difficult location in Antarctica epitomized the Cold War competition to demonstrate the conquest of polar nature. While there was certainly scientific value in conducting research in the far interior of the Antarctic continent, there was no small degree of bravado in this ambition. The two superpowers went about constructing their inland stations in different ways. The United States used airplanes to airlift all the supplies they needed for building the South Pole Station. This led to the curious situation that when the New Zealand adventurer Edmund Hillary led only the third overland expedition ever to arrive at the pole in January 1958 as part of Vivian Fuchs's Commonwealth Trans-Antarctic Expedition, he was greeted by Americans who had simply flown to the bottom of the world.[54] In contrast, the Soviet Union used convoys of large ice-tractors to transport men and materials to the center of the continent to build a station at the Pole of Relative Inaccessibility. Both methods relied on a mixture of technology and human endeavor, but there was perhaps a little more of a brute force mentality behind the Soviet use of tractors.

Alongside the construction of their respective research stations at the South Pole and the Pole of Relative Inaccessibility, the United States and Soviet Union also conducted IGY science in other parts of the Antarctic Continent. Taken together, the international results of IGY science radically changed environmental perceptions of the southern continent. In the years prior to the IGY, a widespread lack of scientific understanding had allowed fantasies to flourish about the economic potential of the southern continent. Nobody knew, for example, how deep the Antarctic ice might be, and there was considerable support for a "thin ice" hypothesis, which held that the ice was little more than several hundred meters thick.[55] This allowed groups such as the Antarctic Colony Associates of Jacksonville, Florida, to present seemingly outlandish plans for melting through the ice to get at the supposedly valuable minerals lying underneath.[56] Rather than being several hundred meters thick, the scientific results of IGY revealed that the Antarctic ice sheet was an average of around 2 km deep, making ideas for drilling look ridiculous. The weather proved as hostile as people imagined, with frequent storms around the edges of the continent and frigid temperatures in the interior. Perhaps most important, almost no mineral resources of any significant economic significance were discovered by IGY scientists despite fairly widespread prospecting.[57]

Several countries, including the United States and Great Britain, treated IGY research as something of an economic survey of Antarctica. A perceived lack of short-to-medium term economic value paved the way for the twelve countries that had participated in IGY Antarctic research to discuss the political future of the southern continent. It is difficult to imagine government officials in London or Washington considering a reduction of their immediate claims and rights in the Antarctic continent if a significant quantity of valuable minerals had been found. As it turned out, however, there was little of immediate value in Antarctica, so the United States and Britain were willing to be flexible in the international discussions of Antarctic sovereignty. In 1958, President Eisenhower of the United States invited the other eleven nations participating in IGY Antarctic science to a conference in Washington, D.C., to discuss the political future of Antarctica. This overlap with the IGY created a strong connection between scientific research and politics. The involvement of the Soviet Union in these negotiations raised the ire of a handful of "cold warrior" politicians, but it raised the possibility of a realistic and comprehensive political settlement for the Antarctic continent.[58]

After eighteen months of preliminary negotiations, representatives of the twelve nations met at State Department offices in Washington, D.C., for a formal Antarctic Conference. Despite numerous disagreements and several occasions when it looked like talks would break down completely, the twelve countries agreed to and signed the Antarctic Treaty on December 1, 1959.[59] The Treaty proclaimed Antarctica to be a "continent dedicated to peace and science." In the context of the conflicting sovereignty claims and reservations of rights of the 1950s, one of the most important parts of the Treaty was Article IV, which effectively suspended the question of sovereignty, neither rejecting nor affirming any of the claims. Other important articles included demilitarization of the continent, with Antarctic to be used exclusively for peaceful purposes. A right to inspection of stations by any signatory country at any time provided a mechanism for guaranteeing this demilitarization. The exchange of information was guaranteed by the Treaty, and the signatories agreed to meet regularly to discuss the affairs of the southern continent. In relation to the wider world, an important part of the Treaty was Article IX, which stipulated that before any country could join the treaty it had to demonstrate a "substantial scientific interest in the southern continent."

In the context of the Cold War, one of the most remarkable aspects of the Treaty was Article V, which stated: "Any nuclear explosions in Antarctica and the disposal there of radioactive waste material shall be prohibited." In effect, this article made the Antarctic Treaty the first nuclear test-ban treaty between the United States and the Soviet Union. The origins of Article V were not purely idealistic. Both the United States and Britain—and quite possibly the Soviet Union—had wanted to keep their options open as far as using Antarctica to test nuclear weapons. Argentine diplomats introduced the idea of banning nuclear explosions into the negotiations, claiming that it was in the interests of southern hemisphere nations.[60] It is possible that another motivation for the Argentine move was to destabilize the negotiations by causing trouble between the United States and the Soviet Union. As it turned out, the ban on nuclear explosions proved acceptable to both superpowers and it was incorporated into the Treaty. Between 1963 and 1973, the United States ran a nuclear power station at McMurdo Station, nicknamed Nukey Poo. Although this did not violate the letter of the Treaty it certainly went against its spirit. After the decommissioning and dismantling of the station, all radioactive material was removed, and Antarctica became a nuclear-free continent, even as nuclear-powered vessels continued to operate in the Southern Ocean.

In drafting the text of the Antarctic Treaty, lawyers and diplomats drew both consciously and unconsciously on precedents that had been set in the Arctic. The Spitsbergen Treaty of 1920 provided something of a model for special legal arrangements in the Polar Regions: when there were no indigenous people and only very small permanent populations, different approaches to sovereignty could be tried. The "sector principle" that had been developed in Canada and Russia offered a way of thinking about sovereignty in the Polar Regions, although it was by no means accepted by everyone. The East Greenland case of 1933 had helped to shape legal thinking about the requirements for "effective occupation" over an uninhabited expanse of ice.[61] In creating a "continent for peace and science," however, the Antarctic Treaty went further in its innovation than anything that had been attempted in the Arctic, or really anywhere else in the world. The idea of "limited internationalization" could be seen as characterizing the Antarctic Treaty, since it definitely created an international governance structure for the continent, but its internationalization was limited in both the reservation of sovereignty rights and the number of participating countries. The Treaty certainly was not the genuine internationalization under the auspices of the United Nations that India had been calling for in the second half of the 1950s.[62]

The Cold War context is vital in understanding why different countries signed and ratified the Antarctic Treaty. For the Soviet Union and the United States, there was a shared feeling that they did not want the full extent of Cold War hostilities to extend to the southern continent.[63] The scientific results of the IGY had proved to both superpowers that Antarctica was not worth fighting over, at least in the short-to-medium term, and there was willingness to compromise. American policymakers also liked the Antarctic Treaty because it helped to diffuse the twenty-year dispute over the sovereignty of the Antarctic Peninsula Region between Britain, Argentina, and Chile, three important Cold War allies. For the British government, the Antarctic Treaty offered a way to put an end to an expensive and distracting conflict without losing face or having to give up completely its claims to the Falkland Islands Dependencies. It was no coincidence therefore that Great Britain was the first country to ratify the Antarctic Treaty. In both Argentina and Chile, the Antarctic Treaty came under intense criticism from nationalists who claimed that it was a surrender of legitimate sovereignty claims.[64] The ratification of the Treaty in these two South American countries can only be fully explained in the context of the Cold War and the fear that without a structure for containing the Soviet Union, the communist superpower could potentially threaten their nations from close proximity.[65] A similar fear of the Soviet Union shaped the decision of the other seven signatories, with Australia in particular being nervous regarding communist intentions in the Australian Antarctic sector.

The Cold War context also makes the Antarctic Treaty all the more remarkable. Over fifty years after its signature the Antarctic Treaty System continues to provide the governing structure for the southern continent. That such an innovative and long-lasting treaty could emerge from the tensions of the Cold War is testament to the creativity of the negotiators as well as to the contingency of history. The Antarctic Treaty is by no means perfect. The requirement of Article IX for a country to be conducting scientific research in Antarctica before it is granted full consultative membership of the Antarctic Treaty System would lead to many poorer nations being excluded on account of not being able to afford the costs of Antarctic research.[66] This requirement also led to much "science" of dubious value being conducted by countries that did manage to join. Another criticism of the Treaty is that rather than resolving the question of Antarctica sovereignty it merely puts off this question through the suspension of claims and assertions of rights. But despite its exclusivity and lack of conclusiveness, it is certainly possible to imagine many scenarios that would have been far worse outcomes, especially given the underlying Cold War tensions.

In relation to the material environment, the 1959 Antarctic Treaty laid the foundations for what the historian Alessandro Antonello has called the "greening of Antarctica."[67] While the environmental consequences of military buildup in the Arctic were generally negative, the environmental consequences of peace and science in Antarctica were generally positive. The Treaty itself made no mention of environmental protection. But it did create a structure through which environmental problems could be discussed and environmental regulations put in place. In the years that followed the ratification in 1961, conservation has provided the Treaty Parties with an ideal sphere for coming together and demonstrating the usefulness of the Antarctic Treaty System, thereby helping to justify the political arrangement. Alongside the obvious divergence from the "Nuclear Arctic," there was also a dramatic contrast between environmental protection on the Antarctic Continent and in the surrounding Southern Ocean, which had been explicitly excluded from the provisions of the Antarctic Treaty. In particular, the Cold War history of whaling was a much less edifying story.

Cold War Whaling

Although the global whaling industry can never be thought of as being exclusively polar, by the mid-twentieth century, the vast majority of the world's commercial whaling was taking place in the Southern Ocean. The history of whaling therefore continues to intersect with an environmental history of the Polar Regions. The development of open-water pelagic whaling in the 1920s and 1930s had revolutionized the industry around Antarctica, and put significant pressure on whale populations through overfishing. Accompanied by a fleet of catcher vessels, large pelagic factory ships were able to follow whales across the ocean and process them where they were killed. This made the whaling industry far more efficient and facilitated the effective hunting of blue whales and fin whales, the world's largest creatures. Pelagic whaling freed the whaling industry from reliance on shore stations to process its catch, which in turn liberated the industry from the taxes and regulations imposed by the sovereign power, which in the Southern Ocean was most often Great Britain. While whaling companies were happy to be freed from these burdens, the open access of pelagic whaling very quickly created a classic fisherman's problem or tragedy of the commons.[68] Any country or company with the means of building or

Figure 17   *Blue whale hauled up on flensing deck of modern Antarctic whaling factory ship. (Source: American Geographical Society Library). [48] 53156 No. 39,852 S]*

purchasing a whaling vessel could participate in pelagic whaling, and there was little incentive to conserve whale populations if other whalers showed no desire to do so.

Just as the Cold War shaped the politics and environment of the terrestrial Arctic and Antarctica, so too did this global conflict have a major impact on the history of commercial whaling and the associated marine ecosystems. In a recent study titled *Whales and Nations* historian Kurk Dorsey argues that international relations played a key role in the twentieth-century history of whaling: the conservation of whale stocks was a diplomatic issue every bit as much as a scientific or technical issue.[69] The essential task for the international whaling community was to put in place a framework for the regulation of whale hunting that would guarantee the long-term sustainability of the industry. The key institution in this effort was the International Whaling Commission (IWC), which was founded in 1946. With both the United States and the Soviet Union involved in the IWC, Cold War tensions pervaded negotiations. Mutual suspicion made it much harder to avoid a tragedy-of-the-commons scenario, since there was little belief that the other side could be trusted. More subtly, ideological differences and rivalries would play important roles in shaping the negotiating positions of the two superpowers, with major implications for the history of whaling.

From an environmentalist perspective, the history of whaling in the second half of the twentieth century is much less edifying than the history of continental Antarctica, where Cold War tensions helped to lay the foundations for the Antarctic Treaty and the conservation measures that followed. The history of whaling in the second half of the twentieth century falls much more readily into the declensionist narrative of wanton destruction of the natural world. The fact that whales were large, charismatic, and seemingly highly intelligent creatures only exacerbated this narrative. Ultimately, however, commercial whaling came to an end in the 1980s before any whale species had become extinct. This result was certainly welcomed by environmentalist organizations, however distraught they were about the history of whaling up to that point. An interesting debate exists as to what factors brought about the end of commercial whaling.[70] Did whaling come to an end as a result of environmentalist pressure, international diplomacy, or simply because the industry became unprofitable? While some combination of all three of these factors seems likely to offer the most satisfactory explanation, the fundamental role of the Cold War in this history cannot be overstated.

In the aftermath of the Second World War, the United States took a lead in constructing a framework for international whaling. Late in 1946, the United States invited interested nations to participate in a conference on whaling in Washington, D.C. Despite no longer having much direct economic interest in the global whaling industry, U.S. politicians, diplomats, and scientists took it upon themselves to establish the it on a sustainable basis. A sustainable whaling industry, they believed, was in the interests of a healthy global economy, and there was a belief that U.S. scientific and managerial expertise would be vital for constructing a workable whaling regime. This was in keeping with various U.S. efforts to design international institutions to govern the postwar world, and fits neatly into a broader Cold War contest for the control of nature.

As the two victorious nations that had played the most active role in modern whaling, Great Britain and Norway were also prominent participants in the postwar whaling negotiations. Despite sharing goals for the future of whaling, differences quickly surfaced between the positions of Britain, Norway, and the United States.[71] While British officials were certainly interested in creating a sustainable whaling industry, they were most concerned with reviving the hunting of whales as quickly as possible to provide food fats to a war-ravaged Britain. Norwegians wanted a return to their prewar position of dominance in the global whaling industry, and argued for whaling quotas based on historical catches. This, they argued, would be the fairest and most efficient way to regulate the industry. Motivated by a free-market ideology, however, U.S. officials rejected the Norwegian position. Although quotas were necessary, the Americans believed that the industry should be open to all, rather than frozen in a situation that favored one nation over others. As a consequence, U.S. officials argued for a quota system that would allow any country to participate, but that would cut off all Antarctic whaling for the season as soon as the quota was reached.

After several weeks of negotiations, the countries present at the Washington Conference signed the International Convention for the Regulation of Whaling on December 2, 1946, and created the International Whaling Commission (IWC) to regulate the industry. This Convention built on regulatory efforts from before the Second World War, but there was optimism that the new international order would make this attempt more effective. The U.S. call for a free-for-all quota system had obvious appeal to every country except Norway, and it is not surprising that this was the policy adopted. The initial quota was set at 16,000 BWU per year, which several scientists at the time (and many since) thought was too high. While the attempt to create a standard unit seemed to make sense, several commentators have criticized this system for encouraging the hunting of blue whales.[72]

Writing a number of years afterwards, Gerald Elliott, a former executive of the British whaling company Salvesen, argued that the ideologically motivated American policy for setting the quota system had a profound impact on the history of post–Second World War whaling.[73] By making the annual whale hunt function on a first-come-first-served basis, the open access system encouraged whaling companies to invest in new technology that would enable them to hunt as many whales as possible, as quickly as possible. This led to innovations such as helicopter spotters being used to search for whales and then radioing their locations to catcher ships.[74] Older, less efficient ships were no longer viable because the quota would likely be reached and all Antarctic whaling cut off before these ships had caught enough to make a profit. The investment in new whaling ships and technology, however, came at a price. After making substantial investments in their whaling companies, owners and shareholders were less willing to contemplate a reduction in the quota, which would almost certainly mean a reduction in annual profits. As a consequence, even when it seemed increasingly necessary for the 16,000 BWU quota to be reduced as the 1950s progressed, most whaling companies rejected this move. A second, more ecological consequence of the first-come-first-served quota system was that it encouraged the hunting of whales early in the season before they had an opportunity to feed for the whole season and put on the layers of fat that whalers were so anxious to obtain.

Another consequence of the first-come-first-served quota system was to open up the Antarctic whaling industry to other interested countries. With support from General MacArthur, Japan resumed Antarctic whaling shortly after the end of the war. Japan was desperate for food, and the U.S. army of occupation reasoned that a resumption of whaling would be one good way of providing sustenance to a hungry nation. The Netherlands began Antarctic whaling for the first time, seeing the industry as a potentially lucrative addition to its postwar economic recovery. Most significant, however, was the entry of the Soviet Union into the Antarctic whaling industry. Before the Second World War, the Soviet Union had hunted whales in the North Pacific, which might be seen as an extension of its maritime interests in the Arctic and sub-Arctic. In the 1946–47 season, the Soviet Union began whaling in the Antarctic using a former German factory ship that was repaired and renamed *Slava*.[75] Soviet whaling operations initially relied upon Norwegian gunners, but they very quickly learned enough about whaling to crew the ship with their own nationals.

The entry of the Soviet Union into Antarctic whaling brought Cold War tensions into the heart of the IWC. Although the private company of Aristotle Onassis became the most notorious "rogue whaler" of the postwar period, the Soviet Union was soon suspected of dishonestly reporting its catch.[76] Sometimes the Soviet whaling fleet would over-report its catch to hasten the end of the international whaling season, with the consequence of leaving more whales for Soviet ships to catch. At other times it would underreport its catch and simply take more whales than the international quota allowed. The full extent of Soviet cheating was only reported after the end of the Cold War in a 1994 *Nature* article by A. V. Yablokov, a Russian whale scientist.[77] The fact that the IWC could do nothing about this dishonesty reveals a fundamental flaw in the regulatory system, which has come in for much criticism.[78] Soviet misreporting had two major consequences. Made-up catch numbers undermined the efforts of whale scientists to estimate whale populations and the attempts to predict the number of whales that could be sustainably caught. Even more fundamentally, misreporting destroyed the basic sense of trust that was fundamental for any international system to function. If the Soviet Union was cheating, other whaling nations reasoned, why should they play by the rules?

Over the course of the 1950s and into the 1960s, Antarctic whale populations declined alarmingly, and it became increasingly clear to almost everybody that the 16,000 BWU quota was too high. In practice, however, a reduction of the quota was not easy to achieve as a result of overinvestment in the industry, a fundamental lack of trust, and the weakness of the IWC as a regulatory system. In all of these ways the politics of the Cold War had an impact on the material environment of the South Ocean. A case could be made that from an environmentalist perspective neither communism nor capitalism emerged with much credit from the history of collapsing global whale populations. Dorsey suggests that 1964 was a nadir for the whaling industry.[79] British whaling companies had given up on the industry and Norwegian companies were about to. The attitude among many whalers, scientists, and officials was that sustainable whaling was a fantasy, and that the industry would continue until it killed so many whales that it destroyed itself.

As a result of its very different economic system, Soviet whaling was not so closely tied to the demand for profit. Soviet authorities would continue to support the whaling fleet as long as there was some combination of economic and political benefit in doing so. The only other nation to continue commercial whaling in Antarctica into the 1970s was Japan. Japanese whaling companies were able to continue Antarctic whaling after the British and Norwegians had quit the industry in large part as a result of the domestic market for whale meat. But it was not uncommon for the Japanese fleet to operate at a loss and require a subsidy from the Japanese government. This support was given in part as a result of the national sentiment that developed around the question of whaling.

The seemingly unstoppable decline of global whale populations served as a stimulus for environmental organizations and the "Save the Whales" campaign.[80] As the world's largest creatures, whales provided ideal "charismatic megafauna" for the growing number of international environmental organizations that were challenging the idea of unfettered economic growth as a universal good. From the mid 1960s onwards, the whaling industry provided an obvious example of humanity's destruction of the natural world. Pictures of harpooned whales with blood pouring into the ocean could create a direct emotional response. This was combined with growing scientific research that seemed to be showing that whales were highly intelligent creatures, which could feel pain and even sadness. For many people, especially in the United States, the growing number of waterparks and aquariums with performing killer whales and other cetaceans helped to create a closer relationship to these creatures. Recordings of whale songs become bestselling albums. In another interesting connection to the Cold War, the environmental organization Greenpeace moved to combat whaling after beginning as an antinuclear group, and played a leading role in the campaign against Antarctic whaling.[81]

By the early 1970s, the US government was beginning to shift its whaling policy away from conservationist ideas of maximum sustainable yield toward a more preservationist goal: suspending or abolishing commercial whaling. In the years that followed, the United States would become one of the driving forces within the IWC pushing for a "zero quota": no commercial whaling. A number of factors account for this shift. There was certainly some genuine environmentalist sentiment within the U.S. government, stimulated in part by the growing political power of environmental groups. Officials in the State Department and other interested agencies looked at the IWC and could clearly see that the regulation of whaling as currently practiced was not working, and therefore they wanted to do something to change it. More cynically, there was also a sense that an antiwhaling policy could hide other less attractive environmental policies, such as continued nuclear testing. And while Cold War politics were not the only motivation behind the U.S. movement against whaling, it certainly did not hurt that one of the major targets of the environmentalist campaign against whaling was the Soviet Union, while the United States itself had nothing to lose economically.

At the first UN Conference on the Environment held in Stockholm in 1972, the United States delegation proposed a moratorium on commercial whaling. In the years that followed, U.S. delegates to the IWC pushed for a "zero quota." The U.S. campaign initially gained little traction and by the middle of the decade it was on the back burner. A change to zero quota required a three-quarter majority in the IWC, and this looked unlikely. But there was nothing to stop the United States from encouraging other nations to join the IWC to make up the necessary numbers for a successful vote on a moratorium. In encouraging new nations to join and adopt an antiwhaling position, the United States was not slow in playing up its importance as a Cold War superpower in *quid pro quo* negotiations.

In an excellent example of the importance of a "bipolar" perspective, a significant complication to the U.S. antiwhaling policy in Antarctica was the question of what should be done about indigenous whaling in Alaska and other parts of the Arctic North.[82] Despite the severe disruptions caused by nineteenth-century commercial whaling, the Inupiat communities of Northern Alaska continued to hunt bowhead whales throughout the twentieth century. As well as supplying food to the community, the annual whale hunt was an important part of their cultural identity. Inupiat whalers, however, had modernized whaling techniques, and there were some reports of muktuk and other whale products being sold to other northern communities. Did this still count as traditional whaling, or was it now commercial? The question of indigenous Arctic whaling caused a disagreement among different U.S. government Departments. On the one hand there was a strong desire for the U.S. antiwhaling stance not to be diluted by what some saw as the minor distraction of traditional whaling. On the other hand, other officials in the U.S. government realized that indigenous northern communities had suffered tremendous disruption in recent decades as a result of U.S. policy, and did not want to add another insult, especially at a time when Inupiat consciousness was growing. Environmentalists tended to have little sympathy for indigenous whaling rights, despite the widespread idea of an "ecological Indian." In the end a compromise was worked out whereby the United States would push for a complete moratorium on whaling, and then seek concessions for a small amount of traditional whaling to continue.

At a meeting of the IWC in 1982, the United States and its anti-whaling allies finally achieved the three-quarters majority of the votes necessary to pass a moratorium on commercial whaling.[83] The vote of twenty-five to seven with five abstentions was very tight, but it was enough to bring about the zero-catch quota from 1986 onwards. Although Iceland left the IWC in 1993 for several years, both the Soviet Union and Japan remained members, despite the Japanese in particular remaining somewhat defiant.[84] In the years following the commercial moratorium, Japanese whalers have exploited a loophole that allows for continued whaling for "scientific purposes," with much of the meat of the whales killed ending up in Japanese markets. This raised the ire of environmental groups such as Greenpeace and Sea Shepherd, which continued their high-profile campaigns against any form of whaling.[85] A decision by the International Court of Justice in March 2014 ruled that that Japanese scientific whaling had little scientific content and was therefore illegal. The end of the Cold War has removed much of the geopolitical tension surrounding the whaling industry, but passions nevertheless remain high.

6

EXPLOITATION AND PRESERVATION
Environmental Conflict

The discovery of oil at Prudhoe Bay on Alaska's Arctic North Slope in December 1967 did not quite conform to the cartoon image of oil gushing unexpectedly from a newly drilled hole in the ground. It was instead part of a drawn-out process by which oil company geologists systematically got closer and closer to the increasingly expected prize.[1] Inupiat communities had long realized that tarry soils from the area could be burned as winter fuel. A nearly twenty-five-million-acre region immediately to the west of Prudhoe Bay had been reserved in 1923 by President Harding as the Navy's Petroleum Reserve Number Four, and by 1967 much of the land at Prudhoe Bay had already been leased to oil companies by the State of Alaska. The question wasn't so much whether oil would be found, but how much. Nevertheless, as geologists and roughnecks from the recently created ARCO Corporation drilled through the shale on December 25 and 26, there was a palpable sense of excitement.[2] In the cold and darkness of the Arctic winter this was tough and difficult work, but reward seemed close at hand. The quantity of oil at Prudhoe Bay would turn out to be similar to the largest oil fields of the Middle East. For oil company shareholders, executives, and workers—and for officials and many residents of the recently created state of Alaska—this was a Christmas present of almost unimaginable generosity.

The Prudhoe Bay oil discovery of 1967 was not to everyone's liking. Many members of the burgeoning environmental movement would have preferred that oil had never been found. Now it had been discovered they wanted it to stay in the ground, but this was a difficult proposition. Oil executives, politicians, and many citizens of Alaska saw oil revenues as a panacea for the economic difficulties that plagued the state in its first decade of existence. Environmentalists, on the other hand, believed that oil extraction would do irreparable damage to the pristine Arctic environment, not least because the location of the oil on Alaska's Arctic North Slope would require the construction of a massive pipeline to get the crude oil to market. The differences in opinion between developers and environmentalists would set the stage for a confrontation that was in many ways typical of the environmental conflicts that have played out throughout the Polar Regions over the past generation.

Close to the center of the conflict between developers and environmentalists in the dispute over Alaska North Slope oil was the Arctic National Wildlife Range (ANWR). This nine-million-acre park had been created by executive order in 1960—almost immediately after the signing of the Antarctic Treaty in Washington, D.C.—in order to protect a natural environment that encompassed the towering peaks of the eastern Brooks Range and the desolate tundra that stretched down to the Arctic Ocean.[3] The Range was home to a large herd of caribou, and some environmentalists had taken to calling it "America's Serengeti." Although ANWR was not directly affected by the Prudhoe Bay oil discovery of 1967, the development of oil in the Alaskan Arctic would prove to be a major threat to the protected area. Some potential pipeline routes would pass through ANWR, and petroleum geologists believed that oil deposits extended eastward from Prudhoe Bay into the northwestern portion of the protected area. The Alaska National Interests Lands Conservation Act (ANILCA) of 1980 changed the name of the protected area to the Arctic National Wildlife Refuge, almost doubled its size, and designated eight million acres as wilderness. But ANILCA also created the so-called 1002 Area in the northwestern portion, which would be investigated for natural resources. Debates over drilling in the 1002 Area have continued up to the present and have become a high-profile environmental conflict in the state of Alaska, as demonstrated by Sarah Palin's 2008 vice presidential campaign slogan: "Drill, baby, drill."

Disputes between developers and environmentalists in northern Alaska had important ramifications on the other side of the world. During the 1960s and 1970s advances in the field of geology were contributing to renewed speculation about the mineral potential of the southern continent.[4] Resource extraction in the Arctic seemed to suggest that with sufficient economic incentives, oil and mining companies could overcome even the most hostile environments, and there was a belief that technology developed for Arctic drilling could be transferred to Antarctica. An increasing belief in the possibility of oil extraction in Antarctica led members of the Antarctic Treaty System to start negotiating a minerals regime for the southern continent, which would regulate mining activities and attempt to develop a system for distributing any profits. The prospect of a financial bonanza in Antarctica led a number of new countries to join the Antarctic Treaty System, and led others to call for an internationalization of the continent through the United Nations. The mineral negotiations also raised the ire of environmental organizations such as Greenpeace, which were taking an increased interest in the southern continent, partly as a result of their antiwhaling campaigns. In the event, the *Exxon Valdez* oil spill in southern Alaska contributed to a change of heart in Antarctica. Instead of ratifying a minerals convention, members of the Antarctic Treaty System instead signed the Madrid Environmental Protocol in 1991, which prohibited any mineral-resource-related activity in Antarctica for a period of at least fifty years. This protocol makes the Antarctic continent by many measures one of the most protected environments anywhere on the planet, and represented a major victory for environmentalists.

During the 1970s and 1980s, environmentalist campaigns to protect the Arctic and Antarctica generally focused on the theme of wilderness.[5] Wilderness was branded a "non-renewable" resource, and the Arctic and Antarctica offered two of the few remaining regions of the world where it could still be protected.[6] In the years that followed the signature of the Madrid Environmental Protocol, however, publicity began to be given to a new potentially more serious threat to the Polar Regions: anthropogenic climate change. Somewhat ironically, the two coldest regions in the world came to be among the places most associated with a warming planet. The Arctic and Antarctica were important locations for climate change research, with the ice itself providing an archive of the Earth's climatic history. At the same time, the Polar Regions have come to be seen as under threat from the consequences of a warming climate. Locally, climate change threatens species such as polar bears and Adelie penguins.[7] Globally, melting polar ice and collapsing ice sheets threaten to raise global sea levels and disrupt climatic patterns throughout the world. Interestingly, the threat of climate change has had quite different political consequences in the two Polar Regions.[8] In the Arctic, warming temperatures and melting ice have contributed to the political destabilization of the region by opening up new areas to potential resource exploitation and sovereignty disputes. In Antarctica, the threat of climate change has functioned to support a political status quo that is based on the idea that it is doing "science for the good of humanity." While warming temperatures are certainly a cause for major concern, these divergent histories suggest that there is nothing inevitable about the future politics of climate change.

The exploitation of fossil fuels in the Polar Regions threatens to create a dangerous feedback loop whereby warming temperatures and melting ice permit further fossil fuel extraction, the burning of which causes additional temperature increase and melting. These concerns have intensified the conflict between developers and environmentalists in the Polar Regions, to a point where there is little common ground. The tension between environmentalism and development, however, is not entirely binary. In both the Arctic and Antarctica, a significant polar tourism industry has developed in recent years, which combines elements of both exploitation and preservation. On the one hand, polar tourism companies burn fossil fuels to bring people into pristine regions or Arctic communities where their presence is likely to have at least some negative impact. On the other hand, it is in the interests of these tourism companies to protect the polar environment and educate their clients in order to maintain the value of their product. There is certainly a tension at the heart of the polar tourism industry, but it is perhaps a tension that offers a middle ground between developers and environmentalists.

Histories of exploitation and preservation are not, of course, confined to the Polar Regions. But the Arctic and Antarctica do offer particularly useful locations for thinking more broadly about these themes because the tensions are often so stark. What is the value of remote wilderness to the world more generally? Is resource extraction inevitably damaging to the environment? How much economic development is too much? How can we respond to the problem of climate change? There are no easy answers to any of these questions, and there are almost always tensions and contradictions. The threat of climate change in many ways presents a problem of unprecedented magnitude, and the full extent of its impact on the Polar Regions has yet to be felt. But the recent histories of ANWR, polar tourism, and, above all, the Madrid Environmental Protocol suggest that the story is not all negative from an environmentalist perspective. Even the divergent political histories of climate change in the Arctic and Antarctica suggest that there is some cause for environmental optimism in the recent history of the Polar Regions.

Environmental Conflict in the Arctic

Early in 1960, just a few weeks after the signing of the Antarctic Treaty in Washington, D.C., the U.S. Secretary of the Interior signed an executive order creating the Arctic National Wildlife Range (ANWR) in northeastern Alaska. This massive withdrawal of public land created the largest conservation unit in the United States. It is difficult to know exactly how much influence the negotiation of the Antarctic Treaty had upon the creation of the ANWR, but the environmental historian Douglas Brinkley speculates that there must have been some connection.[9] At the very least, the signing of the Antarctic Treaty meant that the Polar Regions were very much on the minds of Eisenhower administration officials. In the years that followed the creation of the ANWR there would be a number of connections, direct and indirect, between conservation and exploitation in the Polar Regions. Ecologists and environmentalists in particular continued to draw parallels between the Arctic and Antarctica, culminating in a resolution at the Second World Conference on National Parks held at Yellowstone National Park in 1972 to make Antarctica a World Park.[10]

More directly, the creation of the ANWR was the result of an extended environmentalist campaign both inside and outside Alaska. Major inspirations for the creation of the ANWR were the experiences and writings of the pioneering American environmentalist Bob Marshall. Although he would never visit the Eastern Brooks Range, Marshall, who died tragically early in 1939, wrote poetically about the area of the Central Brooks Range, which would later become Gates of the Arctic National Park, in his book *Arctic Village*.[11] Marshall was the founder of the Wilderness Society, and the creation of ANWR was very much part of the broader campaign for wilderness preservation. Led by veteran campaigners Olaus and Maddy Murie, the list of people who participated in the campaign to found a wildlife refuge in the far north during the 1950s reads as a roll call of the leading environmentalists of the day.[12] Environmentalists viewed Alaska as the last great wilderness and the final opportunity to "get things right the first time." The ANWR campaign was central to this.

The concrete proposal for preserving Alaska's far northeast was suggested by National Park Service official George Collins following a reconnaissance expedition to the region with biologist Lowell Sumner. This led to the writing of a report titled "Arctic Wilderness."[13] Although the idea came from the Park Service, many environmentalists were suspicious of an agency that appeared to be putting roads and development ahead of ecology, highlighted by plans for Mission 66.[14] Wilderness advocates did not see mass visitation as a good thing. Forest Service oversight was quickly dismissed, since the region had relatively few trees. The Bureau of Land Management (BLM) was seen as problematic for a number of reasons, not least of which was the temporary nature of many of its holdings in Alaska. Campaigners gave some consideration to the creation of an entirely new government agency to administer the new protected area along the lines they desired, but this was considered an impractical approach. This left only the U.S. Fish and Wildlife Service as an agency that appeared to offer the best chance of success for what most environmentalists were calling for.[15]

The use of an executive order to create the ANWR was not the environmentalists' favored tool. Alaska had become the forty-ninth state of the Union just over one year earlier, and there was real suspicion about federal interference in the affairs of the new state.[16] The economic viability of Alaska was dependent upon provisions in the Statehood Act for selecting land. The state government in Juneau faced an ever-growing budget deficit as it took on responsibility for costs previously covered by the federal government during the territorial administration. Although some of the ANWR campaigners lived in Alaska and many were familiar with the land, a frequent criticism was that most of the demand for preservation was coming from outside of the state. There was a class dimension to this criticism that alleged that the region was being protected for rich out-of-state tourists who could afford the high costs of travel. Attempts to get Congressional approval failed in the Senate (thanks largely to Alaskan opposition) and environmentalists were more than happy to take what they could get. The creation of ANWR was undoubtedly an environmental success story, but environmentalists themselves recognized that this was part of a very piecemeal and haphazard approach to land planning.[17]

The discovery of oil at Prudhoe Bay early in the winter of 1967–68 made the task of conservationists in Alaska very much more complicated. The State of Alaska, which had just adopted the motto "North to the Future," had come to own the land on which the Prudhoe Bay oil field was located through a combination of good fortune and oil company lobbying, in which the Arctic environment played no small part.[18] At the time of statehood, the federal BLM was the effective owner of virtually all unreserved North Slope land. It was in the process of leasing parcels of land through noncompetitive bids that favored speculators and middlemen. The oil companies preferred to deal directly with the State of Alaska, which could lease the land through competitive auctions, thereby pricing small-time speculators out of the market and considerably simplifying the process. William Egan, the first governor of Alaska, was suspicious of big oil, and preferred the status quo. Before the BLM could lease the land, however, it needed to survey it. This was no easy task in the environmental conditions of the Arctic north, especially in tidal zones where it was difficult to delineate where the land ended and the sea began. "It would take 100 years to effectively survey this area," noted one federal official.[19] A state land claim followed by competitive leasing would bypass the need for a survey. This bureaucratic headache helped to convince Governor Egan to claim the land around Prudhoe Bay for the State of Alaska. The decision would set Alaska on course to becoming the most important oil state in the country.

The most pressing issue faced by oil companies and the State was how to get the billions of barrels of crude oil from the Arctic Slope of

Alaska to markets in the Lower 48 States.[20] Oil tankers from Prudhoe Bay were quickly dismissed as impractical on account of the sea in the Arctic Ocean being frozen for much of the year, and the inherent dangers of navigating in polar waters. This left some sort of pipeline as the only feasible option. A number of routes were discussed, focusing on two possible options. The first option was to pipe oil to an ice-free harbor on the southern coast of Alaska, where it could be transferred to oil tankers and transported to ports along the U.S. west coast. A second option was to build a much larger pipeline across Arctic Alaska and much of Arctic Canada. Neither alternative was particularly appealing to environmentalists, but the second option would pose a much more direct threat to the ANWR and the migration of caribou.

Whichever route the pipeline would take, there was a need to resolve the lingering uncertainties of who owned what land in Alaska. In particular, Alaskan Natives were campaigning for their land claims to be recognized.[21] In much the same way as Native Americans had been dispossessed in other parts of the Western Hemisphere, Alaskan Natives feared that their title to the land would be overlooked in the rush for oil and economic development. But with the help of newspapers such as the *Tundra Times*, Native communities across Alaska organized and developed a sophisticated and largely united demand to have their claims recognized by the state.[22] Sympathetic to the cause of Alaska Natives, Stewart Udall, the Secretary of the Interior, wrote an executive order in 1966 that froze all conveyances of land from the Federal government to the State of Alaska until the Native claims question was settled. The need to resolve this issue intensified with the discovery of oil at Prudhoe Bay.

Partly as a result of the fact that they were standing in the way of development, the demands of the Native communities did not always have the full support of environmental groups. In fact this was quite often a strained relationship. Despite Alaska's tradition of "inhabited wilderness," environmentalists tended to prefer their protected areas to be free from habitation or subsistence use by Native Communities.[23] Environmentalists working for an international wildlife range, for example, often saw the Native question as getting in the way. On the other side, comments from the Inupiat politician Willie Hensley reveal a somewhat disdainful Native attitude toward environmentalists: "The

Iñuit and other Alaska Natives cannot afford to be purists in their views on the environment. We have had to be pragmatic, to judge what is in our best interests. Our perspective on nature is multidimensional, and this is not an easy concept for many activist environmentalists to grasp."[24]

The result of the Alaskan Natives demand for their land claims to be resolved was the Alaskan Native Claims Settlement Act (ANCSA) of December 1971.[25] The Act awarded Native Alaskans title to almost forty million acres of land, to be selected as part of the land conveyance process. It also awarded a monetary settlement of almost one billion dollars in compensation for the lands that they had lost. Many hailed the ANCSA as one of the most enlightened land claims settlements in history. But others accused it of forcing the economic privatization of indigenous society through the creation of Native corporations in which Alaska Natives became shareholders. For conservationists, one of the most important provisions of the ANCSA was the provisional withdrawal of ninety million acres of public land to be considered for environmental protection, which became known as the D-2 Lands.

In the short term, the ANCSA put the legal basis in place for the construction of the Trans-Alaska Pipeline. The prospect of an oil pipeline led environmentalists to take a renewed interest in the ANWR, in order to prevent the Range from being bisected by a pipeline. Led by the Wilderness Society, environmental organizations formed loosely into an alliance that became known as The Alaska Coalition. This coalition utilized what the environmental historian James Morton Turner has identified as an effective new tactic of using lawsuits to pursue their goals.[26] After considerable debate, environmentalists got what most of them regarded as the least bad option: namely the north-south pipeline directly from Prudhoe Bay to Valdez that avoided ANWR. The Alaska Coalition was able to slow down the construction of this pipeline through the use of additional lawsuits, but in the political climate of the mid 1970s there was a limit to how far they could push the issue as a result of the Middle Eastern petroleum crisis.[27]

The construction of the 800-mile Trans-Alaska Pipeline from Prudhoe Bay to the port of Valdez was a tremendous feat of civil engineering, which can be seen as another example of the Cold War struggle to demonstrate environmental authority. It brought many new residents into the state in order to provide labor for the project and provide services for these workers. Some efforts were made to mitigate the environmental impact of pipeline construction. The forty-eight-inch diameter pipeline, for example, was sometimes buried and sometimes elevated in order to avoid direct interference with caribou migration routes and to guard against damage from earthquakes. But some environmental impact was inevitable. In order to build the pipeline a temporary road was constructed from Fairbanks to Prudhoe Bay, which caused damage to the tundra.

When the trans-Alaska pipeline began operations in 1977, the D-2 Lands question remained to be resolved. The Alaska Coalition refocused its objectives to achieve the greatest possible withdrawal of land from development into parks and public land. Environmentalists repeatedly referred to Alaska as "the last chance to do things right the first time." Once again, these efforts were opposed by development-minded politicians who were wary of tying up too much of Alaska's territory into what they regarded as a fundamentally unproductive land use. For a while toward the end of the decade it looked as if Congress might pass a bill that would be to the broad satisfaction of environmental groups. But Alaska's two senators, Mike Gravel and Ted Stevens, spoke persuasively against large-scale permanent withdrawals of land. In 1978, President Carter used the Antiquities Act to create fifty-six million acres of National Monuments in Alaska, and led the way to the passing of ANILCA in 1980. Among its many measures, this act changed the name of the Arctic National Wildlife Range to the Arctic National Wildlife Refuge and more than doubled its size to around nineteen million acres, including around eight million acres of designated wilderness.

Once again, the use of Presidential orders in the process of bringing about the ANILCA was not the preferred tool of environmentalists. This method helps to explain the growing resentment discussed by Turner, and the increasing polarization of environmental politics.[28] In the mid 1970s, for example, plans to create a large international ANWR across the border with Canada had won support from a wide range of businesspeople, environmentalists, and politicians. By the 1980s, such a coalition was becoming more unlikely as a result of the radicalization of both sides. A major cause of controversy was the one-and-a-half-million-acre 1002 Area on the coastal plain.

When the *Exxon Valdez* ran aground shortly after midnight on Good Friday 1989, the Christmas story of the 1967 oil discovery appeared to have come full circle. The oil spill seemed to encapsulate many of the issues that had been at stake in the conflict between environmentalists and developers over the past two decades. For environmentalists, the oil spilled into Prince William Sound offered an all-too-real demonstration that their worst fears could come true. For developers, the disaster was simply a blip in the system, nothing that could not be "made whole again"—in the infamous words of the Exxon chief executive—through a massive cleanup operation and the payment of fines and compensation.

Disputes between environmentalists and developers in the Arctic were not limited to Alaska. But the controversies over ANWR, the Tran-Alaska Pipeline, ANILCA, and the 1002 Area serve as useful models for environmental conflict across the Arctic. In Canada, Greenland, Scandinavia, and Russia, pressure to develop the natural resources of the Arctic have been resisted by environmental organizations, with varying degrees of success. Each part of the Arctic has its own form of environmental politics, and the issues are not always identical. But the desire to make a profit has motivated proponents of economic development across the region, often tied to ideas of political independence and sustainability. For environmentalists, the goal of protecting some of the last remaining expanses of wilderness on the planet is often a motivating factor. Indigenous communities in the Arctic often find themselves caught up in the middle of these resource conflicts, not fitting completely into either side of the argument. Since the foundation of the Arctic Council in 1996, an international forum has existed that seeks to mediate in some of these disputes, especially through the promotion of scientific knowledge. In doing this, the Arctic Council has an effective model from the other side of the world: the Madrid Environmental Protocol.

Environmental Agreement in Antarctica

The *Exxon Valdez* oil spill was not the only marine environmental accident to take place in the Polar Regions in 1989. Earlier in the year, on January 28, the Argentine transport ship *Bahia Paraiso* ran aground and sank near the U.S. Palmer Station on Anvers Island in the Peninsula

Region of Antarctica.[29] Although all passengers and crew were rescued safely, the ship spilled around 600,000 liters of diesel fuel into the Southern Ocean. The amount of fuel that entered the water was sixty times smaller than in Prince William Sound, but the diesel fuel was more toxic than the crude oil. An area of water around 30 square kilometers was covered in an oil slick and numerous seabirds, sea mammals, and other organisms were exposed to the pollution. The direct environmental consequences of the spill were not as dramatic as in the north, but skuas, kelp gulls, and cormorants were among the species affected.

Taken together, the *Bahia Paraiso* and *Exxon Valdez* disasters had a profound impact on the environmental politics of Antarctica. At the time of the two spills the members of the Antarctic Treaty System were coming to the end of an extended period of discussions about how to regulate the mining of the continent's mineral resources. A Minerals Regime had been drawn up, which would permit natural resource extraction in exchange for significant environmental protection measures being put in place to regulate these activities. Any mining activity, for example, would have to undergo an extensive environmental impact assessment before being given permission to operate. Such measures were opposed by environmentalists, who wanted to keep the whole Antarctic continent as a pristine wilderness. They argued that any attempts to regulate mineral resource activities would be ineffective as a result of the hostility of the Antarctic environment: this was not a place where the usual rules applied, and, as a consequence, all mining activities should be prohibited. The two polar marine disasters of early 1989 appeared to offer a vivid demonstration that these fears were perfectly rational.

Over the course of the 1980s, discussions of a Mineral Convention for Antarctica had raised the international profile of the southern continent. It was not only environmentalists who had taken an increased interest in the politics of Antarctica. The number of Antarctic Treaty consultative parties increased from thirteen in 1980 to twenty-five in 1990, with twelve new countries demonstrating a scientific interest in Antarctica, at least in part in order to play a full role in the minerals negotiations.[30] At the United Nations, Prime Minister Mahitir of Malaysia led a campaign against the Antarctic Treaty System.[31] He labeled it a colonial club, and called for jurisdiction over the southern continent to be handed over to the United Nations. The Falklands / Malvinas war between Britain and Argentina in 1982 also raised the profile of the southern continent. As the rest of the world looked on with a sense of bemused horror, many people reasoned that the South Atlantic Region must contain something worth fighting over other than just the bleak moorland of the islands.

In the aftermath of the *Bahia Paraiso* and *Exxon Valdez* oil spills, the governments of Australia and France took a lead in opposing the Convention on the Regulation of Antarctic Mineral Resource Activities (CRAMRA). Both countries had their particular reasons for opposition. In Australia there was a sense that the environmental benefits of not signing CRAMRA—including the appeasement of environmental organizations—outweighed the potential economic benefits of mining in Antarctica. For Australian politicians and scientists, resource extraction in Antarctica did not seem to be a viable proposition, and even if it were viable it would compete with Australian mining. In France, President Mitterrand was a friend of the environmental campaigner Jacques Cousteau, who played a prominent role in the campaign against the Minerals Convention, and this is thought to have influenced French policy. Both France and Australia refused to sign CRAMRA, which caused some consternation among other members of the Antarctic Treaty System after the decade-long negotiations. But when New Zealand took the side of Australia and France and refused to ratify the Minerals Convention, it was effectively dead in the water.[32]

The fairly sudden collapse of CRAMRA raised the question of what should happen next. Environmental organizations were not slow to put forward plans for the comprehensive environmental protection of Antarctica. Since the early 1970s, the idea of an Antarctic World Park had been touted as a possible alternative to the Antarctic Treaty System. When Greenpeace built a station in Antarctica in the late 1980s to campaign against a minerals regime and highlight the lax environmental standards among scientific stations operating on the continent, it was called World Park Base. The creation of an Antarctic World Park, however, threatened to upset the delicate compromise on the question of sovereignty that had been achieved by the Antarctic Treaty System, and few of its members were prepared to go this far. But they were willing to embrace many of the environmental protection measures proposed by organizations such as Greenpeace and the Antarctic and Southern Ocean Coalition, including the proposal to prohibit any activities relating to economic minerals extraction.

In the United States, there was some resentment at the collapse of CRAMRA, which many officials saw as a good "conservationist" compromise in the spirit of Gifford Pinchot. The government of George H. W. Bush was nevertheless willing to contemplate more stringent environmental protection for the Antarctic continent, so long as these policies were not completely binding or permanent. At a hearing before the Senate Committee on Foreign Relations held on July 27, 1990, Senator Al Gore from Tennessee gave support to ideas for comprehensive environmental protection for Antarctica. He called on the U.S. government to "set aside the pending Convention on the Regulation of Antarctic Mineral Resource Activities ... [and] instead support a new round of negotiations ... to craft a new convention that will provide comprehensive protection of Antarctica's environment, including a permanent prohibition on minerals activities." The idea for a prohibition on minerals activities did not come from Al Gore, but he was a strong supporter. In making his case he drew explicitly on the *Exxon Valdez* and *Bahia Paraiso* disasters:

> Last year, the Exxon Valdez disaster in Prince William Sound provided vivid, heartbreaking illustrations of the devastating consequences of an environmental disaster in a pristine wilderness. Also last year, an Argentinian ship, the Bahia Paraiso, ran aground in the waters of Antarctica. This incident did not attract the widespread public attention of the Valdez spill; it wasn't a drama played out nightly on the evening news. It was a smaller spill, but it was disastrous nonetheless, destroying years of research and leaving behind an indelible stain.[33]

Senator Gore clearly recognized the rhetorical power of these two oil spills at opposite ends of the planet, and he sought to use them to push for environmental protection of the Antarctic continent. While it is impossible to measure the impact of Gore's intervention, in the months following his testimony the position he advocated was broadly accepted by the Bush administration.

The *Exxon Valdez* and *Bahia Paraiso* disasters were not the only causes of the international shift from a policy of rational-use conservation in Antarctica to a policy of no-use preservation. The historian Alessando Antonello has identified a shift in Antarctic policy during the 1960s and 1970s that he labels "The Greening of Antarctica."[34] This involved the Antarctic Treaty System passing a series of environmental provisions to protect Antarctica's flora and fauna, with particular attention to seals and krill. While the discussions to negotiate a Minerals Convention for Antarctica certainly fit within this environmental trajectory, so too did calls for a complete prohibition on extractive activities on the continent. The nature of the Antarctic environment also played a role. In much the same way that the failure to find valuable minerals helped to lay the foundations for the signing of the 1959 Antarctic Treaty, it is unlikely that members of the ATS would have completed a prohibition on mining activities if valuable deposits had been found in a location that made their exploitation economically feasible.

In place of a minerals convention, members of the Antarctic Treaty came together in Madrid in October 1991 to sign the Protocol on Environmental Protection, commonly known as the Madrid Protocol. Ratified seven years later in 1998, the provisions of this Protocol contained many of the outcomes that environmental groups had been advocating. It was not quite an Antarctic World Park, but in many ways it came close. The Protocol labeled Antarctica a "natural reserve" and called for the protection of its wilderness and aesthetic values. The most high-profile provision of the Madrid Protocol, Article Seven, prohibited any activity related to mineral resources with the exception of scientific research for at least the next fifty years (unless the Protocol is amended by agreement, or unless a quite elaborate "walkaway" clause is activated by one of the signatories). Even after fifty years the Protocol stipulates that the minerals ban will remain in effect unless a regulatory framework for resource extraction is first put in place. Such a prohibition on mineral exploitation of an entire continent is unprecedented, and on its own makes a major contribution to protecting the Antarctic environment.

In addition to the ban on economically driven mineral activities, the Madrid Protocol contained a number of other articles related to the protection of the Antarctic environment. Article Three calls for wilderness and aesthetic values to be "fundamental considerations" in any activities on the continent. Article Eight requires an environmental impact assessment for all activities on the continent. Article Eleven established a Committee for Environmental Protection to oversee these regulatory efforts. In another profound protection measure, all alien species with the exception of humans are banned from the continent. This marked a major cultural shift, as the husky dogs that had played such a major role in the history of exploration were no longer allowed on the continent. The Madrid Protocol establishes Antarctica as one of the most protected environments anywhere on the planet.

Climate Change

At around the same time as the Madrid Protocol was putting into place unprecedented environmental protection measures on a continental scale, a new and more significant threat was emerging, with the potential to radically change the Antarctic environment. Ideas about climate change had been around for a while, but it was really only in the 1980s and 1990s that the prospect of a warming climate entered the public consciousness as one of the most pressing environmental problems of the modern world.[35] Since the industrial revolution of the late eighteenth and early nineteenth centuries, the emission of greenhouse gases into the atmosphere through the burning of fossil fuels has accelerated. These gases warm the atmosphere by trapping some of the long-wave radiation that would otherwise escape. Some scientists have seen the industrial system as having such a major impact on the global environment that they have labeled it with its own geologic time period: the anthropocene.[36] Whatever it is called, it is indisputable that climate change has had a major impact on the way people think about the environment over the past three decades.[37]

Climate change is a global problem, but the Polar Regions have played a central role in its history and will remain important into the future.[38] Even more than the Cold War, the threat of global climate change has brought the Arctic and Antarctica into the center of international environmental thinking. Over the past fifty years, the Polar Regions have functioned as an important laboratory for the "discovery of global warming."[39] Ice cores drilled in the Arctic and Antarctica have revealed a correlation between warm temperatures and high levels of atmospheric carbon dioxide in the Earth's climatic history; measurements at the South Pole have revealed rising levels of carbon dioxide; the polar regions have played important, if complex, roles in the development of the climate models that are so crucial in understanding and predicting climate change. More than just contributing to the scientific understanding of climate change, the Polar Regions have become research subjects in the search for what the consequences of global climate change will be. These consequences range from fairly local changes of limited significance—falling numbers of polar bears or Adelie penguins—to global and catastrophic shifts—collapsing ice sheets and melting ice raising global sea levels.[40] In relation to climate change, the Polar Regions might be thought of as both canaries in the coal mine and elephants in the room.

In the first half of the twentieth century, scientists began systematically looking to the Polar Regions for clues about changing climate in the Earth's history. The Swedish scientist Hans Ahlmann, for example, developed a theory about climate change in relation to ice ages in which evidence from the Polar Regions was crucial.[41] But it was really with the International Geophysical Year (IGY) of 1957–58 that atmospheric science research in the Polar Regions really began to make major contributions to an understanding of a changing climate. During the IGY, the American scientist David Keeling set up a monitoring station at the South Pole to record changes in atmospheric carbon dioxide. Even within a relatively short period of time he was able to detect an upward trend, which would contribute to the development of the iconic Keeling Curve showing a year-by-year increase in atmospheric carbon dioxide. During the 1960s, ice core researchers at Camp Century in Greenland were able to coordinate their results with ice cores obtained from Antarctica, showing that the Earth's climate functions as a unified system rather than being different in the northern and southern hemisphere.

Advances in the technology of ice core research during the 1970s and 1980s, largely pioneered by the Danish scientist Willi Dansgaard, allowed researchers to ask new questions.[42] The ratio of oxygen isotopes in the ice served as a proxy for temperature at the time the ice was formed. This allowed researchers to use to the ice cores to estimate changing temperatures in the Earth's past. New techniques for extracting tiny air bubbles from the ice enabled scientists to measure the composition of the atmosphere, including the percentage of carbon dioxide and other greenhouse gases, at the time the ice was formed. By putting these two measurements together, scientists were able to show a correlation between periods of warm temperatures and high carbon dioxide. This correlation on its own did not reveal anything about causation, but it did suggest an important connection between temperature and carbon dioxide.

In recent years, data from ice cores has been used to test and calibrate the climate models that today play a central role in scientific understanding of climate change on a global scale.[43] The Polar Regions have proved to be hard to model, and early "General Circulation Models" had difficulty in the far north and far south.[44] But modelers have developed increasingly sophisticated ways of looking at the Polar Regions, finding ways of integrating problematic categories such as darkness and light, snow cover, and sea ice. Taken together, these climate models offer the best means of understanding the global climate and predicting likely future scenarios. Almost without exception, the models are showing a strong anthropogenic fingerprint on recent climate changes and predict that global temperatures will continue to rise as long as atmospheric carbon dioxide continues to increase.

Modeling suggests that climate change will be particularly intense in the Arctic and Antarctica. This is known as "polar amplification," and results from a variety of factors related to snow and ice cover, ocean circulation, heat transport, and net radiation balance. As warming temperatures melt snow and ice, for example, less solar radiation is reflected and more is absorbed into darker-colored land and sea, creating an amplification of temperature and further melting. In many parts of the Polar Regions, polar amplification has been corroborated by recorded temperatures on the Earth's surface. The Antarctic Peninsula region and many parts of the Arctic are among the fastest warming places anywhere on the planet. The major exception to this trend is the large continental mass of East Antarctica, which has generally shown little warming since the beginning of continuous records in the late 1950s. Atmospheric scientists attribute this lack of warming in East Antarctica to an increase in the strength of the winds around Antarctica, known

as the circumpolar vortex, as a result of the ozone hole over the continent. As the ozone hole decreases in size it is expected that the strength
of the circumpolar vortex will weaken, and temperatures across East
Antarctica will rise.

A major difference between the two Polar Regions' climate change
researches has been the use of traditional ecological knowledge in thinking about environmental change over time in the Arctic. Antarctica has
no indigenous population, but local residents in the Arctic often have
much to contribute to understanding climate change as a result of
their longstanding connections with particular environments. Local
peoples have reported changes in the weather, different patterns of ice
formation, and alteration to the migration of animals. The use of local
knowledge, however, can be problematic, as discussed by the anthropologist Julie Cruickshank: "terms like 'co-management' and 'sustainable
development' and 'TEK [Traditional Ecological Knowledge]' are highly
negotiable and have no analogues in Native American languages. To
suggest that they are somehow *bridging concepts* may constitute taking
control of dialogue in ways that mask deep cultural disagreements and
restrict the ways of talking about important issues."[45] All too often an
indigenous perspective is simply added as afterthought to traditional
scientific research as a way of appeasing different interest groups.
But when taken seriously, traditional ecological knowledge has the
capability not only to contribute additional data to an understanding
of environmental change over time but also to radically change ideas
about how the climate is understood by showing that science is not the
only way of understanding the natural world.

Climate research in the Polar Regions has taken place concurrently
with investigation of the stratospheric ozone, which functions to protect the earth from harmful solar radiation. In the mid 1980s, scientists
working at Britain's Halley Bay research station in the Weddell Sea
announced that they had observed a significant increase in the size of
the springtime ozone hole over Antarctica since records had begun
during the IGY. For several years atmospheric chemists had been
predicting that CFCs used in the manufacture of aerosols and refrig-
eration systems would be harmful to the ozone layer, and the Antarctic
observations proved that this was the case. After corroboration by
NASA satellites, the international community fairly rapidly set about

responding to the threat of a growing ozone hole.[46] The Montreal Protocol of 1987 introduced a near-complete ban on the manufacture of CFCs. Since then, the expansion of the ozone hole has slowed and started to decrease. Complete recovery, however, is expected to take at least several more decades.

The immediate response of the international community to the threat posed by the ozone hole contrasts starkly with its response to climate change, where little effective action has so far been forthcoming. Whereas the question of causation was relatively simple in the case of CFCs damaging atmospheric ozone, it is a little more complicated in the case of climate change and greenhouse gases. For a long time, for example, many scientists believed that the oceans would act as a sink for increased atmospheric carbon dioxide, and it has sometimes been difficult to untangle anthropogenic climate change from natural variation. Equally important, a response to the growth in the size of the ozone hole was technologically feasible, and even offered economic opportunities in replacing CFC products with non-CFC products.[47] In contrast, there is no technology in place that can immediately replace the abundant use of energy that currently comes from fossil fuels. Reductions of greenhouse gas emissions are usually presented as a barrier to economic growth, rather than an economic opportunity. As a consequence, global debates about global warming connect to the concept of the tragedy of the commons: why should any one country take a lead in reducing greenhouse gases if other countries will benefit from not doing so? The general result is political inertia as greenhouse gas emissions increase and temperatures continue to rise.

The politics of climate change are often presented as a conflict between those who believe in global warming and want to do something to reduce greenhouse gas emissions and the "climate deniers," who refuse to believe the science and have no interest in changing their energy-rich lifestyles. This conflict is undoubtedly important, but it only scrapes the surface of the political implications of a warming planet. The recent history of both the Arctic and Antarctica offer useful locations for expanding the environmental history of climate change and thinking about its political consequences.[48] In some ways the recent history of climate change in the Arctic and Antarctica have much in common, but in other ways they are quite different.

In facing the threat of climate change, the Polar Regions share with the rest of the world a sense of political impotence. There is little that can be done in the Arctic or Antarctica alone that can change the trend of increasing atmospheric greenhouse gases and warming temperatures. For the continent of Antarctica and much of the Arctic, this sense of powerlessness is exacerbated by the fact that these are regions with almost no industrial production, and that the climate change that they are experiencing is caused almost exclusively by human actions in other parts of the world. Even for the industrialized regions of the Arctic, the amount of greenhouse gas emissions is generally so small relative to the rest of the world that there is little sense that internal changes could have much of an impact. Unlike the Madrid Environmental Protocol, through which members of the Antarctic Treaty took it upon themselves to protect the environment, it is impossible to imagine a regional solution to the problem of climate change in either of the Polar Regions.

In the Arctic, an argument can be made that climate change is contributing to a destabilization of the political status quo.[49] The reduction of Arctic sea ice is opening new sea routes through the Arctic, which raises questions about sovereignty that did not exist when there was way no way through.[50] Since the passage of the U.S. oil tanker *Manhattan* through the Northwest Passage in 1969, there have been disputes between Canada and the United States about whether this route constitutes open ocean or whether it is an internal Canadian waterway. Climate change also has the potential to help facilitate the extraction of natural resources by making prospecting, mining, and transportation easier. An argument that climate change exacerbates political disputes cannot be taken too far. Many of the changes in accessibility are as much about developing technology such as powerful icebreakers as about a changing environment. And there is no way of knowing what political relations would be like if the Arctic were not steadily warming. But it is not outlandish to look at the recent history of political tension in the Arctic and suggest that the instability of the environment has played at least a partial role.

In Antarctica, in contrast, a strong case can be made that climate change is strengthening the political status quo.[51] The Antarctic Treaty is a political system based on the authority of science. The member states have used scientific research and the useful knowledge it generates to justify the existing political system. During debates on the "Question of Antarctica" in the United Nations in the 1980s, members of the Antarctic System repeatedly pointed to the importance of their scientific research for "the good of humanity" in their ultimately successful argument against UN interference. As a major threat to the future of humanity, climate change serves to strengthen the justification of members of the Antarctic Treaty System that they are doing science for "the good of humanity" and accusations that the Antarctic Treaty is an exclusive club have generally faded into the background in recent years.

While there is much that is deeply depressing for environmentalists about the recent history of climate change, there is perhaps something in the different experiences of the Polar Regions that might offer a glimmer of hope. The fact that the politics of climate change have in some ways played out quite differently in two regions that are in part defined by their cold climate suggests that there is nothing inevitable about the politics of climate change. On their own, the political histories of climate change in both the Arctic and Antarctica might be seen as negative. In the Arctic, climate change appears to be contributing to political destabilization at a number of different scales. In Antarctica, climate change might be seen as supporting a political status quo that is in some ways exclusive. When taken together, however, these histories reveal that different possibilities certainly exist, and this is a positive message for a global climate debate that is often mired in the language of impossibility and inevitability.

Polar Tourism

For a skeleton crew on board the *Ocean Nova* polar tourist vessel, extreme climate change is a biannual reality. Twice a year, the ship endures an unpleasantly hot crossing of the equator en route from Antarctica to the Arctic and back again. The ship was built for ferry service in Greenland, and its designers saw no need to install air conditioning. The strengthened ice-resistant hull is temporarily redundant in the ice-free mid-Atlantic, and navigation is usually much less strenuous there than its accustomed routes in the bays and channels of the

Antarctic Peninsula or Spitsbergen. There are no tourists on board, and this means there is less work to do. But reduction of the regular work-load offers little respite from the intense sunlight and the muggy heat of the tropics. The crew eats, sleeps, and spends as much time as possible in the shaded observation lounge on the upper deck with the windows open and fans whirring. By choice or requirement, most crew members take this period as their annual leave.

The *Ocean Nova's* twice-yearly equatorial crossing is part of an annual migration of tourist vessels from one Polar Region to the other. Polar tour companies work the far south from November through March and the far north from May through September. Much polar tourism is marine-based, with the ships providing accommodation as well as a means of transport to visit a variety of different places. In Antarctica maritime tourism also gets around the thorny issue of sovereignty, since there is no need for hotels or taxes. Ship-based tourism is only possible in the summer, when sea ice breaks up and sunlight allows tourists to spot the wildlife they have come to see. As a result of this seasonality, the crew on ships like the *Ocean Nova* live a perpetual summer of near-constant daylight, broken only by the necessary hemispheric transitions and by the brief periods of nighttime darkness early and late in the respective seasons.

The history of tourism in the Polar Regions is complicated by the question of definition. What makes a polar tourist? A case could be made that many of the explorers who headed to the Arctic and Antarctica in the late nineteenth and early twentieth centuries repre-sented an early generation of adventure tourists. Some—such as the English aristocrat Apsley Cherry Garrard, who accompanied Captain Scott on the *Terra Nova* expedition—even paid handsomely to be there.[52] Chile's President Gabriel González Videla sailed with his family to the Antarctic Peninsula region early in 1948; ten years later Britain's Prince Philip visited the same area during the IGY. Since then, there have been frequent "distinguished visitor" trips to Antarctica and the Arctic by politicians and government officials from numerous nations. In 2006, when he was still leader of the opposition, Britain's Prime Minister David Cameron famously traveled to northern Spitsbergen in 2006 to "hug a husky" and demonstrate his concern about climate change. Do these trips constitute tourism? Even for contemporary scientists and logistics staff, a trip to Antarctica is not all about work. Are they "temporary tourists" if they go hiking or skiing on their days off? In regions where tourism has often been bracketed off and treated as a separate and often less worthy activity, it is important to acknowledge these grey areas.

A useful definition of tourism is that it is an activity that involves paying guests in a moneymaking enterprise. Using this definition, it is possible to identify trips to Spitsbergen in the late nineteenth century that might have been some of the first examples of polar tourism. A trip to the far north offered rich Victorians an opportunity to experience a sublime polar landscape, and maybe to shoot some polar bears. Although some paying passengers certainly traveled to Antarctica before then, organized commercial tourism to Antarctica is usually dated to 1966 with the expedition of Lars-Eric Lindblad.[53] In both Polar Regions, a great stimulus to tourism was the end of the Cold War. The collapse of the Soviet Union suddenly made available a large number of icebreakers and ice-strengthened vessels that were chartered by tourism companies such as Quark to take tourists to parts of the Arctic and Antarctica that had previously never been visited by commercial operations. It even became possible to pay for a voyage to the North Pole without ever needing to leave your ship.

The history of polar tourism presents a fascinating juxtaposition of exploitation and conservation. Its business model might be characterized as the financial exploitation of pristine wilderness, with tourists willing to pay large amounts of money to experience places most people only get to see in pictures and on television programs such as *Frozen Planet*. The industry has grown exponentially in recently years and has become big business. South of the Antarctic Circle, tourism has overtaken fishing as the most significant moneymaking activity. In the far north, tourism remains significantly behind extractive industries in terms of the wealth it generates, but its contribution is increasingly significant, especially for many of the small communities visited by tourist vessels.

A useful model for thinking about the history of tourism in the Polar Regions is the so-called dual mandate of the U.S, National Park Service.[54] On the one hand, it is the job of park staff to bring tourists into national parks so that they can enjoy the landscapes, learn about the environment and its history, and participate in recreation activities such as hiking and climbing. On the other hand, park staff are charged with protecting the natural environment so that it might be visited and enjoyed by future generations. These two mandates are often seen as being in opposition to each other, with visitors and their activities being viewed as one of the greatest threats to the environment. Something similar could be said for tourism in the Polar Regions. In the 1950s, one of the reasons environmentalists gave for not wanting the National Park Service to be put in charge of the Arctic National Wildlife Range was that the agency might encourage additional visitation. Wilderness advocates preferred their wild areas to be difficult to visit so that the environment would remain "untrammeled" by human activity.

Visitors to the Arctic and Antarctica undoubtedly have some impact on the material environment, but the extent of this impact is much debated. At the height of the Antarctic summer, popular landing spots around the Peninsula Region might receive several visits a day from the passengers of different cruise ships, with the potential for disturbance to wildlife, trampling of soils, and the leaving behind of litter. The impact of tourism on polar ecosystems, however, is difficult to predict. Anecdotal results from a long-term study of penguin colonies at Port Lockroy, for example, suggest that penguin numbers actually benefit from tourism, since the presence of tourists scares away the skuas that eat the penguin chicks. Whether this is positive or negative depends on your preference for penguins or skuas. In the Arctic, an additional problem is the potential for disruption to local communities, with tour companies unloading large numbers of money-spending tourists for short periods of time. Locals have to endure their towns being inundated with visitors and frequent requests for photos. But these visits also offer contact with the outside world and commercial opportunities for the local population. Again, whether this is a good thing or a bad thing depends on your perspective.

At the same time that their activities affect the material environment of the Polar Regions, the industry as a whole goes to great lengths to preserve the polar environment and perceptions of wilderness upon which its profits rely. In Antarctica, tour operators have established a voluntary association known as the International Association of Antarctic Tour Operators (IAATO) to organize and regulate their activities.[55] Elaborate planning goes into ensuring that there is as little contact as possible between different ships, thereby preserving the sense of isolation expected by polar tourists. But environmental concern is usually a lot more than a facade. Many of the people attracted to work in the polar tourism industry do so out of a genuine passion for these extreme environments, and they are keen to share their interest with the paying passengers. The environmental regulations voluntarily adopted by IAATO in Antarctica are often more stringent than those followed by scientists and support staff working for national polar programs. Few things can generate an environmental concern more strongly than direct personal experience of a place, and much emphasis is placed on creating "polar advocates" who will go back home and support causes related to the Arctic and Antarctica.

As part of their work to safeguard the environment, most polar cruise companies have an active enrichment program with talks from guest lecturers. The more people can know about the places they are visiting, the more they will understand the issues and take care of the environment. Alongside overviews of the history, biology, geology, and politics of the Polar Regions, most ships have a lecture or two on the causes and consequences of climate change. Many lecturers have worked in the Arctic and Antarctica for several decades, and they are able to describe and show pictures of the environmental changes they have seen over this time. Glaciers have retreated in parts of both Polar Regions; in the Arctic polar bears have often drastically reduced in numbers; in many of the frequently visited areas of the Antarctic Peninsula Adelie penguins have been replaced by Gentoo penguins as a result of a changing climate.[56]

The image of a rich tourist sitting in a warm lounge on board a tourist vessel in the Arctic or Antarctica and listening to a lecture on the threat of climate change encapsulates much about the contemporary reality of the Polar Regions. There is certainly an irony to people paying to go to the Polar Regions to be lectured about climate change. Polar tourism is an energy-rich activity, made possible by the global oil economy of which Prudhoe Bay and the Trans-Alaska Pipeline are integral parts. In the Arctic in particular, some voyages, such as trips through the Northwest Passage or to the North Pole, are made possible by the melting sea ice. At the same time, wanting to learn about and experience the polar environment is difficult to criticize, especially if this experience leads to a change in behavior or greater activism against climate change upon return home. There is a danger, of course, that a "see it before it disappears" tourism might be the new tragedy of the commons in the Polar Regions (a bit like the whaling industry of the 1960s and 1970s). But in representing both exploitation and preservation, polar tourism connects to a long history of darkness and light in the Polar Regions that has proved remarkably resilient.

CONCLUSION

GEOGRAPHIES OF DESPAIR AND HOPE

In November 1977 Justice Thomas R. Berger of the Supreme Court of British Columbia gave an address to the Arctic Institute of North America titled "The Geography of Hope."[1] Berger had spent the past several years as Commissioner of the Mackenzie Valley Pipeline Inquiry, traveling across the north listening to testimony from both sides of the debate as to whether Canada should follow the lead of the United States in building a pipeline to get Arctic hydrocarbon resources to market. By the end of the inquiry, the Justice's own sympathies lay broadly with conservationists. Much to the chagrin of the oil industry and development-minded politicians in Ottawa, Berger recommended a ten-year moratorium on the construction of a pipeline. This, he argued, would give an opportunity to deal with the complex issues it raised, not least the fact that the region was home to many local communities who would have their lives changed by the construction of the pipeline. In place of the immediate construction of the Mackenzie Valley Pipeline, Berger recommended the establishment of a Canadian National Wilderness Park that would border the Arctic National Wildlife Range in the United States to constitute "a magnificent area of 18 million acres spanning the international boundary."[2]

The title of Justice Berger's talk borrowed from a phrase in the famous "wilderness letter" written by the environmentalist and Western

writer Wallace Stegner in 1960. In his lecture Berger elaborated on the
conflict between wilderness and development that had been raised by
the pipeline controversy. In agreeing that any gas pipeline would have
to follow a route along the Alaska Highway instead of opening up a new
area of Arctic wilderness, Berger believed, the governments of Canada
and the United States had recognized "that industrial goals do not at all
times and in all places take precedence over environmental values and
rights."[3] He was at pains to point out that he did not consider himself
as anti-industrial per se, but that he saw wilderness as a nonrenewable
resource, and that great care had to be taken whenever there was a proposal to develop previously undeveloped regions. "So we stand on the
leading edge of history," he concluded, "driven by forces that require
greater and greater and greater use of energy, and greater and greater
consumption of dwindling resources. Can we change direction? Upon
that question depends the future of the world we know and of our
environment."[4]

Berger's critics accused him of going into the inquiry with his mind
already made up, but it is clear that several years of traveling through
the Arctic and meeting its people had a profound impact on his thinking. His lecture to the Arctic Institute of North America provides an
example of the fine line between hope and despair in the environmental
history of the Polar Regions. If the Commission's findings had been
interpreted differently or rejected, it is difficult to believe that Berger
would have been giving a talk titled "the geography of hope." It is
also not difficult to imagine that for many of the supporters of the
Mackenzie Valley Pipeline proposal the dominant emotional response
to the ten-year moratorium would have been despair at lost economic
opportunities rather than hope in the retention of wilderness. The history of the Polar Regions looks very different from the perspective of
developers, environmentalists, scientists or local communities.

It is easy to pick a side, and then divide the environmental history of
the Polar Regions into geographies of despair and geographies of hope.
Taking the perspective of even a relatively moderate environmentalist,
it is difficult to do anything but despair at the recent histories of sealing
and whaling in both Polar Regions, or at the pollution and displacement
of local communities that often accompanied development projects and
military buildup in the twentieth-century Arctic. The threat of climate

change, and the seeming inability up to now of the international community to do anything about it, is for many a cause of urgent despair. Yet at the same time, the environmental history of the Polar Regions offers environmentalists plenty of causes for hope. At the height of the Cold War, the 1959 Antarctic Treaty laid the foundations for making the southern continent one of the most protected environments on the planet. Even in the Arctic, despite the intense military buildup, there are many examples of successful campaigns to preserve wilderness and protect the environment. As demonstrated perhaps most starkly by the connection between the *Exxon Valdez* disaster and the signing of the Madrid Protocol in Antarctica, positive environmental outcomes have come out of the most negative environmental catastrophes.

Similar lists of desperation and hopefulness could be made for any group in the history of the Arctic and Antarctica at any given time. The perspectives of an indigenous Arctic community, for example, would likely be quite different from those of environmentalist from outside the region, and the view from the 1950s might look quite different from today. But there would still be elements of despair and hope in all these viewpoints. While the complexity of the environmental history of the Polar Regions does not fit neatly into binaries, such an exercise is nevertheless useful. The contradictory histories of the Arctic and Antarctica suggest that they are dynamic rather than static places, and that their futures abound in possibilities. Far from stifling debate in resigned inertia, an approach that emphasizes contrasts and contradictions creates a space for constructive discussion. As we look to the future, the challenge will be to maximize the good and minimize the bad, while recognizing that there will always be a multiplicity of perspectives and that perfect solutions will likely remain elusive.

Geographies of Despair

It is difficult for an environmentalist to think about the recent history of the Polar Regions and not feel some sense of despair. Over the past three centuries, the Arctic and Antarctica have been the locations for some of the worst examples of human exploitation of the natural world. From the late eighteenth and early nineteenth centuries, the commercial butchering of seals in both the far north and the far south caused the extinction of at least one species, and left several others on the brink. In the abstract, the remorseless logic of the resource frontier is easy to grasp, and can even have an element of romance. As sealers destroyed seal populations in one colony they needed to find new colonies to exploit, and this often put them at the forefront of the history of exploration. But the reality of the industry involved seals being beaten to death, blood-soaked beaches, and the crying of orphaned pups. In the second half of the twentieth century, environmental organizations such as Greenpeace were able to draw upon these emotive images to win support for their cause. But in the eighteenth and nineteenth centuries, it was the near-destruction of seal populations, to the point of making seal hunting uneconomic, rather than any moral or ethical considerations that brought an end to the industry.

Perhaps the greatest tragedy of eighteenth- and nineteenth-century sealing was that lessons were not learned, and that a similar commercial butchery continued into the twentieth century in both Polar Regions with the history of the modern whaling industry. Modern whaling combined the logic of the resource frontier with the power of the modern industrial system. Steam-powered catcher ships, hydraulic winches, and the grenade harpoon left even blue whales and fin whales—the world's largest creatures—with little chance of survival. The transition to pelagic whaling from the 1920s onwards freed the industry from traditional regulation and created a distinctly twentieth-century version of the tragedy of the commons. Cold War politics exacerbated the problem by infusing international discussions with ideological discord and mistrust. While environmentalist campaigns undoubtedly had some influence on bringing the industry to an end, it was the decimation of whale populations to the point of extinction that arguably played the most significant role.

In places like Deception Island in Antarctica and Spitsbergen in the Arctic, evidence of failed development projects scar the landscape in the form of rusting and decaying buildings. Many of the structures from the DEW Line remain across Arctic North America as a legacy of the Cold War hubris and paranoia.[5] In Antarctica, McMurdo Station continues to be described by many as a blot on the landscape, despite significant efforts to improve its environmental record, including the removal of the Nukey Poo nuclear reactor. Like the residual oil from the *Exxon Valdez* disaster, the true environmental legacy of these efforts to harness polar nature is often hidden beneath the surface. This is especially the case with the radioactive waste that remains in many parts of the Arctic. The human dimensions of these environmental disasters are often the most disturbing. Many Inuit today face limitations on the number of marine mammals they can hunt and eat, not because populations are low but because the buildup of mercury and other toxins makes this traditional food a significant health risk.[6]

In the last few decades, the Polar Regions have become central to the science and politics of global climate change, arguably the most threatening environmental crisis of the twenty-first century. If taken seriously, images of collapsing glaciers, graphics of shrinking Arctic sea ice, and statistics for dying penguins and polar bears cannot help but cause despair. For all the concern about distant environments for their own sake, the Arctic and Antarctica matter for what they mean for people around the world and their local environments. Melting polar ice threatens to raise sea levels around the world with dire consequences, especially for those living in coastal communities. Warming temperatures in the Arctic are melting tundra and releasing the stored carbon dioxide into the atmosphere, accelerating warming. Perhaps most scary of all is the idea of an anthropogenic feedback loop being created in the Polar Regions as warming temperatures and melting ice make additional fossil fuel extraction possible, and as the burning of these fuels further increases temperatures and melts polar ice.

Climate change can be seen as a tragedy of the commons on a global scale. Why should any one country, region, or organization take a lead in reducing greenhouse gas emissions when others might not do the same? Such a question gets at the heart of the difficulties faced in getting a global agreement to reduce emissions. Historical inequalities and the political imperative of economic development further complicate the situation. The lessons from smaller-scale examples of open access resource problems from the Polar Regions are not promising. Although broader economic and political considerations played a role, sealing and whaling industries in both the Arctic and Antarctica generally came to an end not as the result of an enlightened change of heart, but because stocks had been hunted to the point of extinction. While such an outcome cannot readily be extrapolated to climate change, it might be worth asking a somewhat desperate question: what would constitute the point equivalent to near extinction sufficient to change behavior in the case of a warming planet?

Geographies of Hope

Alongside depressing declensionist narratives, environmental histories of the Arctic and Antarctica offer a number of sometimes quite surprising positive examples of environment protection and restoration. Some of these were deliberate, but others were unplanned. One of the less discussed side effects of the twentieth-century whaling industry in the Southern Ocean was that it quite possibly aided the recovery of fur seal and elephant seal populations decimated by nineteenth-century hunting. A reduction in the number of krill-feeding rorqual whales likely made more krill available to other predators, thereby increasing food supplies for seals both directly and indirectly. Although it is impossible to know the pre-exploitation populations of elephant seals and fur seals, by the end of the twentieth century their populations had recovered substantially. Today there are some beaches on the island of South Georgia where it is again difficult to move around during the fur seal breeding season as a result of such large numbers of seals.

In retrospect, it is quite remarkable that Cold War political tensions helped to bring about the signing of the 1959 Antarctic Treaty, which created a continent dedicated to peace and science in the midst of one of the most threatening conflicts in history. The Antarctic Treaty in turn helped to lay the foundations for the environmental protection of the southern continent that culminated in the signing of the 1991 Madrid Environmental Protocol, which by many measures made Antarctica the most protected environment anywhere on the planet. The Antarctic Treaty is not perfect, and it is possible to identify recurring political exclusion in the question of which countries get to participate. But it is certainly possible to imagine many alternative outcomes, political and environmental, that would have been much worse than the current status quo. It is certainly difficult to imagine a much better system for protecting the environment, at least for the next few decades.

Despite greater environmental contamination as a result of the intensity of the Cold War conflict, there have been numerous environmental success stories in the recent history of the Arctic. A quick glance at the International Union for Conservation of Nature's (IUCN) world map of protected areas reveals that much of the Arctic has today some sort of status as a protected area. Although Justice Berger's dreams for a jointly managed international Arctic park spanning the Alaska-Canada border have not quite come true, this region currently enjoys protection with the ANWR on the U.S. side and Ivvavik National Park on the Canadian side. Despite population fluctuations, the region's Porcupine caribou herd appears to be doing well, and judged by the distance of the caribou migration, this is one of the wildest places in North America. The 1002 Area in the ANWR is of continued concern for environmentalists, and there is fear that drilling will begin with the next major oil crisis. While it is not good news for environmentalists in general, however, the emergence of hydraulic fracturing (or fracking) across much of North America has taken some of the pressure off drilling in the ANWR, at least temporarily.

Perhaps one of the greatest causes for hope in the Polar Regions comes from the fact that positive environmental outcomes have emerged from some of the most serious threats to the polar environment. In Alaska, the campaign against Operation Chariot's plans for geo-engineering a deepwater harbor with a nuclear explosion in the late 1950s helped to mobilize Alaska's Native communities. This mobilization contributed to the creation of an effective political organization that campaigned throughout the 1960s for recognition of the land claims of Alaska Natives. Although the Alaska Native Claims Settlement Act (ANCSA) of 1971 has been criticized for imposing a free-market system on Alaska's indigenous communities, it can also be seen as a successful outcome for the Alaska Natives' campaign, especially when compared to many other attempts in North America to compensate Native Americans for the land lost to colonialism. The urgency of the need to settle the land claims in order to construct the Trans-Alaska Pipeline played a significant role in the rapid negotiation of the Alaska Natives' claims. In turn the D-2 section of the ANCSA laid the foundations for the environmentalist campaigns during the 1970s to protect Arctic wilderness. Although the Alaska National Interest Lands Claims Act of 1980 was by no means perfect, it did result in a large part of Arctic Alaska coming under federal protection and administration.

Despite the multiple threats posed by climate change, the scientific research that is taking place in the Polar Regions offers another cause for hope. Much remains to be learned about the precise mechanisms through which greenhouse gases warm the atmosphere, and more still remains to be known about what the consequences of a warming planet will be. But scientific research in the Arctic and Antarctica has already made a major contribution to climate change research, and the basic mechanisms through which greenhouse gases contribute to a warming climate are now well known. There are certainly many legitimate questions to debate in discussing the political response to climate change, but as a result of the atmospheric science research in places such as the Arctic and Antarctica, the basic causes of a warming climate are not in doubt. Scientific research in the Polar Regions continues to ask important questions and contribute to global scientific discussions. Ecological research in the McMurdo Dry Valleys region of Antarctica, for example, is investigating ecosystem response to climate change; numerous studies in the Arctic are investigating the impacts of climate change on local communities.[7] Science alone cannot solve the problem of climate change, but it is extremely important to have a basic understanding of what is happening.

Darkness and Light

Historians should be wary about drawing clear lessons from the histories we study. Circumstances change, and things are rarely as simple as they sometimes seem. While a wide variety of sources can give us insights into what has happened in the past, they cannot easily be used to predict the future. But neither can historians stick our heads in the sand and pretend to have no concern for the question of what happens next. For environmental historians in particular, the scope and scale of contemporary environmental problems—the geographies of despair—demand an engagement with the present and future as well as the past. There are some suggestions that the threat of climate change, in particular, is already changing the way we think about history, not only by raising new questions but also by changing the nature of the historical process.[8] It may not be long before burning fossil fuels to travel to archives, attend conferences, and visit the places we study looks like wasteful extravagance. Maybe it already does. In order to justify continued historical research, we may find ourselves having to think more carefully about the utility of our work.

Theologians sometimes talk about "thin places" where there is a particularly strong connection between the immanent and the transcendent, and there are plenty of examples of people experiencing the Polar Regions in this way.[9] But a theological perspective is not necessary for the concept of thin places to be a useful way of thinking about the Arctic and Antarctica. Justice Berger's talk to the Arctic Institute of North America demonstrates that the Polar Regions offer good locations for asking big questions. These are places where extreme beauty coexists with life-threatening hostility. They take us out of our comfort zones, and they help us to see the world from a different perspective. At the same time, the questions we ask in the Arctic and Antarctica are similar to those we ask in other parts of the world. Physical, intellectual, and political connections with the rest of the planet mean that the Arctic and Antarctica are not "poles apart." The environmental histories of the Polar Regions have much to contribute to our understanding of contemporary environmental problems.

There is a saying at McMurdo Station that you do not really know Antarctica until you have spent a winter there. Locals in northern Alaska are fond of telling summer tourists that they are not really experiencing the real Arctic unless they live through a real winter. Neither Polar Region is complete without both the darkness of winter and the sunlight of summer. One possible lesson to draw from the environmental history of the Polar Regions is that darkness and light have coexisted throughout history, both physically and metaphorically. The Arctic and Antarctica are places where positives and negatives exist together, sometimes starkly and sometimes subtly. Environmental historians are becoming more nuanced in dealing with contradiction. Yet there is still a tendency to emphasize declensionist narratives or to tell triumphalist stories about conservation successes. On one end of the scale, environmental despair can easily lead to paralysis. At the other end, anthropocentric hubris can believe that every problem has a solution. When these two tendencies are put together there is a very real danger that dire threats of contemporary environmental problems might be used to justify nondemocratic politics and massive geo-engineering projects. The inherent contradictions of the environmental history of the Polar Regions encourage a more humble approach. While both the Arctic and Antarctica have certainly been modified by the presence of humans, polar environments retain a visceral hostility that reminds us that nature can never be fully conquered. As we move forward, history reminds us that we do not have all the answers, but that does not mean we should stop trying to make the world a better place. For as long as a spinning earth revolves around the sun, the Polar Regions will continue to be lands of darkness and light.

NOTES

Introduction: Lands of Darkness and Light

1 There are a number of books on the *Exxon Valdez* oil spill. For a local perspective see, for example, Sharon Bushell and Stan Jones, *The Spill: Personal Stories from the Exxon Valdez Disaster* (Kenmore, WA: Epicenter Press, 2009).

2 Riki Ott, "They Have No Ears," in *Arctic Voices: Resistance at the Tipping Point*, ed. Subhankar Banerjee (New York: Seven Stories Press, 2012), 58–59.

3 For the difficulty in attributing ecological causation, see Ryan Tucker Jones, *Empire of Extinction: Russians and the North Pacific's Strange Beasts of the Sea, 1741–1867* (2014).

4 Peter Coates, *The Trans-Alaska Pipeline Controversy: Technology, Conservation, and the Frontier* (Bethlehem, PA: Lehigh University Press, 1991).

5 Dermot Cole, *North to the Future: The Alaska Story, 1959–2009*, Alaska Book Adventures (Kenmore, WA: Epicenter Press, 2008).

6 Donald Mitchell, *Take My Land, Take My Life: The Story of Congress's Historic Settlement of Alaska Native Land Claims, 1960–1971* (Fairbanks: University of Alaska Press, 2001).

7 Jack Roderick, *Crude Dreams: A Personal History of Oil & Politics in Alaska* (Fairbanks, AK: Epicenter Press, 1997).

8 See, for example, Proposal for Finding of Final Phase of the Wilderness Society Portion of the Alaska Pipeline Case (Wilderness Society et al. v. Morton) May 1973. USA Denver Public Library (DPL) CONS 86 Harry B. Crandell Papers. Box 20. FF29 Pipeline Litigation: Proposal for Funding.

9 See, for example, Tom Griffiths, *Slicing the Silence: Voyaging to Antarctica* (Cambridge, MA: Harvard University Press, 2007).

10 United Nations Organization, *Question of Antarctica: Study Requested under General Assembly Resolution 38/77 Report of the Secretary General*, 4 vols. (New York: United Publications, 1984).

11 Remarks of Senator Al Gore. Hearing on Legislation Relating to Protection of the Antarctic Environment. Committee on Foreign Relations. U.S. Senate, July 27 1990. USA Denver Public Library (DPL) Wilderness Society CONS 130 Series 5 Box 16. FF23—November 1990—Alliance for Antarctica: press packet.

12 William Cronon, "Landscapes of Abundance and Scarcity," in *The Oxford History of the American West*, ed. Clyde A. Milner, Carol A. O'Connor, and Martha A. Sandweiss (New York: Oxford University Press, 1994), 634.

13 *Frozen Planet*, first broadcast 2011. Popular interest in polar-themed documentaries is nothing new: the American filmmaker Robert Flaherty received critical acclaim for his 1923 documentary *Nanook of the North*. Hugh Brody, *Living Arctic: Hunters of the Canadian North* (Vancouver: Douglas & McIntyre, 1987), 19.

14 See, for example, the website and blog that accompanied the failed attempt made by Sir Ranulph Fiennes to cross Antarctica during the winter in 2012: http://www.thecoldestjourney.org [Accessed Nov 26, 2014].

15 http://www.worldatlas.com/webimage/countrys/polar/arctic.htm. See also University of the Arctic.

16 See, for example, Julie Cruikshank, *Do Glaciers Listen?: Local Knowledge, Colonial Encounters, and Social Imagination*, Brenda and David McLean Canadian Studies Series (Vancouver: UBC Press, 2005).

17 See, for example, Adrian Howkins, "Icy Relations: The Emergence of South American Antarctica During the Second World War," *Polar Record* 42, no. 2 (2006).

18 Sherrill Grace, *Canada and the Idea of North* (Montreal, London: McGill–Queen's University Press, 2002).

19 Francis Spufford, *I May Be Some Time: Ice and the English Imagination* (London: Faber and Faber, 1996).

20 Robert McGhee, *The Last Imaginary Place: A Human History of the Arctic World* (Oxford, New York: Oxford University Press, 2005), 31–32. For an interesting discussion of South African interest in Antarctica see Peder Roberts, Klaus Dodds, and Lize-Marie van der Watt, "'But Why Do You Go There?' Norway and South Africa in the Antarctic During the 1950s," in *Science, Geopolitics and Culture in the Polar Region: Norden Beyond Borders*, ed. Sverker Sörlin (Farnham: Ashgate, 2013).

21 See, for example, the excellent essays, stories, poems, and pictures in Anne Hanley and Carolyn Kremers, *The Alaska Reader: Voices from the North* (Golden, CO: Fulcrum, 2005). For a slightly different perspective, see William L. Iġġiaġruk Hensley, *Fifty Miles from Tomorrow: A Memoir of Alaska and the Real People* (New York: Sarah Crichton Books, 2009).

22 Stephen J. Pyne, *The Ice* (London: Weidenfeld & Nicolson, 2003), 2.

23 For an early use of this term see Günter Oskar Dyhrenfurth, *To the Third Pole: The History of the High Himalaya* (London: W. Laurie, 1955).

24 James D. Hansom and John E. Gordon, *Antarctic Environments and Resources: A Geographical Perspective* (New York: Longman, 1998).

25 See discussion in Charles Emmerson, *The Future History of the Arctic* (New York: PublicAffairs, 2010).

26 Terence Armstrong, George William Rogers, and Graham Rowley, *The Circumpolar North: A Political and Economic Geography of the Arctic and Sub-Arctic* (London: Methuen, 1978).

27 While Peter Davidson's *The Idea of North* (2005) is an excellent book, it largely ignores the southern hemisphere. See also Grace, *Canada and the Idea of North*.

28 Barry Holstun Lopez, *Arctic Dreams: Imagination and Desire in a Northern Landscape* (New York: Scribner, 1986); "Informed by Indifference: A Walk in Antarctica," *Harper's Magazine*, May (1988).

29 This goes back to the discussion in Spufford, *I May Be Some Time: Ice and the English Imagination.*

30 Adrian Howkins, "Appropriating Space: Antarctic Imperialism and the Mentality of Settler Colonialism," in *Making Settler Colonial Space: Perspectives on Race, Place and Identity*, ed. Tracey Banivanua Mar and Penelope Edmonds (Houndmills, Basingstoke: Palgrave Macmillan, 2010). Many of the essays in this collection touch on the themes of "empty space" and "wilderness."

31 Dolly Jørgensen and Sverker Sörlin, *Northscapes: History, Technology, and the Making of Northern Environments* (Vancouver: UBC Press, 2013), 1. See also Brody, *Living Arctic: Hunters of the Canadian North*, 173.

32 David G. Anderson and Mark Nuttall, *Cultivating Arctic Landscapes: Knowing and Managing Animals in the Circumpolar North* (New York: Berghahn Books, 2004), 2.

33 Tracey Banivanua Mar and Penelope Edmonds, eds., *Making Space: Settler Colonial Perspectives on Place, Race and Identity* (Houndmills, Basingstoke: Palgrave Macmillan, 2010).

34 Adrian Howkins, "The Significance of the Frontier in Antarctic History: How the U.S. West Has Shaped the Geopolitics of the Far South," *The Polar Journal* (2013). {AQ: do you need any further citation info here?}

35 Jørgensen and Sörlin, *Northscapes: History, Technology, and the Making of Northern Environments*, 5.

36 This phrase is taken from Donald Worster, "Appendix: Doing Environmental History," in *The Ends of the Earth: Perspectives on Modern Environmental History*, ed. Donald Worster (Cambridge: Cambridge University Press, 1989).

37 Carlo Ginzburg, "Making Things Strange: The Prehistory of a Literary Device," *Representations* 56, Special Issue: The New Erudition (1996).

38 William Cronon, "The Trouble with Wilderness; or, Getting Back to the Wrong Nature," in *Uncommon Ground: Rethinking the Human Place in Nature*, ed. William Cronon (New York: W.W. Norton & Co., 1995). See also Michael L. Lewis, *American Wilderness: A New History* (Oxford: Oxford University Press, 2007).

39 Philip W. Quigg, *A Pole Apart: The Emerging Issue of Antarctica* (New York: New Press, 1983).

40 Tom Griffiths, *Slicing the Silence: Voyaging to Antarctica* (Cambridge, MA: Harvard University Press, 2007), 257.

41 Mark Fiege, *The Republic of Nature: An Environmental History of the United States* (Seattle: University of Washington Press, 2012).

42 John Robert McNeill and Corinna R. Unger, *Environmental Histories of the Cold War*, Publications of the German Historical Institute (Washington, D.C.: Cambridge University Press, 2010).

43 Richard Harry Drayton, *Nature's Government: Science, Imperial Britain, and the "Improvement" of the World* (New Haven, CT: Yale University Press, 2000).

44 For a discussion of this concept, see Adrian Howkins, "Melting Empires? Climate Change and Politics in Antarctica since the International Geophysical Year," *Osiris* 26, no. 1 (2011).

45 Garrett Hardin, "The Tragedy of the Commons," *Science* 162 (1968); Harold Adams Innis, *The Fur Trade in Canada: An Introduction to Canadian Economic History* (Toronto: University of Toronto Press, 1999).

46 J. Donald Hughes, *What Is Environmental History?* (Cambridge: Polity, 2006).

1. Myth and History

1 See, for example, Stephen Martin, *A History of Antarctica* (Sydney: State Library of New South Wales Press, 1996).

2 Although he cannot be accused of embellishment, the scholar that did most to establish the myth of Captain Cook was the New Zealander J. C. Beaglehole. See J. C. Beaglehole, *The Life of Captain James Cook* (Stanford, CA: Stanford University Press, 1974).

3 For a discussion see Hughes, *What Is Environmental History?*

4 Jared M. Diamond, *Collapse: How Societies Choose to Fail or Succeed* (New York: Viking, 2005).

5 Knud Rasmussen, *Intellectual Culture of the Iglulik Eskimos (Report of the Fifth Thule Expedition, 1921–24)*, trans. W. Worster, vol. 7, no.1 (Gyldendalske Boghandel, 1929), 253.

6 Conforms to what Kirsten Thisted says about Rasmussen only giving the first names of his informants. See Kirsten Thisted, "The

Power to Represent: Intertextuality and Discourse in *Smilla's Sense of Snow*," in *Narrating the Arctic: A Cultural History of Nordic Scientific Practices*, ed. Michael Bravo and Sverker Sörlin (Canton, MA: Science History Publications, 2002).

7 Brody, *Living Arctic: Hunters of the Canadian North*, 99.

8 For a discussion of the attractions of winter, see ibid., 47.

9 See Chapter 2.

10 Terrence Cole, "Introduction," in *Across Arctic America*, ed. Knud Rasmussen (Fairbanks: University of Alaska Press, 1999), xi.

11 Quoted in ibid., xvi.

12 Quoted in ibid., xx.

13 Richard White, *The Middle Ground: Indians, Empires, and Republics in the Great Lakes Region, 1650–1815*, Cambridge Studies in North American Indian History (Cambridge, New York: Cambridge University Press, 1991).

14 See the movie *The Journals of Knud Rasmusen* (2006) http://www.isuma.tv/isuma-productions/jkr

15 Knud Rasmussen, *Across Arctic America: Narrative of the Fifth Thule Expedition*, Classic Reprint Series (Fairbanks: University of Alaska Press, 1999), 63.

16 A classic example of an environmentalist seeking purity in the Polar Regions is the Canadian Farley Mowat. His name would be given to one of the ships used by the Sea Shepherd environmental group in their campaign against Japanese whaling in Antarctica.

17 See, for example, Jean Comaroff and John L. Comaroff, *Of Revelation and Revolution: Christianity, Colonialism, and Consciousness in South Africa* (Chicago: University of Chicago Press, 1991).

18 George P. Kanaqlak Charles, "Cultural Identity through Yupiaq Narrative," in *The Alaska Native Reader*, ed. Maria Sháa Tláa Williams (Durham, NC: Duke University Press, 2009), 58.

19 David Damas, *Handbook of North American Indians Volume 5: Arctic*, ed. W. C. Sturtevant (Smithsonian Insitution 1984).

20 Rasmussen, *Across Arctic America: Narrative of the Fifth Thule Expedition*, 118.

21 Ibid., 124.

22 For example, the Alaska Museum in Anchorage has a Tlingit mask with images of a fox and a raven.

23 Cole, "Introduction," xi.

24 Ibid., xxi.

25 Ibid.

26 McGhee, *The Last Imaginary Place: A Human History of the Arctic World*, 104.

27 Quoted in ibid., 105.

28 Brody, *Living Arctic: Hunters of the Canadian North*, 7.

29 McGhee, *The Last Imaginary Place: A Human History of the Arctic World*, 112.

30 Ibid., 26.

31 Ibid., 112.

32 Ibid., 47.

33 Ibid., 44.

34 Ibid.

35 Ibid., 45.

36 Ibid., 53.

37 Ibid., 122.

38 Ibid., 121.

39 See, for example, Vine Deloria, *Custer Died for Your Sins: An Indian Manifesto* (Norman: University of Oklahoma Press, 1988).

40 See, for example, displays at the Anchorage Museum and the University of Alaska's Museum of the North in Fairbanks.

41 Hugh Robert Mill, *The Siege of the South Pole: The Story of Antarctic Exploration* (London: Alston Rivers, 1905), 3.

42 Ibid.

43 Ibid., 4.

44 See, for example, Martin, *A History of Antarctica*.

45 McGhee, *The Last Imaginary Place: A Human History of the Arctic World*, 22.

46 Ibid., 23.

47 Apsley Cherry-Garrard, *The Worst Journey in the World, Antarctic, 1910–1913* (London,: Constable, 1922); Frank Hurley, *Argonauts of the South* (New York: Putnam's, 1925).

48 For an interesting discussion of the culture of the heroic era see Max Jones, *The Last Great Quest: Captain Scott's Antarctic Sacrifice* (Oxford: Oxford University Press, 2003).

49 Mill, *The Siege of the South Pole: The Story of Antarctic Exploration*, 3.

50 Avan Judd Stallard, "Origins of the Idea of Antipodes: Errors, Assumptions, and a Bare Few Facts," *Terrae Incognitae* 42 (2010).

51 Elizabeth Leane, *Antarctica in Fiction: Imaginative Narratives of the Far South* (New York: Cambridge University Press, 2012), 24–25.

52 Ibid., 25.

53 Ruben Stehberg and Liliana Nilo, "Procedencia Antartica Inexacta De Dos Puntos De Proyectil," *Instituto Antártico Chileno Serie Científica* 30 (1983).

54 Karen Oslund, *Iceland Imagined: Nature, Culture, and Storytelling in the North Atlantic*, Weyerhaeuser Environmental Books (Seattle: University of Washington Press, 2011).

55 Diamond, *Collapse: How Societies Choose to Fail or Succeed*.

56 Oslund, *Iceland Imagined: Nature, Culture, and Storytelling in the North Atlantic*.

57 Diamond, *Collapse: How Societies Choose to Fail or Succeed*, 217.

58 Ibid., 179.

59 Ibid., 21.

60 Ibid., 193.

61 See introduction in Patricia Ann McAnany and Norman Yoffee, *Questioning Collapse: Human Resilience, Ecological Vulnerability, and the Aftermath of Empire* (Cambridge, New York: Cambridge University Press, 2010).

62 Diamond, *Collapse: How Societies Choose to Fail or Succeed*, 213.

63 Ibid., 179.

64 McAnany and Yoffee, *Questioning Collapse: Human Resilience, Ecological Vulnerability, and the Aftermath of Empire*, 6.

65 Ibid.

66 Diamond, *Collapse: How Societies Choose to Fail or Succeed*, 179.

67 Joel Berglund, "Did the Medieval Norse Society in Greenland Really Fail?," in *Questioning Collapse: Human Resilience, Ecological Vulnerability, and the Aftermath of Empire*, ed. Patricia Ann McAnany and Norman Yoffee (2010).

68 Ibid., 60.

69 Drayton, *Nature's Government: Science, Imperial Britain, and the "Improvement" of the World*.

70 Lynn White, Jr., "The Historical Roots of Our Ecologic Crisis," *Science* 155, no. 3767 (1967).

71 John Gascoigne, *Science in the Service of Empire: Joseph Banks, the British State and the Uses of Science in the Age of Revolution* (Cambridge: Cambridge University Press, 1998).

72 Alan Gurney, *Below the Convergence: Voyages toward Antarctica, 1699–1839*, 1st ed. (New York: Norton, 1997).

73 Ibid.

74 Beaglehole, *The Life of Captain James Cook.*

75 Quoted in James Cook, J. C. Beaglehole, and R. A. Skelton, *The Journals of Captain James Cook on His Voyages of Discovery* (Rochester, NY: Boydell Press, 1999), 625.

76 *Robert Burton, Southern Horizons: The History of the British Antarctic Territory (London: United Kingdom Antarctic Heritage Trust, 2008)*, 7.

77 Cook, Beaglehole, and Skelton, *The Journals of Captain James Cook on His Voyages of Discovery*, 626.

2. Scarcity and Abundance

1 Damas, *Handbook of North American Indians Volume 5: Arctic.*

2 Brody, *Living Arctic: Hunters of the Canadian North*, 97.

3 Jørgensen and Sörlin, *Northscapes: History, Technology, and the Making of Northern Environments*, 5.

4 Ibid., 178.

5 Hardin, "The Tragedy of the Commons."

6 See, for example, Elinor Ostrom, *Governing the Commons: The Evolution of Institutions for Collective Action*, The Political Economy of Institutions and Decisions (Cambridge, New York: Cambridge University Press, 1990).

7 See discussion in William Cronon, "Foreword," in *Whales and Nations: Environmental Diplomacy on the High Seas*, ed. Kurkpatrick Dorsey (Seattle: University of Washington Press, 2013).

8 For a discussion of the idea of a resource frontier see Innis, *The Fur Trade in Canada: An Introduction to Canadian Economic History.*

9 Quoted in Gurney, *Below the Convergence: Voyages Toward Antarctica, 1699–1839.*

10 One of the most authoritative accounts of the history of Antarctica in the nineteenth century remains Mill, *The Siege of the South Pole: The Story of Antarctic Exploration.*

11 Dag Avango, Louwrens Hacquebord, and Urban Wråkberg,

"Industrial Extraction of Arctic Natural Resources Since the Sixteenth Century: Technoscience and Geo-Economics in the History of Northern Whaling and Mining," *Journal of Historical Geography* 44 (2014).

12 Andrés Zarankín and M. Ximena Senatore, *Historias De Un Pasado En Blanco: Arqueología Histórica Antártica* (Belo Horizonte: Argumentum, 2007).

13 Maria Ximena Senatore, "Antártida Como Narrativa," *Vestígios: Revista Latino-Americana de Arqueologia Histórica* 5, no. 2 (2011).

14 McGhee, *The Last Imaginary Place: A Human History of the Arctic World*, 173.

15 Brody, *Living Arctic: Hunters of the Canadian North*, 45.

16 McGhee, *The Last Imaginary Place: A Human History of the Arctic World*, 115.

17 See, for example, Aqqalu Rosing-Asvid, *Seals of Greenland* (Gylling: Narayana Press, 2010).

18 Erik W. Born, *The Walrus in Greenland* (Nuuk: Ilinniusiorfik Education, 2005).

19 Jones, *Empire of Extinction: Russians and the North Pacific's Strange Beasts of the Sea, 1741–1867*.

20 Brody, *Living Arctic: Hunters of the Canadian North*, 57–59.

21 Diamond, *Collapse: How Societies Choose to Fail or Succeed*.

22 Brody, *Living Arctic: Hunters of the Canadian North*, 73.

23 Ibid., 75.

24 Shepard Krech, *The Ecological Indian: Myth and History*, 1st ed. (New York: W.W. Norton, 1999); Michael Eugene Harkin and David Rich Lewis, *Native Americans and the Environment: Perspectives on the Ecological Indian* (Lincoln: University of Nebraska Press, 2007).

25 Eric R. Wolf, *Europe and the People without History* (Berkeley: University of California Press, 1982).

26 McGhee, *The Last Imaginary Place: A Human History of the Arctic World*, 38.

27 See, for example, Craig Campbell, "A Genealogy of the Concept of 'Wanton Slaughter' in Canadian Wildlife Biology," in *Cultivating Arctic Landscapes: Knowing and Managing Animals in the Circumpolar North*, ed. David G. Anderson and Mark Nuttall (New York: Berghahn Books, 2004). The anthropologist Hugh Brody takes

issue with this claim, Brody, *Living Arctic: Hunters of the Canadian North*, 79. For a non-polar example of environmental destruction being used to justify colonialism, see Diana K. Davis, *Resurrecting the Granary of Rome: Environmental History and French Colonial Expansion in North Africa* (Athens: Ohio University Press, 2007).

28 Brody, *Living Arctic: Hunters of the Canadian North*, 77.

29 Pamela R. Stern and Lisa Stevenson, *Critical Inuit Studies: An Anthology of Contemporary Arctic Ethnography* (Lincoln: University of Nebraska Press, 2006).

30 White, *The Middle Ground: Indians, Empires, and Republics in the Great Lakes Region, 1650–1815.*

31 McGhee, *The Last Imaginary Place: A Human History of the Arctic World*, 102.

32 Ibid., 93.

33 Richard Vaughan, *The Arctic: A History* (Dover, NH: A. Sutton, 1994), 79.

34 William Cronon, *Changes in the Land: Indians, Colonists, and the Ecology of New England* (New York: Hill and Wang, 2003).

35 While Vaughan rejects the idea of including the Aleutian Islands in a strict definition of the Arctic, a looser definition of the circumpolar north certainly allows for their inclusion, Vaughan, *The Arctic: A History.*

36 Jones, *Empire of Extinction: Russians and the North Pacific's Strange Beasts of the Sea, 1741–1867*, 79.

37 Ibid., 85.

38 Ibid., 81.

39 Ibid., 88.

40 Ibid., 84.

41 Fredericka I. Martin, *The Hunting of the Silver Fleece, Epic of the Fur Seal* (New York: Greenberg, 1946).

42 Jones, *Empire of Extinction: Russians and the North Pacific's Strange Beasts of the Sea, 1741–1867*, 95.

43 Ibid., 197.

44 An exception is Martin, *The Hunting of the Silver Fleece, Epic of the Fur Seal.*

45 Jones, *Empire of Extinction: Russians and the North Pacific's Strange Beasts of the Sea, 1741–1867.*

46 Cook, Beaglehole, and Skelton, *The Journals of Captain James Cook on His Voyages of Discovery*, 622.

47 Quoted in Martin, *A History of Antarctica*, 54.

48 Robert Headland, *A Chronology of Antarctic Exploration: A Synopsis of Events and Activities from the Earliest Times until the International Polar Years, 2007–09* (London: Bernard Quaritch, 2009), 97. Christie suggests that that the exact date is unknown, Eric William Hunter Christie, *The Antarctic Problem; an Historical and Political Study* (London: Allen & Unwin, 1951), 64.

49 Kenneth John Bertrand, *Americans in Antarctica, 1775–1948* (New York: American Geographical Society, 1971), 29.

50 Ibid.

51 For detailed figures, see Bjørn Basberg and Robert Headland, "The 19th Century Antarctic Sealing Industry. Sources, Data and Economic Significance," *NHH Dept. of Economics Discussion Paper*, no. 21 (2008).

52 Headland, *A Chronology of Antarctic Exploration: A Synopsis of Events and Activities from the Earliest Times until the International Polar Years, 2007–09*, 118.

53 Gurney, *Below the Convergence: Voyages toward Antarctica, 1699–1839*, 149.

54 Ibid.

55 Ibid.

56 Ibid., 147.

57 Ibid., 152.

58 For an important discussion of work and nature see Richard White, "'Are You an Environmentalist or Do You Work for a Living?' Work and Nature," in *Uncommon Ground: Rethinking the Human Place in Nature*, ed. William Cronon (New York: Norton, 1996). See also, Thomas G. Andrews, *Killing for Coal: America's Deadliest Labor War* (Cambridge, MA: Harvard University Press, 2008).

59 It is testimony to the low status of the sealers that there are no accurate figures for mortality in the early nineteenth-century Antarctic sealing industry. See broader discussion in Basberg and Headland, "The 19th Century Antarctic Sealing Industry. Sources, Data and Economic Significance."

60 Gurney, *Below the Convergence: Voyages toward Antarctica, 1699–1839*, 148.

61 Anthony Bertram Dickinson, *Seal Fisheries of the Falkland Islands and Dependencies: An Historical Review*, Research in Maritime History (St. John's, Nfld.: International Maritime Economic History Association, 2007), 75.

62 For a classic discussion of this theme see Arthur F. McEvoy, *The Fisherman's Problem: Ecology and Law in the California Fisheries, 1850–1980* (Cambridge: Cambridge University Press, 1986).

63 Andrews, *Killing for Coal: America's Deadliest Labor War*.

64 Bertrand, *Americans in Antarctica, 1775–1948*, 133.

65 Headland, *A Chronology of Antarctic Exploration: A Synopsis of Events and Activities from the Earliest Times Until the International Polar Years, 2007–09*, 122.

66 This point is made in Adolfo E. Quevedo Paiva, *Medio Siglo Del Ejército Argentino En Nuestra Antártida: 1951–2001* (Buenos Aires: Editorial Dunken, 2001).

67 Bertrand, *Americans in Antarctica, 1775–1948*, 122.

68 Gurney, *Below the Convergence: Voyages toward Antarctica, 1699–1839*, 178.

69 Ibid., 202.

70 Ibid., 193.

71 Martin, *A History of Antarctica*, 72.

72 James Weddell, *A Voyage Towards the South Pole, Performed in the Years 1822–'24. Containing ... A Visit to Tierra Del Fuego, with a Particular Account of the Inhabitants* (London: Longman, Hurst, Rees, Orme, Brown, and Green, 1825).

73 Thaddeus Bellingshausen and Frank Debenham, *The Voyage of Captain Bellingshausen to the Antarctic Seas 1819–1821* (London: Hakluyt Society, 1945), 425–26.

74 Ibid.

75 Jones, *Empire of Extinction: Russians and the North Pacific's Strange Beasts of the Sea, 1741–1867*.

76 Vaughan, *The Arctic: A History*, 77.

77 Ibid., 93.

78 Ibid., 95.

79 Ibid., 89.

80 Ibid., 85.

81 Ibid., 93.

82 Peter Nichols, *Final Voyage: A Story of Arctic Disaster and One Fateful Whaling Season* (New York: G.P. Putnam's Sons, 2009).

83 Vaughan, *The Arctic: A History*, 178.

84 Brody, *Living Arctic: Hunters of the Canadian North*, 191–93.

85 Vaughan, *The Arctic: A History*, 181.

86 Nichols, *Final Voyage: A Story of Arctic Disaster and One Fateful Whaling Season*.

87 Vaughan, *The Arctic: A History*, 272.

88 Nichols, *Final Voyage: A Story of Arctic Disaster and One Fateful Whaling Season*.

89 The most comprehensive book on the history of modern whaling is J. N. Tønnessen and Arne Odd Johnsen, *The History of Modern Whaling* (Berkeley: University of California Press, 1982).

90 W. G. Burn Murdoch and William Speirs Bruce, *From Edinburgh to the Antarctic* (London and New York: Longmans, Green, 1894).

91 Ian B. Hart, *Whaling in the Falkland Islands Dependencies, 1904–1931* (Newton St. Margarets, Herefordshire: Pequena, 2006).

92 For an interesting discussion of this expedition and its legacy, see Aant Elzinga, *Antarctic Challenges: Historical and Current Perspectives on Otto Nordenskjöld's Antarctic Expedition, 1901–1903* (Göteborg: Royal Society of Arts and Sciences, 2004).

93 Ian B. Hart, *Pesca: The History of Compañia Argentina De Pesca Sociedad Anónima of Buenos Aires: An Account of the Pioneer Modern Whaling and Sealing Company in the Antarctic*, rev. ed. (Salcombe: Aidan Ellis, 2002).

94 For a thorough discussion of Britain's legal claim to the Falkland Islands Dependencies, see Christie, *The Antarctic Problem; an Historical and Political Study*.

95 Peder Roberts, *The European Antarctic: Science and Strategy in Scandinavia and the British Empire* (New York: Palgrave Macmillan, 2011); D. Graham Burnett, *The Sounding of the Whale: Science & Cetaceans in the Twentieth Century* (Chicago: The University of Chicago Press, 2012).

96 Robert Headland, *The Island of South Georgia* (Cambridge: Cambridge University Press, 1984), 66.

97 Daniel Simberloff, *Invasive Species: What Everyone Needs to Know*, text.{AQ: What does "text" signify here?}

98 Kurkpatrick Dorsey, *Whales and Nations: Environmental Diplomacy on the High Seas*, 18.

3. Nature Conquered, Nature Unconquered

1 Beau Riffenburgh, *The Myth of the Explorer: The Press, Sensationalism, and Geographical Discovery* (Oxford: Oxford University Press, 1994).

2 With a handful of important exceptions such as Donald Worster, *A River Running West: The Life of John Wesley Powell* (Oxford, New York: Oxford University Press, 2001); Aaron Sachs, *The Humboldt Current: A European Explorer and His American Disciples* (Oxford: Oxford University Press, 2007); Jared Orsi, *Citizen Explorer: The Life of Zebulon Pike* (New York: Oxford University Press, 2014). In the Arctic, Christina Adcock has done important work on the environmental history of exploration: "Tracing Warm Lines: Northern Canadian Exploration, Knowledge, and Memory, 1905–1965" (Cambridge University, 2010).

3 Hughes, *What Is Environmental History?*

4 For a discussion of the science conducted during the heroic era of exploration relative to the scientific research that followed, see G. E. Fogg, *A History of Antarctic Science*, Studies in Polar Research (Cambridge: Cambridge University Press, 1992).

5 Adcock, "Tracing Warm Lines: Northern Canadian Exploration, Knowledge, and Memory, 1905–1965."

6 Orsi, *Citizen Explorer: The Life of Zebulon Pike*.

7 See, for example, Mill, *The Siege of the South Pole: The Story of Antarctic Exploration*.

8 Willy Schuyesmans, *El Invierno Del Bélgica: Prisioneros De La Antártica* (Santiago de Chile: RIL, 2010).

9 Jones, *The Last Great Quest: Captain Scott's Antarctic Sacrifice*.

10 Orsi, *Citizen Explorer: The Life of Zebulon Pike*.

11 Spufford, *I May Be Some Time: Ice and the English Imagination*.

12 See, for example, The American Geographical Society's influential 1928 publication titled *Problems of Polar Research*, which considered the Arctic and Antarctic together. W. L. G. Joerg, *Problems of Polar Research* (New York: American Geographical Society, 1928).

13 Roald Amundsen, *Roald Amundsen: My Life as an Explorer* (Garden City, NY: Doubleday, Page, 1927).

14 Frederick Albert Cook, *Through the First Antarctic Night, 1898–9* ([S.l.]: Heinemann, 1900).{AQ: What is [S.I.] here? }

15 The "Northern Sea Route" north of Russia will be investigated in more detail in Chapter 5.

16 Brody, *Living Arctic: Hunters of the Canadian North*, 16.

17 McGhee, *The Last Imaginary Place: A Human History of the Arctic World*, 26.

18 Vaughan, *The Arctic: A History*, 144.

19 Ibid., 142.

20 Leane, *Antarctica in Fiction: Imaginative Narratives of the Far South*.

21 See, for example, discussion of Jeremiah Reynolds in Sachs, *The Humboldt Current: A European Explorer and His American Disciples*.

22 Brody, *Living Arctic: Hunters of the Canadian North*, 61.

23 Vaughan, *The Arctic: A History*, 147.

24 Fergus Fleming, *Barrow's Boys* (London: Granta Books, 1998).

25 Vaughan, *The Arctic: A History*, 152.

26 G. A. Mawer, *South by Northwest: The Magnetic Crusade and the Contest for Antarctica* (Edinburgh: Birlinn, 2006).

27 Ibid.

28 Vaughan, *The Arctic: A History*, 155.

29 Ibid., 156.

30 Vilhjalmur Stefansson and Explorers Club, *Unsolved Mysteries of the Arctic* (New York: Macmillan, 1938).

31 Vaughan, *The Arctic: A History*. 168

32 Ibid., 185.

33 A further four men lost their lives in Antarctica during this period as a result of illnesses that cannot be directly attributed to being in the southern continent. And two others died on route.

34 John Oldfield Chadwick, "Perseverance in Arctic Exploration: An Enquiry Whether the Advantages Which May Be Expected to Result from a Successful Expedition to the North Pole Are Sufficient to Justify Further Efforts in the Attempt," (London, 1877).

35 James C. Scott, *Seeing Like a State: How Certain Schemes to Improve*

the Human Condition Have Failed (New Haven, CT: Yale University Press, 1998).

36 Vaughan, *The Arctic: A History*, 192.

37 Matthew Alexander Henson, *Henson at the North Pole* (Mineola, NY: Dover, 2008).

38 See for example, Ted Leitzell, "Peary's Conspiracy Against Dr. Cook: The inside Story of the Famous Polar Controversy," *Real America*, October (1935); Russell W. Gibbons, "Dr Cook: An American Dreyfus in the Arctic," *North* 15, no. 2 (1968).

39 The historiography of this period of Antarctic history is extensive. For an interesting recent example see, Edward J. Larson, *An Empire of Ice: Scott, Shackleton, and the Heroic Age of Antarctic Science* (New Haven, CT: Yale University Press, 2011).

40 Mill, *The Siege of the South Pole: The Story of Antarctic Exploration*.

41 Roland Huntford, *Scott and Amundsen*, (New York: Atheneum, 1984). Also see discussion of this book in Griffiths, *Slicing the Silence: Voyaging to Antarctica*.

42 For an extended discussion, see Spufford, *I May Be Some Time: Ice and the English Imagination*.

43 Vaughan, *The Arctic: A History*, 194.

44 Marionne Cronin, "Technological Heroes: Images of the Arctic in the Age of Polar Exploration," in *Northscapes: History, Technology, and the Making of Northern Environments*, ed. Jørgensen and Sörlin.

45 Jones, *The Last Great Quest: Captain Scott's Antarctic Sacrifice*.

46 Cronin, "Technological Heroes: Images of the Arctic in the Age of Polar Exploration," 58.

47 Simon Nasht, *The Last Explorer: Hubert Wilkins, Hero of the Great Age of Polar Exploration*, (New York: Arcade, 2006).

48 See, for example, Evans to Bowman, Jan. 30, 1926 (Dic't Jan 29). AGS Archive Expedition Files, Box 3. Wilkins, Hubert, Detroit Arctic Expedition, 1926–28, correspondence 1926. USA AGS Library (AGS) Expedition Files Box 3. Arctic. Wilkins, Hubert, Detroit Arctic Expedition, 1926–28, correspondence 1926.

49 See, for example, Evans to Bowman, Jan. 26, 1926. USA AGS Library (AGS) Expedition Files Box 3. Arctic. Wilkins, Hubert, Detroit Arctic Expedition, 1926–28, correspondence 1926.

50 Nasht, *The Last Explorer: Hubert Wilkins, Hero of the Great Age of Polar Exploration*.

51 Ibid.

52 Quoted in Cronin, "Technoloigcal Heroes: Images of the Arctic in the Age of Polar Exploration," 63.

53 *The Polar Times* 4, December, 1936, 6.

54 Paul R. Josephson, *The Conquest of the Russian Arctic* (2014), text. {AQ: "text"?}

55 Jean Clark Potter, *The Flying North* (New York: Macmillan, 1947).

4. Dreams and Realities

1 Amundsen, *Roald Amundsen: My Life as an Explorer*.

2 Quoted in Statement with Reference to Amundsen's Criticism of Stefansson. Undated. USA AGS Library (AGS) Expedition Files Box 3. Arctic. George H. Wilkins, Reaction to R. Amundsen's criticism of V. Stefansson, 1927, undated.

3 Ibid.

4 Bowman [?] to Wilkins, November 15, 1927. AGS Archive Expedition Files, Box 3. Arctic, George H. Wilkins, Reaction to R. Amundsen's criticism of V. Stefansson, 1927, undated. USA AGS Library (AGS) Expedition Files Box 3. Arctic. George H. Wilkins, Reaction to R. Amundsen's criticism of V. Stefansson, 1927, undated.

5 Wilkins Report/Letter. Written from his house in California. Undated. AGS Archive Expedition Files, Box 3. Arctic, George H. Wilkins, Reaction to R. Amundsen's criticism of V. Stefansson, 1927, undated. USA AGS Library (AGS) Expedition Files Box 3. Arctic. George H. Wilkins, Reaction to R. Amundsen's criticism of V. Stefansson, 1927, undated.

6 Dolly Jørgensen and Sverker Sörlin, "Making the Action Visible: Making Environments in Northern Landscapes," in *Northscapes: History, Technology, and the Making of Northern Environments*, ed. Jørgensen and Sörlin, 1.

7 Vilhjalmur Stefansson, *The Friendly Arctic; the Story of Five Years in Polar Regions* (New York: Macmillan, 1921), 6.

8 For example, Anderson and Nuttall seem to side with Stefansson: "The contributors to this volume see it as their task to make this possible by directing our attention to the symbols and words that

make us imagine the North as a warm, populated place." Anderson and Nuttall, *Cultivating Arctic Landscapes: Knowing and Managing Animals in the Circumpolar North*, 15.

9 Howkins, "The Significance of the Frontier in Antarctic History: How the U.S. West Has Shaped the Geopolitics of the Far South."

10 Quoted in Nancy LeBlond, January 1982 Memo to Board of Directors of the AIWRS, Jan. 5, 1982. USA UA Fairbanks Archives (UAF) George L Collins Paper, Series 3: Arctic International Wildlife Range Society. BOX 5. File 33. AIWRS – 1982

11 Libby Robin, *The Future of Nature: Documents of Global Change* (New Haven, CT: Yale University Press, 2013), text. See also http://www.arcticfutures.se/ {AQ: "text"?}

12 Louwrens Hacquebord, *Lashipa: History of Large Scale Resource Exploitation in Polar Areas* (Groningen: Barkhuis Pub., 2012). For an extended discussion of economic development in Arctic Canada, see Graeme Wynn, *Canada and Arctic North America: An Environmental History*, Abc-Clio's Nature and Human Societies Series (Santa Barbara, CA: ABC-CLIO, 2007).

13 See Hanley and Kremers, *The Alaska Reader: Voices from the North*, 59.

14 Scott, *Seeing Like a State: How Certain Schemes to Improve the Human Condition Have Failed.*

15 Brody, *Living Arctic: Hunters of the Canadian North.*

16 Stefansson, *The Friendly Arctic; the Story of Five Years in Polar Regions.*

17 *The Northward Course of Empire* (New York: Harcourt, 1922), 22. "With the initial advantage of knowing what the reader or listener thinks he knows about the North for I knew those things myself once and believed them until I went North and they were not true), I proceed as follows to demolish his misknowledge [sic]."

18 See, for example, introduction in Emmerson, *The Future History of the Arctic.*

19 Gísli Pálsson, *Travelling Passions: The Hidden Life of Vilhjalmur Stefansson* (Hanover, NH: Dartmouth College Press: University Press of New England, 2005), 76.

20 Ibid.

21 Quoted in ibid., 121.

22 Vilhjalmur Stefansson and Rudolph Martin Anderson, *My Life with the Eskimo* (New York: Macmillan, 1913).

23 Pálsson, *Travelling Passions: The Hidden Life of Vilhjalmur Stefansson*, 126.

24 For a full discussion of the *Karluk* disaster, see Jennifer Niven, *The Ice Master: The Doomed 1913 Voyage of the Karluk* (New York: Hyperion, 2000).

25 James Murray, *British Antarctic Expedition 1907–9 Reports on the Scientific Investigations. Volume 1: Biology* (London: William Heinemann, 1911).

26 Pálsson, *Travelling Passions: The Hidden Life of Vilhjalmur Stefansson*.

27 Stefansson, *The Friendly Arctic; the Story of Five Years in Polar Regions*, 16.

28 Ibid., 5.

29 Stefansson, *Northward Course of Empire*.

30 Ibid., 19.

31 Stefansson to Mr. Kenneth Kenneth-Smith, Jan 14 192. USA Byrd Polar (BPRC) Byrd Collection. Box 67, Folder 3067. Byrd Polar Research Center.

32 Jennifer Niven, *Ada Blackjack: A True Story of Survival in the Arctic*, 1st ed. (New York: Hyperion, 2003).

33 Lorne Knight Letter Feb 8 1923 Wrangel Island Arctic Ocean. AGS Archive Expedition Files, Box 3. Stefansson, Vilhjamur, Wrangell Island Expedition 1921–23, Correspondence, 1922–23. USA AGS Library (AGS) Expedition Files Box 3. Arctic.

34 Robert P. Wishart, "A Story About a Muskox: Some Implications of Tetlit Gwih'in Human-Animal Relationships," in *Cultivating Arctic Landscapes: Knowing and Managing Animals in the Circumpolar North*, ed. David G. Anderson and Mark Nuttall (New York Berghahn Books, 2004), 94.

35 Pálsson, *Travelling Passions: The Hidden Life of Vilhjalmur Stefansson*.

36 Brigid Hains, *The Ice and the Inland: Mawson, Flynn, and the Myth of the Frontier* (Carlton South, Vic.: Melbourne University Press, 2002).

37 See, for example, Stefansson to Railey, Jan. 17, 1929. USA Byrd Polar (BPRC) Byrd Collection. Box 67, Folder 3067.

38 Lisle Abbott Rose, *Explorer: The Life of Richard E. Byrd* (Columbia: University of Missouri Press, 2008).

39 R. B. M. Barton to Admiral Byrd, March 19, 1946. USA Byrd Polar (BPRC) Byrd Collection. Box 9, Folder 345.

40 Nasht, *The Last Explorer: Hubert Wilkins, Hero of the Great Age of Polar Exploration.*

41 Howkins, "The Significance of the Frontier in Antarctic History: How the U.S. West Has Shaped the Geopolitics of the Far South."

42 Early H. Balch to Byrd, Dec 4, 1930. USA Byrd Polar (BPRC) Byrd Collection. Box 39, Folder 1706.

43 Clara A. Hanson (words and music), "Hail, Little America." Dedicated to Richard E. Byrd. Undated. USA Byrd Polar (BPRC) Byrd Collection. Box 101, Folder 4028.

44 Copy of Book. USA Byrd Polar (BPRC) Byrd Collection. Box 90, Folder 3833.

45 Copy of Book. USA Byrd Polar (BPRC) Byrd Collection. Box 90, Folder 3833.

46 Richard Evelyn Byrd, *Alone* (New York: G. P. Putnam's Sons, 1938).

47 See, for example, Bertrand, *Americans in Antarctica, 1775–1948.*

48 Oscar Pinochet de la Barra, *La Antártica Chilena* (Santiago de Chile: Editorial del Pacífico, 1948), 164.

49 Frigga Kruse, "Frozen Assets: British Mining, Exploration, and Geopolitics on Spitsbergen, 1904–53" (Rijksuniversiteit Groningen, 2013).

50 A situation not dissimilar from Thomas Andrew's discussion of the Roosevelt mining interests in Colorado; Andrews, *Killing for Coal: America's Deadliest Labor War.*

51 Emmerson, *The Future History of the Arctic*, 90.

52 Jorge Berguño, "Intellectual Sources of the Antarctic Treaty," *Boletin Antartico Chileno*, (2009).

53 For a contemporary portrayal of life in Barentsburg, see the Adrian Briscoe movie *Dream Town*: http://vimeo.com/83736303

54 Michael Bravo and Sverker Sörlin, *Narrating the Arctic: A Cultural History of Nordic Scientific Practices* (Canton, MA: Science History Publications, 2002).

55 Adrian Howkins, "Reluctant Collaborators: Argentina and Chile in Antarctica During the IGY," *Journal of Historical Geography* 34 (2008).

56 See, for example, Juan Carlos Puig, *La Antártida Argentina Ante El Derecho* (Buenos Aires: R. Depalma, 1960).

57 Howkins, "Icy Relations: The Emergence of South American Antarctica During the Second World War."

58 "Address of the Minister of Foreign Relations, Raúl Juliet Gomez, Before the Chilean Senate on the Government's Foreign Policy, 21 January 1947, RREE Antártico, 1939–52." Chilean translation.

59 See, for example, Enrique Cordovez Madariaga, *La Antártida Sudamericana* (Santiago, Chile: Nascimento, 1945).

60 Luis Ortiz Behety, *Antartida Argentina: Poemas De Las Tierras Procelares* (Buenos Aires, 1948).

61 Miguel Serrano, *La Antártica Y Otros Mitos* (Santiago de Chile: Titania, 1948).

62 See, for example, Ramón Cañas Montalva, *El Valor Geopolitico De La Posicion Antartica De Chile* (1953).

63 For an extended discussion of this visit, see Gabriel González Videla, *Memorias*, (Santiago de Chile: Gabriela Mistral, 1975).

64 Eugenio A. Genest, *Pujato Y La Antártida Argentina En La Década Del Cincuenta* (Buenos Aires: H. Senado de la Nación, Secretaría Parlamentaria, Dirección Publicaciones, 1998); Susana Rigoz, *Hernán Pujato: El Conquistador Del Desierto Blanco* (Buenos Aires: Editorial María Ghirlanda, 2002).

65 Jorge Edgard Leal, *Operación 90* (Buenos Aires: Instituto Antártico Argentino, 1971).

66 Louis Bobe, "Greenland—A Two Hundredth Anniversary," *The American-Scandinavian Review* 9, no. 10 (1921): 659.

67 See for example, McGhee, *The Last Imaginary Place: A Human History of the Arctic World*. Emmerson calls it "colonial rule with a light touch," Emmerson, *The Future History of the Arctic*, 275.

68 Trevor Lloyd, "Progress in West Greenland," *The Journal of Geography* 49, no. 8 (1950): 329.

69 Bobe, "Greenland—A Two Hundredth Anniversary," 664.

70 V. Borum, "Greenland—Denmark's Colony," *Danish Foreign Office Journal*, nos. 1 and 2 (1948): 10.

71 Herman Ralph Friis, "Greenland: A Productive Arctic Colony," (1937), 84.

72 Borum, "Greenland—Denmark's Colony," 7.

73 McGhee, *The Last Imaginary Place: A Human History of the Arctic World*, 109.

74 For a broader discussion of Inuit relocation schemes, see Alan R. Marcus, *Relocating Eden: The Image and Politics of Inuit Exile in the Canadian Arctic*, Arctic Visions (Hanover: Dartmouth College: University Press of New England, 1995).

75 Finn Nielsen, "Planned Reforms in Greenland," *Arctic* 4, no. 1 (1951): 12.

76 Friis, "Greenland: A Productive Arctic Colony," 88.

77 Norway, "Norway and East Greenland, a Short Survey" (Oslo: A/S Norwegian Publications, 1931), 3.

78 Peder Roberts, "Nordic or National? Post-War Visions of Polar Conflict and Cooperation," in *Science, Geopolitics and Culture in the Polar Regions*, ed. Sverker Sörlin (Farnham, Surrey: Ashgate, 2013).

79 Norway, "Norway and East Greenland, a Short Survey," 3.

80 Ibid., 20.

81 Ibid., 23.

82 Bobe, "Greenland—A Two Hundredth Anniversary," 664.

83 Sydney H. Ball, *The Mineral Resources of Greenland* (Copenhagen: Bianco Lunos Bogtrykkeri, 1922), 1.

84 Friis, "Greenland: A Productive Arctic Colony," 90.

85 Lloyd, "Progress in West Greenland."

86 For an example from another part of the world see Davis, *Resurrecting the Granary of Rome: Environmental History and French Colonial Expansion in North Africa.*

87 Scott, *Seeing Like a State: How Certain Schemes to Improve the Human Condition Have Failed.*

88 Brody, *Living Arctic: Hunters of the Canadian North.*

89 Earl P. Hanson, "Should We Buy Greenland?," *Harper's Magazine* 180, May (1940).

90 Erling Porsild, "Greenland at the Crossroads," *Arctic* 1, no. 1 (1948).

5. War and Peace

1 See, for example, John Robert McNeill, *Something New Under the Sun: An Environmental History of the Twentieth-Century World* (New York: W.W. Norton, 2000). McNeill and Unger, *Environmental Histories of the Cold War*.

2 Scott, *Seeing Like a State: How Certain Schemes to Improve the Human Condition Have Failed*.

3 Anderson and Nuttall, *Cultivating Arctic Landscapes: Knowing and Managing Animals in the Circumpolar North*, 3.

4 Emmerson, *The Future History of the Arctic*, 110.

5 A good summary of much of this literature can be found in Ronald E. Doel, Urban Wråkberg, and Suzanne Zeller, "Science, Environment, and the New Arctic," *Journal of Historical Geography* 44 (2014).

6 See, for example, Emmerson, *The Future History of the Arctic*, 41.

7 See, for example, John Grierson, *Air Whaler* (London: Low, 1949).

8 See, for example, Dorsey, *Whales and Nations: Environmental Diplomacy on the High Seas*.

9 Robert L. Friedheim, *Toward a Sustainable Whaling Regime* (Seattle: University of Washington Press, 2001).

10 Pálsson, *Travelling Passions: The Hidden Life of Vilhjalmur Stefansson*.

11 Josephson, *The Conquest of the Russian Arctic*. For other discussions of the Soviet Arctic, see Pier Horensma, *The Soviet Arctic* (London, New York: Routledge, 1991); John McCannon, *Red Arctic: Polar Exploration and the Myth of the North in the Soviet Union, 1932–1939* (New York: Oxford University Press, 1998).

12 Josephson, *The Conquest of the Russian Arctic*.

13 Emmerson, *The Future History of the Arctic*, 40.

14 Ibid.

15 Ibid., 31.

16 Josephson, *The Conquest of the Russian Arctic*, 19.

17 Emmerson, *The Future History of the Arctic*, 42.

18 Josephson, *The Conquest of the Russian Arctic*, 141.

19 Emmerson, *The Future History of the Arctic*, 44.

20 Ibid., 41.

21 McNeill, *Something New Under the Sun: An Environmental History of the Twentieth-Century World*, 86.

22 Andrews, *Killing for Coal: America's Deadliest Labor War*.

23 Yuri Slezkine, *Arctic Mirrors: Russia and the Small Peoples of the North* (Ithaca, NY: Cornell University Press, 1994).

24 B. Grant, "Siberia Hot and Cold: Reconstructing the Image of Siberian Indigenous Peoples," in *Between Heaven and Hell: The Myth of Siberia in Russian Culture*, ed. Galya Diment and Yuri Slezkine (New York: St. Martin's Press, 1993); Patty A. Gray, "Chukotkan Reindeer Husbandry in the Twentieth Century: In the Image of the Soviet Economy," in *Cultivating Arctic Landscapes: Knowing and Managing Animals in the Circumpolar North*, ed. David G. Anderson and Mark Nuttall (New York: Berghahn Books, 2004).

25 Quoted in Emmerson, *The Future History of the Arctic*, 52.

26 Josephson, *The Conquest of the Russian Arctic*, 171.

27 Ibid., 89.

28 Emmerson, *The Future History of the Arctic*, 52.

29 Ibid., 159.

30 Josephson, *The Conquest of the Russian Arctic*, 190.

31 Emmerson, *The Future History of the Arctic*, 52.

32 Josephson, *The Conquest of the Russian Arctic*, 104.

33 *The Polar Times* 5, Oct. (1937), 1.

34 Emmerson, *The Future History of the Arctic*, 119.

35 Ibid.

36 Ibid., 114.

37 McNeill, *Something New Under the Sun: An Environmental History of the Twentieth-Century World*, 343.

38 Matthias Heymann et al., "Exploring Greenland: Science and Technology in Cold War Settings," *Scientia Canadensis* 33, no. 2 (2012).

39 Janet Martin-Nielsen, "The Other Cold War: The United States and Greenland's Ice Sheet Environment, 1948–1966," *Journal of Historical Geography* 38, no. 1 (2012).

40 See Chapter 6.

41 Emmerson, *The Future History of the Arctic*.

42 Stacey Anne Fritz, *DEW Line Passage: Tracing the Legacies of Arctic Militarization* (Fairbanks: University of Alaska Press, 2010), 4.

43 Ronald Doel, "Cold Conflict: The Pentagon's Fascination with the Arctic (and Climate Change) in the Early Cold War," in

Lashipa: History of Large Scale Resource Exploitation in Polar Areas, ed. Louwrens Hacquebord (Groningen: Barkhuis, 2012).

44 Matthew Farish, "The Lab and the Land: Overcoming the Arctic in Cold War Alaska," *Isis* 104(2013).

45 Dan O'Neill, *The Firecracker Boys: H-Bombs, Inupiat Eskimos, and the Roots of the Environmental Movement* (New York: Basic Books, 2007).

46 Lael Morgan, *Art and Eskimo Power: The Life and Times of Alaskan Howard Rock* (1988, 2008)

47 Richard Sale and Eugene Potapov, *The Scramble for the Arctic: Ownership, Exploitation and Conflict in the Far North* (London: Frances Lincoln, 2010).

48 Finn Ronne, *Antarctic Conquest; the Story of the Ronne Expedition, 1946–1948* (New York: Putnam's Sons, 1949).

49 See, for example, Rip Bulkeley, "Bellingshausen's First Accounts of His Antarctic Voyage of 1819–1821," *Polar Record* 49, no. 1 (2013).

50 Roger D. Launius, James Roger Fleming, and David H. DeVorkin, eds., *Globalizing Polar Science: Reconsidering the Social and Intellectual Implications of the International Polar and Geophysical Years* (New York: Palgrave, 2010); Susan Barr and Cornelia Luedecke, *The History of the International Polar Years (Ipys)* (Heidelberg: Springer, 2010).

51 Walter Sullivan, *Assault on the Unknown; the International Geophysical Year* (New York: McGraw-Hill, 1961).

52 For a firsthand account of this episode see Oscar Pinochet de la Barra, *Medio Siglo De Recuerdos Antárticos: Memorias* (Santiago de Chile: Editorial Universitaria, 1994).

53 Emmerson, *The Future History of the Arctic*, 54.

54 Vivian Fuchs and Edmund Hillary, *The Crossing of Antarctica: The Commonwealth Trans-Antarctic Expedition, 1955–1958* (London: Cassell, 1958).

55 Frank A. Simpson, ed., *The Antarctic Today: A Mid-Century Survey by the New Zealand Antarctic Society* (Wellington: A.H. and A.W. Reed in conjunction with the NZ Antarctic Society, 1952).

56 Howkins, "Appropriating Space: Antarctic Imperialism and the Mentality of Settler Colonialism."

57 For a partisan discussion of the results of the IGY from an American perspective, see Richard S. Lewis, *A Continent for Science: the Antarctic Adventure* (New York: Viking Press, 1965).

58 Christopher C. Joyner, *Eagle Over the Ice: The U.S. In the Antarctic* (Hanover, NH: University Press of New England, 1997).

59 For a complete text of the treaty see http://www.state.gov/t/avc/trty/193967.htm

60 Adolfo Scilingo, *El Tratado Antártico: Defensa De La Soberanía Y La Proscripción Nuclear* (Buenos Aires: Librería Hachette, 1963).

61 Berguño, "Intellectual Sources of the Antarctic Treaty," *Boletin Antartico Chileno*.

62 Adrian Howkins, "Defending Polar Empire: Opposition to India's Proposal to Raise the 'Antarctic Question' at the United Nations in 1956," *Polar Record* 44, no. 1 (2008); Sanjay Chaturvedi, "Rise and Decline of Antarctica in Nehru's Geopolitical Vision: Challenges and Opportunities of the 1950s," *The Polar Journal* 3, no. 2 (2013).

63 Frank Klotz, *America on the Ice: Antarctic Policy Issues* (Washington, DC: National Defense University Press, 1990); Joyner, *Eagle Over the Ice: The U.S. In the Antarctic*.

64 Alberto M. Candioti, *Nuestra Antártida No Es Tierra Conquistada Ni Anexada. El Tratado Antártico No Debe Ratificarse* (Buenos Aires, 1960).{AQ: Press?}

65 Howkins, "Reluctant Collaborators: Argentina and Chile in Antarctica During the IGY."

66 "Melting Empires? Climate Change and Politics in Antarctica Since the International Geophysical Year."{AQ: Author?}

67 Alessandro Antonello, "The Greening of Antarctica: Environment, Science and Diplomacy" (Australian National University, 2014). {AQ: Dissertation?} See also "Nature Conservation and Antarctic Diplomacy, 1959–1964," *The Polar Journal* 4, no. 2 (2014).

68 McEvoy, *The Fisherman's Problem: Ecology and Law in the California Fisheries, 1850–1980*.

69 Dorsey, *Whales and Nations: Environmental Diplomacy on the High Seas*.

70 Burnett, *The Sounding of the Whale: Science & Cetaceans in the Twentieth Century*.

71 Dorsey, *Whales and Nations: Environmental Diplomacy on the High Seas*, 92.

72 Mark Cioc, "The Antarctic Whale Massacre," in *The Game of*

Conservation: International Treaties to Protect the World's Migratory Animals (Athens: Ohio University Press, 2009).

73 Gerald Elliot, *A Whaling Enterprise: Salvesen in the Antarctic* (Wilby, Norwich: Michael Russell, 1998).

74 Grierson, *Air Whaler.*

75 Dorsey, *Whales and Nations: Environmental Diplomacy on the High Seas.*

76 Ibid., 130–31.

77 Ibid., 156.

78 Friedheim, *Toward a Sustainable Whaling Regime.*

79 Dorsey, *Whales and Nations: Environmental Diplomacy on the High Seas,* 163–64.

80 See, for example, Charlotte Epstein, *The Power of Words in International Relations: Birth of an Anti-Whaling Discourse* (Cambridge, MA: MIT Press, 2008). There is also an extended discussion in Burnett, *The Sounding of the Whale: Science & Cetaceans in the Twentieth Century.*

81 Frank S. Zelko, *Make It a Green Peace!: The Rise of Countercultural Environmentalism* (New York: Oxford University Press, 2013).

82 Dorsey, *Whales and Nations: Environmental Diplomacy on the High Seas,* 249.

83 Ibid., 267.

84 Ibid., 284.

85 Peter Heller, *The Whale Warriors: The Battle at the Bottom of the World to Save the Planet's Largest Mammals* (New York: Free Press, 2007).

6. Exploitation and Preservation

1 Roderick, *Crude Dreams: A Personal History of Oil & Politics in Alaska.*

2 Ibid., 217.

3 Roger Kaye, *Last Great Wilderness: The Campaign to Establish the Arctic National Wildlife Refuge* (Fairbanks: University of Alaska Press, 2006).

4 For a detailed discussion of Antarctic geology, see Hansom and Gordon, *Antarctic Environments and Resources: A Geographical Perspective.*

5 See, for example, May 2, 1990, Statement of James N. Barnes to the House Subcommittee on Human Rights and International

Organizations of the Committee on Foreign Affairs Concerning Antarctica [CHECK FF]{AQ: is this ready? Do you need to do this check?} USA Denver Public Library (DPL) Wilderness Society CONS 130 Series 5 Box 16. FF2 TWS Teare, John. Antarctica, HR 3977, HR 4210 Antarctic Environmental Protection: Notes, Statements, Testimony, Text of Bill.

6 Justice Thomas R. Berger [Supreme Court of B.C. and Commissioner of the Mackenzie Valley Pipeline Inquiry], "The Geography of Hope" address to the Arctic Institute of North America, Monday, Nov. 21, 1977, Fawcett Center for Tomorrow at Ohio State University. USA UA Fairbanks Archives (UAF) George L Collins Paper, Series 3: Arctic International Wildlife Range Society. Box 3. File 21. AIWRS – 1977.

7 See, for example, Meredith Hooper, *The Ferocious Summer: Palmer's Penguins and the Warming of Antarctica* (London: Profile Books, 2007).

8 Howkins, "Melting Empires? Climate Change and Politics in Antarctica since the International Geophysical Year; Brandon Luedtke and Adrian Howkins, "Polarized Climates: The Distinctive Histories of Climate Change and Politics in the Arctic and Antarctica since the Beginning of the Cold War," *Wiley Interdisciplinary Reviews: Climate Change* 3, no. 2 (2012).

9 Douglas Brinkley, *The Quiet World: Saving Alaska's Wilderness Kingdom, 1879–1960* (New York: Harper, 2011).

10 Hugh F. I. Elliott, *Second World Conference on National Parks* (Morges, Switzerland: International Union for Conservation of Nature and Natural Resources, 1974).

11 Robert Marshall, *Arctic Village* (New York: H. Smith and R. Haas, 1933).

12 See, for example, Margaret E. Murie, *Two in the Far North* (New York: Knopf, 1962).

13 George L. Collins and Lowell Sumner, A Proposed Arctic Wilderness International Park: A Preliminary Report Concerning Its Values, Alaska Recreation Survey, Preliminary Statement, Nov. 1952, Arctic Wilderness International Park, U.S. Department of the Interior, National Park Service, Region Four, 20. George Collins Papers (University of Alaska Fairbanks Archive)

14 Paul Sutter, *Driven Wild: How the Fight Against Automobiles Launched the Modern Wilderness Movement*, Weyerhaeuser Environmental Books (Seattle: University of Washington Press, 2002).

15 See discussion in Kaye, *Last Great Wilderness: The Campaign to Establish the Arctic National Wildlife Refuge*.

16 Cole, *North to the Future: The Alaska Story, 1959–2009*; Claus-M. Naske and Herman E. Slotnick, *Alaska: A History* (Norman: University of Oklahoma Press, 2011).

17 Kaye, *Last Great Wilderness: The Campaign to Establish the Arctic National Wildlife Refuge*.

18 See discussion in Roderick, *Crude Dreams: A Personal History of Oil & Politics in Alaska*.

19 Ibid., 168.

20 Coates, *The Trans-Alaska Pipeline Controversy: Technology, Conservation, and the Frontier*.

21 Hensley, *Fifty Miles from Tomorrow: A Memoir of Alaska and the Real People*.

22 Elizabeth James, "Toward Alaska Native Political Organization," *The Western Historical Quarterly* 41, no. 3 (2010). For a broader discussion see O'Neill, *The Firecracker Boys: H-Bombs, Inupiat Eskimos and the Roots of the Environmental Movement*.

23 Theodore Catton, *Inhabited Wilderness: Indians, Eskimos, and National Parks in Alaska*, New American West Series (Albuquerque: University of New Mexico Press, 1997).

24 Hensley, *Fifty Miles from Tomorrow: A Memoir of Alaska and the Real People*.

25 Mitchell, *Take My Land, Take My Life: The Story of Congress's Historic Settlement of Alaska Native Land Claims, 1960–1971*.

26 James Morton Turner, *The Promise of Wilderness: American Environmental Politics since 1964* (Seattle: University of Washington, 2012).

27 Fiege, *The Republic of Nature: An Environmental History of the United States*.

28 Turner, *The Promise of Wilderness: American Environmental Politics since 1964*.

29 http://www.antarcticmarc.com/bahia.html

30 Hansom and Gordon, *Antarctic Environments and Resources: A Geographical Perspective*.

31 Organization, *Question of Antarctica: Study Requested Under General Assembly Resolution 38/77 Report of the Secretary General.*

32 For an interesting discussion of this episode, see Griffiths, *Slicing the Silence: Voyaging to Antarctica.*

33 Remarks of Senator Al Gore. Hearing on Legislation Relating to Protection of the Antarctic Environment. Committee on Foreign Relations. U.S. Senate, July 27, 1990. USA Denver Public Library (DPL) Wilderness Society CONS 130 Series 5 Box 16. FF23 – November 1990 – Alliance for Antarctica: press packet.

34 Antonello, "Nature Conservation and Antarctic Diplomacy, 1959–1964."

35 Spencer R. Weart, *The Discovery of Global Warming*, rev. and expanded ed. (Cambridge, MA: Harvard University Press, 2008).

36 Mark Carey et al., "Forum Introduction," *Environmental History* 19, no. 2 (2014).

37 M. Hulme, *Why We Disagree About Climate Change: Understanding Controversy, Inaction and Opportunity* (Cambridge: Cambridge University Press, 2009).

38 Luedtke and Howkins, "Polarized Climates: The Distinctive Histories of Climate Change and Politics in the Arctic and Antarctica since the Beginning of the Cold War."

39 Weart, *The Discovery of Global Warming.*

40 Hooper, *The Ferocious Summer: Palmer's Penguins and the Warming of Antarctica.*

41 Sverker Sörlin, "The Anxieties of a Science Diplomat: Field Co-Production of Climate Knowledge and the Rise and Fall of Hans Ahlmann's 'Polar Warming'," *Osiris* 26 (2011).

42 See discussion in Weart, *The Discovery of Global Warming.*

43 Paul N. Edwards, *A Vast Machine: Computer Models, Climate Data, and the Politics of Global Warming* (Cambridge, MA: MIT Press, 2010).

44 BAS Archives.

45 Sörlin, "The Anxieties of a Science Diplomat: Field Co-Production of Climate Knowledge and the Rise and Fall of Hans Ahlmann's 'Polar Warming'."

46 Richard Elliot Benedick, *Ozone Diplomacy: New Directions in*

Safeguarding the Planet (Cambridge, MA: Harvard University Press, 1998).

47 Maureen Christie, *Ozone Layer: A Philosophy of Science Perspective* (Cambridge: Cambridge University Press, 2001).

48 Howkins, "Melting Empires? Climate Change and Politics in Antarctica Since the International Geophysical Year."

49 Many discussions exist of contemporary Arctic politics. See, for example, Kristine Offerdal and Rolf Tamnes, *Geopolitics and Security in the Arctic: Regional Dynamics in a Global World*, Routledge Global Security Studies (2014), text.{AQ: Give standard publication information please}

50 Hannes Gerhardt et al., "Contested Sovereignty in a Changing Arctic," *Annals of the Association of American Geographers* 100, no. 4 (2010).

51 Howkins, "Melting Empires? Climate Change and Politics in Antarctica since the International Geophysical Year."

52 Sara Wheeler, *Cherry: A Life of Apsley Cherry-Garrard* (New York: Random House, 2002).

53 Joan N. Boothe, *The Storied Ice: Exploration, Discovery, and Adventure in Antarctica's Peninsula Region* (Berkeley, CA: Regent Press, 2011).

54 Richard West Sellars, *Preserving Nature in the National Parks: A History* (New Haven, CT: Yale University Press, 2009).

55 http://iaato.org/home

56 BAS, *Antarctic Peninsula: A Visitor's Guide* (London: Natural History Museum, 2012).

Conclusion

1 Justice Thomas R. Berger [Supreme Court of B.C. and Commissioner of the Mackenzie Valley Pipeline Inquiry], "The Geography of Hope" address to the Arctic Institute of North America, Monday, Nov. 21, 1977, Fawcett Center for Tomorrow at Ohio State University. USA UA Fairbanks Archives (UAF) George L Collins Paper, Series 3: Arctic International Wildlife Range Society. Box 3. File 21. AIWRS – 1977.

2 Quoted in Nancy LeBlond, January 1982 Memo to Board of Directors of the AIWRS, Jan. 5, 1982 USA UA Fairbanks Archives

(UAF) George L Collins Paper, Series 3: Arctic International Wildlife Range Society. BOX 5. File 33. AIWRS – 1982

3 Berger, 22.

4 Berger, 24

5 Fritz, *DEW Line Passage: Tracing the Legacies of Arctic Militarization.*

6 Subhankar Banerjee, *Arctic Voices: Resistance at the Tipping Point* (New York: Seven Stories Press, 2012).

7 Julie Cruikshank, "Uses and Abuses of 'Traditional Knowledge': Perspectives from the Yukon Territory," in *Cultivating Arctic Landscapes: Knowing and Managing Animals in the Circumpolar North,* ed. David G. Anderson and Mark Nuttall (New York: Berghahn Books, 2004), 31; Carey et al., "Forum Introduction."

8 "Forum Introduction." Julia Adeney Thomas, "Comment: Not Yet Far Enough," *The American Historical Review* 117, no. 3 (2012).

9 See, for example, Adam M. Sowards, *The Environmental Justice: William O. Douglas and American Conservation* (Corvallis: Oregon State University Press, 2009).

BIBLIOGRAPHY

Adcock, Christina. "Tracing Warm Lines: Northern Canadian Exploration, Knowledge, and Memory, 1905–1965." Cambridge: Cambridge University, 2010.

Amundsen, Roald. *Roald Amundsen: My Life as an Explorer*. Garden City, NY: Doubleday, Page, 1927.

Anderson, David G., and Mark Nuttall. *Cultivating Arctic Landscapes: Knowing and Managing Animals in the Circumpolar North*. New York: Berghahn Books, 2004.

Andrews, Thomas G. *Killing for Coal: America's Deadliest Labor War*. Cambridge, MA: Harvard University Press, 2008.

Antonello, Alessandro. "The Greening of Antarctica: Environment, Science and Diplomacy." Canberra: Australian National University, 2014.

———. "Nature Conservation and Antarctic Diplomacy, 1959–1964." *The Polar Journal* 4, no. 2 (2014): 335–53.

Armstrong, Terence, George William Rogers, and Graham Rowley. *The Circumpolar North: A Political and Economic Geography of the Arctic and Sub-Arctic*. London: Methuen, 1978.

Avango, Dag, Louwrens Hacquebord, and Urban Wråkberg. "Industrial Extraction of Arctic Natural Resources Since the Sixteenth Century: Technoscience and Geo-Economics in the History of Northern

Whaling and Mining." *Journal of Historical Geography* 44 (2014): 15–30.

Ball, Sydney H. Ball. "The Mineral Resources of Greenland." Copenhagen: Bianco Lunos Bogtrykkeri, 1922.

Banerjee, Subhankar. *Arctic Voices: Resistance at the Tipping Point.* New York: Seven Stories Press, 2012.

Barr, Susan, and Cornelia Luedecke. *The History of the International Polar Years (Ipys).* Heidelberg: Springer, 2010.

BAS. *Antarctic Peninsula: A Visitor's Guide.* London: Natural History Museum, 2012.

Basberg, Bjørn, and Robert Headland. "The 19th Century Antarctic Sealing Industry: Sources, Data and Economic Significance." *NHH Dept. of Economics Discussion Paper,* no. 21 (2008): 1–26.

Beaglehole, J. C. *The Life of Captain James Cook.* Stanford, CA: Stanford University Press, 1974.

Bellingshausen, Thaddeus, and Frank Debenham. *The Voyage of Captain Bellingshausen to the Antartic Seas 1819–1821.* London: Hakluyt Society, 1945.

Benedick, Richard Elliot. *Ozone Diplomacy: New Directions in Safeguarding the Planet.* Cambridge, MA: Harvard University Press, 1998.

Berglund, Joel. "Did the Medieval Norse Society in Greenland Really Fail?" In *Questioning Collapse: Human Resilience, Ecological Vulnerability, and the Aftermath of Empire,* ed. Patricia Ann McAnany and Norman Yoffee, 2010.

Berguño, Jorge. "Intellectual Sources of the Antarctic Treaty." *Boletin Antartico Chileno* (2009).

Bertrand, Kenneth John. *Americans in Antarctica, 1775–1948.* New York: American Geographical Society, 1971.

Bobe, Louis. "Greenland: Two Hundredth Anniversary." *The American-Scandinavian Review* 9, no. 10 (1921): 659–65.

Boothe, Joan N. *The Storied Ice: Exploration, Discovery, and Adventure in Antarctica's Peninsula Region.* Berkeley, CA: Regent Press, 2011.

Born, Erik W. *The Walrus in Greenland.* Nuuk: Ilinniusiorfik Education, 2005.

Borum, V. "Greenland: Denmark's Colony." *Danish Foreign Office Journal,* nos. 1 and 2 (1948): 1–16.

Bravo, Michael, and Sverker Sörlin. *Narrating the Arctic: A Cultural*

History of Nordic Scientific Practices. Canton, MA: Science History Publications, 2002.

Brinkley, Douglas. *The Quiet World: Saving Alaska's Wilderness Kingdom, 1879–1960.* New York: Harper, 2011.

Brody, Hugh. *Living Arctic: Hunters of the Canadian North.* Vancouver: Douglas & McIntyre, 1987.

Bulkeley, Rip. "Bellingshausen's First Accounts of His Antarctic Voyage of 1819–1821." *Polar Record* 49, no. 1 (2013): 9–25.

Burn Murdoch, W. G., and William Speirs Bruce. *From Edinburgh to the Antarctic.* London and New York: Longmans, Green, 1894.

Burnett, D. Graham. *The Sounding of the Whale: Science and Cetaceans in the Twentieth Century.* Chicago: The University of Chicago Press, 2012.

Burton, Robert. *Southern Horizons: The History of the British Antarctic Territory.* London: United Kingdom Antarctic Heritage Trust, 2008.

Bushell, Sharon, and Stan Jones. *The Spill: Personal Stories from the Exxon Valdez Disaster.* Kenmore, WA: Epicenter Press, 2009.

Byrd, Richard Evelyn. *Alone.* New York: G. P. Putnam's sons, 1938.

Campbell, Craig. "A Genealogy of the Concept of 'Wanton Slaughter' in Canadian Wildlife Biology." In *Cultivating Arctic Landscapes: Knowing and Managing Animals in the Circumpolar North,* ed. David G. Anderson and Mark Nuttall. New York: Berghahn Books, 2004.

Cañas Montalva, Ramón. *El Valor Geopolitico De La Posicion Antartica De Chile.* 1953.{AQ: more info needed? See also next entry.}

Candioti, Alberto M. *Nuestra Antártida No Es Tierra Conquistada Ni Anexada. El Tratado AntáRtico No Debe Ratificarse.* Buenos Aires, 1960.

Carey, Mark, Philip Garone, Adrian Howkins, Georgina Endfield, Lawrence Culver, Sherry Johnson, Sam White, and James Rodger Fleming. "Forum Introduction." *Environmental History* 19, no. 2 (2014): 282–364.

Catton, Theodore. *Inhabited Wilderness: Indians, Eskimos, and National Parks in Alaska.* New American West Series. Albuquerque: University of New Mexico Press, 1997.

Chadwick, John Oldfield. "Perseverance in Arctic Exploration: An Enquiry Whether the Advantages Which May Be Expected to Result from a Successful Expedition to the North Pole Are

Sufficient to Justify Further Efforts in the Attempt." London, 1877. {AQ: Press?}

Chaturvedi, Sanjay. "Rise and Decline of Antarctica in Nehru's Geopolitical Vision: Challenges and Opportunities of the 1950s." *The Polar Journal* 3, no. 2 (2013): 301–15.

Cherry-Garrard, Apsley. *The Worst Journey in the World, Antarctic, 1910–1913.* London: Constable, 1922.

Christie, Eric William Hunter. *The Antarctic Problem: an Historical and Political Study.* London: Allen & Unwin, 1951.

Christie, Maureen. *Ozone Layer: A Philosophy of Science Perspective.* Cambridge: Cambridge University Press, 2001.

Cioc, Mark. "The Antarctic Whale Massacre." In *The Game of Conservation: International Treaties to Protect the World's Migratory Animals.* Athens: Ohio University Press, 2009.

Coates, Peter. *The Trans-Alaska Pipeline Controversy: Technology, Conservation, and the Frontier.* Bethlehem, PA: Lehigh University Press, 1991.

Cole, Dermot. *North to the Future: The Alaska Story, 1959–2009.* Alaska Book Adventures. Kenmore, WA: Epicenter Press, 2008.

Cole, Terrence. "Introduction." In *Across Arctic America,* ed. Knud Rasmussen. Fairbanks: University of Alaska Press, 1999.

Comaroff, Jean, and John L. Comaroff. *Of Revelation and Revolution: Christianity, Colonialism, and Consciousness in South Africa.* Chicago: University of Chicago Press, 1991.

Cook, Frederick Albert. *Through the First Antarctic Night, 1898–9.* [S.l.]: Heinemann, 1900.

Cook, James, J. C. Beaglehole, and R. A. Skelton. *The Journals of Captain James Cook on His Voyages of Discovery.* Rochester, NY: Boydell Press, 1999.

Cordovez Madariaga, Enrique. *La Antártida Sudamericana.* Santiago, Chile: Nascimento, 1945.

Cronin, Marionne. "Technological Heroes: Images of the Arctic in the Age of Polar Exploration." In *Northscapes: History, Technology, and the Making of Northern Environments,* ed. Dolly Jørgensen and Sverker Sörlin. Vancouver: UBC Press, 2013.

Cronon, William. *Changes in the Land: Indians, Colonists, and the Ecology of New England.* New York: Hill and Wang, 2003.

———. "Foreword." In *Whales and Nations: Environmental Diplomacy on the High Seas*, ed. Kurkpatrick Dorsey. Seattle: University of Washington Press, 2013.

———. "Landscapes of Abundance and Scarcity." In *The Oxford History of the American West*, ed. Clyde A. Milner, Carol A. O'Connor and Martha A. Sandweiss. Oxford, New York: Oxford University Press, 1994.

———. "The Trouble with Wilderness; or, Getting Back to the Wrong Nature." In *Uncommon Ground: Rethinking the Human Place in Nature*, ed. William Cronon, 69–90. New York: W.W. Norton, 1995.

Cruikshank, Julie. *Do Glaciers Listen?: Local Knowledge, Colonial Encounters, and Social Imagination*. Brenda and David Mclean Canadian Studies Series. Vancouver: UBC Press, 2005.

———. "Uses and Abuses of 'Traditional Knowledge': Perspectives from the Yukon Territory." In *Cultivating Arctic Landscapes: Knowing and Managing Animals in the Circumpolar North*, ed. David G. Anderson and Mark Nuttall. New York: Berghahn Books, 2004.

Damas, David. *Handbook of North American Indians Volume 5: Arctic*. Handbook of North American Indians, ed. W. C. Sturtevant. Vol. 5: Arctic Smithsonian Insitution 1984.

Davis, Diana K. *Resurrecting the Granary of Rome: Environmental History and French Colonial Expansion in North Africa*. Athens: Ohio University Press, 2007.

Deloria, Vine. *Custer Died for Your Sins: An Indian Manifesto*. Norman: University of Oklahoma Press, 1988.

Diamond, Jared M. *Collapse: How Societies Choose to Fail or Succeed*. New York: Viking, 2005.

Dickinson, Anthony Bertram. *Seal Fisheries of the Falkland Islands and Dependencies: An Historical Review*. Research in Maritime History, St. John's, Nfld.: International Maritime Economic History Association, 2007.

Doel, Ronald. "Cold Conflict: The Pentagon's Fascination with the Arctic (and Climate Change) in the Early Cold War." In *Lashipa: History of Large Scale Resource Exploitation in Polar Areas*, ed. Louwrens Hacquebord. Groningen: Barkhuis, 2012.

Doel, Ronald E., Urban Wråkberg, and Suzanne Zeller. "Science,

Environment, and the New Arctic." *Journal of Historical Geography* 44 (2014): 2–14.

Dorsey, Kurkpatrick. *Whales and Nations: Environmental Diplomacy on the High Seas.* Weyerhaeuser Environmental Books. 2013.{AQ: this googles as a University of Washington Press book. Which is it, and if it's Weyerhaeuser, what is the city of publication?}

Drayton, Richard Harry. *Nature's Government: Science, Imperial Britain, and the "Improvement" of the World.* New Haven, CT: Yale University Press, 2000.

Dyhrenfurth, Günter Oskar. *To the Third Pole: The History of the High Himalaya.* London: W. Laurie, 1955.

Edwards, Paul N. *A Vast Machine: Computer Models, Climate Data, and the Politics of Global Warming.* Cambridge, MA: MIT Press, 2010.

Elliot, Gerald. *A Whaling Enterprise: Salvesen in the Antarctic.* Wilby, Norwich: Michael Russell, 1998.

Elliott, Hugh F. I. *Second World Conference on National Parks.* Morges, Switzerland: International Union for Conservation of Nature and Natural Resources, 1974.

Elzinga, Aant. *Antarctic Challenges: Historical and Current Perspectives on Otto Nordenskjöld's Antarctic Expedition, 1901–1903.* Göteborg: Royal Society of Arts and Sciences, 2004.

Emmerson, Charles. *The Future History of the Arctic.* New York: PublicAffairs, 2010.

Epstein, Charlotte. *The Power of Words in International Relations: Birth of an Anti-Whaling Discourse.* Politics, Science, and the Environment. Cambridge, MA: MIT Press, 2008.

Farish, Matthew. "The Lab and the Land: Overcoming the Arctic in Cold War Alaska." *Isis* 104 (2013): 1–29.

Fiege, Mark. *The Republic of Nature: An Environmental History of the United States.* Seattle: University of Washington Press, 2012.

Fleming, Fergus. *Barrow's Boys.* London: Granta Books, 1998.

Fogg, G. E. *A History of Antarctic Science.* Studies in Polar Research. Cambridge: Cambridge University Press, 1992.

Friedheim, Robert L. *Toward a Sustainable Whaling Regime.* Seattle: University of Washington Press, 2001.

Friis, Herman Ralph. "Greenland: A Productive Arctic Colony." 1937. {AQ: Publication info here?}

Fritz, Stacey Anne. "Dew Line Passage: Tracing the Legacies of Arctic Militarization." University of Alaska Fairbanks, 2010.{AQ: Publication info here?}

Fuchs, Vivian, and Edmund Hillary. *The Crossing of Antarctica; the Commonwealth Trans-Antarctic Expedition, 1955–1958.* London: Cassell, 1958.

Gascoigne, John. *Science in the Service of Empire: Joseph Banks, the British State and the Uses of Science in the Age of Revolution.* Cambridge: Cambridge University Press, 1998.

Genest, Eugenio A. *Pujato Y La Antártida Argentina En La Década Del Cincuenta.* Buenos Aires, Argentina: H. Senado de la Nación, Secretaría Parlamentaria, Dirección Publicaciones, 1998.

Gerhardt, Hannes, Philip E. Steinberg, Jeremy Tasch, Sandra J. Fabiano, and Rob Shields. "Contested Sovereignty in a Changing Arctic." *Annals of the Association of American Geographers* 100, no. 4 (2010): 992–1002.

Gibbons, Russell W. "Dr Cook: An American Dreyfus in the Arctic." *North* 15, no. 2 (1968).

Ginzburg, Carlo. "Making Things Strange: The Prehistory of a Literary Device." *Representations* 56, Special Issue: The New Erudition (1996): 8–28.

González Videla, Gabriel. *Memorias.* Santiago de Chile: Gabriela Mistral, 1975.

Grace, Sherrill. *Canada and the Idea of North.* Montreal, London: McGill-Queen's University Press, 2002.

Grant, B. "Siberia Hot and Cold: Reconstructing the Image of Siberian Indigenous Peoples." In *Between Heaven and Hell: The Myth of Siberia in Russian Culture*, ed. Galya Diment and Yuri Slezkine: St. Martin's Press, 1993.

Gray, Patty A.. "Chukotkan Reindeer Husbandry in the Twentieth Century: In the Image of the Soviet Economy." In *Cultivating Arctic Landscapes: Knowing and Managing Animals in the Circumpolar North*, ed. David G. Anderson and Mark Nuttall, xvi, 238. New York: Berghahn Books, 2004.

Grierson, John. *Air Whaler.* London: Low, 1949.

Griffiths, Tom. *Slicing the Silence: Voyaging to Antarctica.* Cambridge, MA: Harvard University Press, 2007.

Gurney, Alan. *Below the Convergence: Voyages toward Antarctica, 1699–1839*. New York: Norton, 1997.

Hacquebord, Louwrens. *Lashipa: History of Large Scale Resource Exploitation in Polar Areas*. Groningen: Barkhuis Pub., 2012.

Hains, Brigid. *The Ice and the Inland: Mawson, Flynn, and the Myth of the Frontier*. Carlton South, Vic.: Melbourne University Press, 2002.

Hanley, Anne, and Carolyn Kremers. *The Alaska Reader: Voices from the North*. Golden, CO: Fulcrum, 2005.

Hansom, James D., and John E. Gordon. *Antarctic Environments and Resources: A Geographical Perspective*. New York: Longman, 1998.

Hanson, Earl P. "Should We Buy Greenland?" *Harper's Magazine* 180, May (1940).

Hardin, Garrett. "The Tragedy of the Commons." *Science* 162 (1968): 1243–48.

Harkin, Michael Eugene, and David Rich Lewis. *Native Americans and the Environment: Perspectives on the Ecological Indian*. Lincoln: University of Nebraska Press, 2007.

Hart, Ian B. *Pesca: The History of Compañia Argentina De Pesca Sociedad Anónima of Buenos Aires: An Account of the Pioneer Modern Whaling and Sealing Company in the Antarctic*. Rev. ed. Salcombe: Aidan Ellis, 2002.

———. *Whaling in the Falkland Islands Dependencies, 1904–1931*. Newton St. Margarets, Herefordshire: Pequena, 2006.

Headland, Robert. *A Chronology of Antarctic Exploration: A Synopsis of Events and Activities from the Earliest Times until the International Polar Years, 2007–09*. London: Bernard Quaritch, 2009.

———. *The Island of South Georgia*. Cambridge: Cambridge University Press, 1984.

Heller, Peter. *The Whale Warriors: The Battle at the Bottom of the World to Save the Planet's Largest Mammals*. New York: Free Press, 2007.

Hensley, William L. Iġġiaġruk. *Fifty Miles from Tomorrow: A Memoir of Alaska and the Real People*. New York: Sarah Crichton Books, 2009.

Henson, Matthew Alexander. *Henson at the North Pole*. Mineola, NY: Dover, 2008.

Heymann, Matthias, Henrik Knudsen, Lykke Maiken, Henry Nielsen, Kristian Hvidtfelt Nielsen, and Christopher Jocob Ries. "Exploring Greenland: Science and Technology in Cold War Settings." *Scientia Canadensis* 33, no. 2 (2012): 11–42.

Hooper, Meredith. *The Ferocious Summer: Palmer's Penguins and the Warming of Antarctica*. London: Profile Books, 2007.

Horensma, Pier. *The Soviet Arctic*. London, New York: Routledge, 1991.

Howkins, Adrian. "Appropriating Space: Antarctic Imperialism and the Mentality of Settler Colonialism." In *Making Settler Colonial Space: Perspectives on Race, Place and Identity*, ed. Tracey Banivanua Mar and Penelope Edmonds. Houndmills, Basingstoke: Palgrave Macmillan, 2010.

————. "Defending Polar Empire: Opposition to India's Proposal to Raise the 'Antarctic Question' at the United Nations in 1956." *Polar Record* 44, no. 1 (2008): 35–44.

————. "Icy Relations: The Emergence of South American Antarctica During the Second World War." *Polar Record* 42, no. 2 (2006): 153–65.

————. "Melting Empires? Climate Change and Politics in Antarctica since the International Geophysical Year." *Osiris* 26, no. 1 (2011): 180–97.

————. "Reluctant Collaborators: Argentina and Chile in Antarctica During the IGY." *Journal of Historical Geography* 34 (2008): 596–617.

————. "The Significance of the Frontier in Antarctic History: How the U.S. West Has Shaped the Geopolitics of the Far South." *The Polar Journal* (2013): 1–22.{AQ: Publication info?}

Hughes, J. Donald. *What Is Environmental History?* Cambridge: Polity, 2006.

Hulme, M. *Why We Disagree About Climate Change: Understanding Controversy, Inaction and Opportunity*. Cambridge: Cambridge University Press, 2009.

Huntford, Roland. *Scott and Amundsen*. 1st American ed. New York: Atheneum, 1984.

Hurley, Frank. *Argonauts of the South*. New York: Putnam's, 1925.

Innis, Harold Adams. *The Fur Trade in Canada: An Introduction to Canadian Economic History*. Toronto: University of Toronto Press, 1999.

James, Elizabeth. "Toward Alaska Native Political Organization." *The Western Historical Quarterly* 41, no. 3 (2010): 285–303.

Joerg, W. L. G. *Problems of Polar Research*. New York: American Geographical Society, 1928.

Jones, Max. *The Last Great Quest: Captain Scott's Antarctic Sacrifice.* Oxford: Oxford University Press, 2003.

Jones, Ryan Tucker. *Empire of Extinction: Russians and the North Pacific's Strange Beasts of the Sea, 1741–1867.* 2014.{AQ: Publication info?}

Jørgensen, Dolly, and Sverker Sörlin. "Making the Action Visible: Making Environments in Northern Landscapes." In *Northscapes: History, Technology, and the Making of Northern Environments,* ed. Dolly Jørgensen and Sverker Sörlin. Vancouver: UBC Press, 2013.

———. *Northscapes: History, Technology, and the Making of Northern Environments.* Vancouver: UBC Press, 2013..

Josephson, Paul R. *The Conquest of the Russian Arctic.* 2014. text.{AQ: Publication info?}

Joyner, Christopher C. *Eagle over the Ice: The U.S. In the Antarctic.* Hanover, NH: University Press of New England, 1997.

Kanaqlak Charles, George P. "Cultural Identity through Yupiaq Narrative." In *The Alaska Native Reader,* ed. Maria Sháa Tláa Williams. Durham: Duke University Press, 2009.

Kaye, Roger. *Last Great Wilderness: The Campaign to Establish the Arctic National Wildlife Refuge.* Fairbanks: University of Alaska Press, 2006.

Klotz, Frank. *America on the Ice: Antarctic Policy Issues.* Washington, DC: National Defense University Press, 1990.

Krech, Shepard. *The Ecological Indian: Myth and History.* New York: W.W. Norton, 1999.

Kruse, Frigga. "Frozen Assets: British Mining, Exploration, and Geopolitics on Spitsbergen, 1904–53." Rijksuniversiteit Groningen, 2013.

Larson, Edward J. *An Empire of Ice: Scott, Shackleton, and the Heroic Age of Antarctic Science.* New Haven, CT: Yale University Press, 2011.

Launius, Roger D., James Roger Fleming, and David H. DeVorkin, eds. *Globalizing Polar Science: Reconsidering the Social and Intellectual Implications of the International Polar and Geophysical Years.* New York: Palgrave, 2010.

Leal, Jorge Edgard. *"Operación 90".* Buenos Aires: Instituto Antártico Argentino, 1971.

Leane, Elizabeth. *Antarctica in Fiction: Imaginative Narratives of the Far South.* New York: Cambridge University Press, 2012.

Leitzell, Ted. "Peary's Conspiracy Against Dr. Cook: The Inside Story of the Famous Polar Controversy." *Real America*, October (1935).

Lewis, Michael L. *American Wilderness: A New History*. Oxford: Oxford University Press, 2007.

Lewis, Richard S. *A Continent for Science: the Antarctic Adventure*. New York: Viking Press, 1965.

Lloyd, Trevor. "Progress in West Greenland." *The Journal of Geography* 49, no. 8 (1950): 319–29.

Lopez, Barry Holstun. *Arctic Dreams: Imagination and Desire in a Northern Landscape*. New York: Scribner, 1986.

————. "Informed by Indifference: A Walk in Antarctica." *Harper's Magazine*, May (1988).

Luedtke, Brandon, and Adrian Howkins. "Polarized Climates: The Distinctive Histories of Climate Change and Politics in the Arctic and Antarctica Since the Beginning of the Cold War." *Wiley Interdisciplinary Reviews: Climate Change* 3, no. 2 (2012): 145–59.

Mar, Tracey Banivanua, and Penelope Edmonds, eds. *Making Space: Settler Colonial Perspectives on Place, Race and Identity*. Houndmills, Basingstoke, England: Palgrave Macmillan, 2010.

Marcus, Alan R. *Relocating Eden: The Image and Politics of Inuit Exile in the Canadian Arctic*. Arctic Visions. Hanover: University Press of New England, 1995.

Marshall, Robert. *Arctic Village*. New York: H. Smith and R. Haas, 1933.

Martin, Fredericka I. *The Hunting of the Silver Fleece: Epic of the Fur Seal*. New York: Greenberg, 1946.

Martin, Stephen. *A History of Antarctica*. Sydney: State Library of New South Wales Press, 1996.

Martin-Nielsen, Janet. "The Other Cold War: The United States and Greenland's Ice Sheet Environment, 1948–1966." *Journal of Historical Geography* 38, no. 1 (2012): 69–80.

Mawer, G. A. *South by Northwest: The Magnetic Crusade and the Contest for Antarctica*. Edinburgh: Birlinn, 2006.

McAnany, Patricia Ann, and Norman Yoffee. *Questioning Collapse: Human Resilience, Ecological Vulnerability, and the Aftermath of Empire*. Cambridge, New York: Cambridge University Press, 2010.

McCannon, John. *Red Arctic: Polar Exploration and the Myth of the North in the Soviet Union, 1932–1939.* New York: Oxford University Press, 1998.

McEvoy, Arthur F. *The Fisherman's Problem: Ecology and Law in the California Fisheries, 1850–1980.* Cambridge: Cambridge University Press, 1986.

McGhee, Robert. *The Last Imaginary Place: A Human History of the Arctic World.* Oxford, New York: Oxford University Press, 2005.

McNeill, John Robert. *Something New Under the Sun: An Environmental History of the Twentieth-Century World.* New York: W.W. Norton, 2000.

McNeill, John Robert, and Corinna R. Unger. *Environmental Histories of the Cold War.* Publications of the German Historical Institute. Washington, DC: Cambridge University Press, 2010.

Mill, Hugh Robert. *The Siege of the South Pole: The Story of Antarctic Exploration.* London: Alston Rivers, 1905.

Mitchell, Donald. *Take My Land, Take My Life: The Story of Congress's Historic Settlement of Alaska Native Land Claims, 1960–1971.* Fairbanks: University of Alaska Press, 2001.

Murie, Margaret E. *Two in the Far North.* New York,: Knopf, 1962.

Murray, James. *British Antarctic Expedition 1907–9 Reports on the Scientific Investigations. Volume 1: Biology* London: William Heinemann, 1911.

Nasht, Simon. *The Last Explorer: Hubert Wilkins, Hero of the Great Age of Polar Exploration.* New York: Arcade, 2006.

Naske, Claus-M., and Herman E. Slotnick. *Alaska: A History.* 3rd ed. Norman: University of Oklahoma Press, 2011.

Nichols, Peter. *Final Voyage: A Story of Arctic Disaster and One Fateful Whaling Season.* New York: G.P. Putnam's Sons, 2009.

Nielsen, Finn. "Planned Reforms in Greenland." *Arctic* 4, no. 1 (1951): 12–17.

Niven, Jennifer. *Ada Blackjack: A True Story of Survival in the Arctic.* New York: Hyperion, 2003.

———. *The Ice Master: The Doomed 1913 Voyage of the Karluk.* New York: Hyperion, 2000.

Norway. "Norway and East Greenland a Short Survey." Oslo: A/S Norwegian Publications, 1931.

O'Neill, Dan. *The Firecracker Boys: H-Bombs, Inupiat Eskimos and the Roots of the Environmental Movement.* New York: Basic Books, 2007.

Offerdal, Kristine, and Rolf Tamnes. *Geopolitics and Security in the Arctic: Regional Dynamics in a Global World*. Routledge Global Security Studies. 2014. text.

Organization, United Nations. *Question of Antarctica: Study Requested under General Assembly Resolution 38/77 Report of the Secretary General*. 4 vols. New York: United Publications, 1984.

Orsi, Jared. *Citizen Explorer: The Life of Zebulon Pike*. New York: Oxford University Press, 2014.

Ortiz Behety, Luis. *Antartida Argentina: Poemas De Las Tierras Procelares*. Buenos Aires, 1948.

Oslund, Karen. *Iceland Imagined: Nature, Culture, and Storytelling in the North Atlantic*. Weyerhaeuser Environmental Books. Seattle: University of Washington Press, 2011.

Ostrom, Elinor. *Governing the Commons: The Evolution of Institutions for Collective Action*. The Political Economy of Institutions and Decisions. Cambridge, New York: Cambridge University Press, 1990.

Ott, Riki. "They Have No Ears." In *Arctic Voices: Resistance at the Tipping Point*, ed. Subhankar Banerjee. New York: Seven Stories Press, 2012.

Pálsson, Gísli. *Travelling Passions: The Hidden Life of Vilhjalmur Stefansson*. Hanover, NH: Dartmouth College Press, University Press of New England, 2005.

Pinochet de la Barra, Oscar. *La Antártica Chilena*. Santiago de Chile: Editorial del Pacífico, 1948.

———. *Medio Siglo De Recuerdos Antárticos: Memorias*. Santiago de Chile: Editorial Universitaria, 1994.

Porsild, Erling. "Greenland at the Crossroads." *Arctic* 1, no. 1 (1948).

Potter, Jean Clark. *The Flying North*. New York: Macmillan, 1947.

Puig, Juan Carlos. *La Antártida Argentina Ante El Derecho*. Buenos Aires: R. Depalma, 1960.

Pyne, Stephen J. *The Ice*. London: Weidenfeld & Nicolson, 2003.

Quevedo Paiva, Adolfo E. *Medio Siglo Del Ejército Argentino En Nuestra Antártida: 1951–2001*. Buenos Aires: Editorial Dunken, 2001.

Quigg, Philip W. *A Pole Apart: The Emerging Issue of Antarctica*. New York: New Press, 1983.

Rasmussen, Knud. *Across Arctic America: Narrative of the Fifth Thule Expedition*. Classic Reprint Series. Fairbanks: University of Alaska Press, 1999.

———. *Intellectual Culture of the Iglulik Eskimos (Report of the Fifth Thule Expedition, 1921–24)*. Trans. W. Worster. Vol. 7, No. 1: Gyldendalske Boghandel, 1929.

Riffenburgh, Beau. *The Myth of the Explorer: The Press, Sensationalism, and Geographical Discovery*. Oxford: Oxford University Press, 1994.

Rigoz, Susana. *Hernán Pujato: El Conquistador Del Desierto Blanco*. Buenos Aires: Editorial María Ghirlanda, 2002.

Roberts, Peder. *The European Antarctic: Science and Strategy in Scandinavia and the British Empire*. New York: Palgrave Macmillan, 2011.

———. "Nordic or National? Post-War Visions of Polar Conflict and Cooperation." In *Science, Geopolitics and Culture in the Polar Regions*, ed. Sverker Sörlin. Farnham, Surrey: Ashgate, 2013.

Roberts, Peder, Klaus Dodds, and Lize-Marie van der Watt. "'But Why Do You Go There?' Norway and South Africa in the Antarctic Duuring the 1950s." In *Science, Geopolitics and Culture in the Polar Region: Norden Beyond Borders*, ed. Sverker Sörlin. Farnham: Ashgate, 2013.

Robin, Libby. *The Future of Nature: Documents of Global Change*. New Haven: Yale University Press, 2013.

Roderick, Jack. *Crude Dreams: A Personal History of Oil & Politics in Alaska*. Fairbanks, AK: Epicenter Press, 1997.

Ronne, Finn. *Antarctic Conquest; the Story of the Ronne Expedition, 1946–1948*. New York: Putnam's Sons, 1949.

Rose, Lisle Abbott. *Explorer: The Life of Richard E. Byrd*. Columbia: University of Missouri Press, 2008.

Rosing-Asvid, Aqqalu. *Seals of Greenland*. Gylling: Narayana Press, 2010.

Sachs, Aaron. *The Humboldt Current: A European Explorer and His American Disciples*. Oxford: Oxford University Press, 2007.

Sale, Richard, and Eugene Potapov. *The Scramble for the Arctic: Ownership, Exploitation and Conflict in the Far North*. London: Frances Lincoln, 2010.

Schuyesmans, Willy. *El Invierno Del Bélgica: Prisioneros De La Antártica*. Santiago de Chile: RIL, 2010.

Scilingo, Adolfo. *El Tratado Antártico; Defensa De La Soberanía Y La Proscripción Nuclear*. Buenos Aires: Librería Hachette, 1963.

Scott, James C. *Seeing Like a State: How Certain Schemes to Improve the Human Condition Have Failed.* New Haven, CT: Yale University Press, 1998.

Sellars, Richard West. *Preserving Nature in the National Parks: A History.* New Haven, CT: Yale University Press, 2009.

Senatore, Maria Ximena. "Antártida Como Narrativa." *Vestígios: Revista Latino-Americana de Arqueologia Histórica* 5, no. 2 (2011): 159–84.

Serrano, Miguel. *La Antártica Y Otros Mitos.* Santiago de Chile: Titania, 1948.

Simberloff, Daniel. *Invasive Species: What Everyone Needs to Know.* text. {AQ: Publication info?}

Simpson, Frank A. (ed.). *The Antarctic Today: A Mid-Century Survey by the New Zealand Antarctic Society.* Wellington: A.H. and A.W. Reed in conjunction with the NZ Antarctic Society, 1952.

Slezkine, Yuri. *Arctic Mirrors: Russia and the Small Peoples of the North.* Ithaca, NY: Cornell University Press, 1994.

Sörlin, Sverker. "The Anxieties of a Science Diplomat: Field Co-Production of Climate Knowledge and the Rise and Fall of Hans Ahlmann's 'Polar Warming'." *Osiris* 26 (2011): 66–88.

Sowards, Adam M. *The Environmental Justice: William O. Douglas and American Conservation.* Corvallis: Oregon State University Press, 2009.

Spufford, Francis. *I May Be Some Time: Ice and the English Imagination.* London: Faber and Faber, 1996.

Stallard, Avan Judd. "Origins of the Idea of Antipodes: Errors, Assumptions, and a Bare Few Facts." *Terrae Incognitae* 42 (2010): 34–51.

Stefansson, Vilhjalmur. *The Friendly Arctic; the Story of Five Years in Polar Regions.* New York: Macmillan, 1921.

———. *The Northward Course of Empire.* New York: Harcourt, 1922.

Stefansson, Vilhjalmur, and Rudolph Martin Anderson. *My Life with the Eskimo.* New York: Macmillan, 1913.

Stefansson, Vilhjalmur, and Explorers Club. *Unsolved Mysteries of the Arctic.* New York: Macmillan, 1938.

Stehberg, Ruben, and Liliana Nilo. "Procedencia Antartica Inexacta De Dos Puntos De Proyectil." *Instituto Antártico Chileno Serie Científica* 30 (1983): 77–86.

Stern, Pamela R., and Lisa Stevenson. *Critical Inuit Studies: An Anthology of Contemporary Arctic Ethnography*. Lincoln: University of Nebraska Press, 2006.

Sullivan, Walter. *Assault on the Unknown: The International Geophysical Year*. New York: McGraw-Hill, 1961.

Sutter, Paul. *Driven Wild: How the Fight Against Automobiles Launched the Modern Wilderness Movement*. Weyerhaeuser Environmental Books. Seattle: University of Washington Press, 2002.

Thisted, Kirsten. "The Power to Represent: Intertextuality and Discourse in *Smilla's Sense of Snow*." In *Narrating the Arctic: A Cultural History of Nordic Scientific Practices*, edited by Michael Bravo and Sverker Sörlin. Canton, MA: Science History Publications, 2002.

Thomas, Julia Adeney. "Comment: Not Yet Far Enough." *The American Historical Review* 117, no. 3 (2012): 794–803.

Tønnessen, J. N., and Arne Odd Johnsen. *The History of Modern Whaling*. Berkeley: University of California Press, 1982.

Turner, James Morton. *The Promise of Wilderness: American Environmental Politics since 1964*. Seattle: University of Washington Press, 2012.

Vaughan, Richard. *The Arctic: A History*. Dover, NH: A. Sutton, 1994.

Weart, Spencer R. *The Discovery of Global Warming*. Rev. and expanded ed. Cambridge, MA: Harvard University Press, 2008.

Weddell, James. *A Voyage Towards the South Pole, Performed in the Years 1822–'24. Containing ... A Visit to Tierra Del Fuego, with a Particular Account of the Inhabitants*. London: Longman, Hurst, Rees, Orme, Brown, and Green, 1825.

Wheeler, Sara. *Cherry: A Life of Apsley Cherry-Garrard*. New York: Random House, 2002.

White, Lynn, Jr. "The Historical Roots of Our Ecologic Crisis." *Science* 155, no. 3767 (1967): 1203–7.

White, Richard. "'Are You an Environmentalist or Do You Work for a Living?' Work and Nature." In *Uncommon Ground: Rethinking the Human Place in Nature*, ed. William Cronon, 171–85. New York: Norton, 1996.

———. *The Middle Ground: Indians, Empires, and Republics in the Great Lakes Region, 1650–1815*. Cambridge Studies in North American Indian History. Cambridge, New York: Cambridge University Press, 1991.

Wishart, Robert P. "A Story About a Muskox: Some Implications of Tetlit Gwih'in Human-Animal Relationships." In *Cultivating Arctic Landscapes: Knowing and Managing Animals in the Circumpolar North*, ed. David G. Anderson and Mark Nuttall. New York: Berghahn Books, 2004.

Wolf, Eric R. *Europe and the People Without History*. Berkeley: University of California Press, 1982.

Worster, Donald. "Appendix: Doing Environmental History." In *The Ends of the Earth: Perspectives on Modern Environmental History*, ed. Donald Worster, 289–308. Cambridge: Cambridge University Press, 1989.

———. *A River Running West: The Life of John Wesley Powell*. Oxford, New York: Oxford University Press, 2001.

Wynn, Graeme. *Canada and Arctic North America: An Environmental History*. Abc-Clio's Nature and Human Societies Series. Santa Barbara, CA: ABC-CLIO, 2007.

Zarankín, Andrés, and M. Ximena Senatore. *Historias De Un Pasado En Blanco: Arqueología Histórica Antártica*. Belo Horizonte: Argumentum, 2007.

Zelko, Frank S. *Make It a Green Peace!: The Rise of Countercultural Environmentalism*. New York: Oxford University Press, 2013.